THE K FACTOR
A Proven Stock Strategy

THE K FACTOR

A PROVEN STOCK STRATEGY

by

Jerome Krumholz

Abben Publishing Company
SINCE 1969
New York, New York

The K Factor A Proven Stock Strategy

Library of Congress Catalog Card Number: 89-85804

ISBN: 0-9624000-8-4

Book Design by Cheryl Mirkin

(∞) This book is printed on acid free paper.

Abben Publishing Company
since 1969
Box 463, Flushing, N.Y. 11365

TO MY WIFE ROSE

. . . who insisted that I dedicate this book . . .
to the many millions of investors
who so desperately reach out
for help.

Preface by the Author

This book is to stocks and bonds what the bible is to religion. This book is your bible for investing. It will instruct you on how to make money. It explains how to stop your losing ways. Its premise is the protection of your savings, your retirement funds, your investment profits!

It's a case study of how I took $2000 to Wall Street and made over ½ million dollars. How I built my retirement fund. It takes exception to accepted Wall Street dogma and frees you from its manacles. It teaches you how to think and to act and to make your own investment decisions.

To do this you must get right down to the basics . . . to the fundamentals of the stock market itself . . . to the very heart and definition of investing . . . which is what this book does!

I wrote this book with great enthusiasm. Throughout its chapters, I jumped up with excitement after explaining how and why and when I made my investment decisions and how you should follow suit.

After reading this book through for the first time, several months after writing the last chapter, I excitedly exclaimed to my wife, "It's a really good book! It is going to help lots of people!"

That's how enthusiastic I was and still am about the contents, facts and help which are between the covers. You can't read one chapter by itself. You must read this book, cover to cover starting with page one.

Like the bible, this book was written on sheer inspiration. I was angered for many, many years at conventional Wall Street for advocating buy. .buy. .buy. .when they should have been saying sell. .sell. .sell.

So when the stock market crashed on October 19,

1987, and I started to read about the devastating losses that investors were suffering, my heart went out to those helpless people. Here I was sitting on my profits and out of the stock market completely. I had not ten cents in stocks!!

I can cry when I read of the sixty-five-year-old retiree who invested his life savings of $55,000 in a AAA municipal bond only to have it go bankrupt shortly thereafter!

It makes me sad when I read of the thirty-year-old who invested $20,000 among five mutual funds in 1986 only to suffer large losses after the crash!

I feel badly when an over-seventy client visits my office and asks for help because he can't survive on $5200 dividend income after his portfolio of over forty years has shrunk because of bear markets!

That's why I was inspired to write this book. I felt an obligation to help those people who wanted to invest in stocks and bonds.

I'm an ordinary guy and I did it! You can do it too! But you have to work at it . . . or otherwise keep your money in Treasuries!

You are pitting your savings against brilliant brains, untold wealth, much greed, extremely knowledgeable and tough minded people.

You are also risking your money on your own emotions. That is why it is imperative that you keep this book on your desk. It's your bible!

I know it's mine!

—Jerome Krumholz

About the Author

Pick up books on investing in the stock market and the chances are that the authors all fit into a single category. They became rich . . . working on Wall Street . . . and not by investing in the stock market solely with their money as you and I do.

They work at telling you . . . how they *think* that you should invest . . . your . . . money.

This author is the exception to the rule! I am from the "grass roots". I tell you how to invest your money because I became rich investing . . . my savings . . . in the stock market!!!

First I practiced what I'm writing about! I experienced what I'm writing about! I successfully tested what I'm writing about! And—I disagree with accepted Wall Street theory.

Several years ago when I first contemplated writing a book, I was asked by a publisher for my qualifications. I stated that I had many years of successful investing experience and that I had made some $100,000.

To which the publisher snapped, "That's no money. I just lost $400,000."

I quickly asked, "Then tell me who do you think should write this book? You, who lost $400,000 or I, who made $100,000?"

The publisher replied, "You are qualified. Send in your material." Since that time I have made fivefold as much.

So now I'm telling you how to invest your money!!!

I graduated from Pace College, cum laude and am registered as an investment adviser under the Investment Act of 1940.

Prologue

CAUTION!

You are preparing to invest. . . .

THOUSANDS! THOUSANDS! THOUSANDS OF DOLLARS!!!

so read these pages thoughtfully!

* * *

Ode to the Stock Market Investor

If you will not see, then truly you are blind
If you will not hear, then truly you are deaf
If you cannot decide, then truly you are not prepared
If you will not *THINK*, then surely you will fail!

—Jerome Krumholz

* * *

Now join with me! Welcome! Try to see it my way!

Contents

THE K FACTOR
A Proven Stock Strategy

COGITARE EST PROSPERARE

1

How To Avoid Market Crashes: Monday, October 19, 1987

"Wall Street Crashes $91.55!" Wow!!

It's Tuesday, October 6, 1987 . . .

After a meaningless rally the next day, the Dow Jones average falls $34.44 on Thursday only to be followed by another fall of $34.43 on Friday!

Sitting on the patio of my hotel room in Virginia Beach I was watching and listening to the ocean waves as they rolled up on the beach just beneath me and thinking of the stock market report I had just heard over the radio.

Another down day on Wall Street!

I shifted uncomfortably in my chair. Here I was on a nine day vacation attending a regional bridge tournament and instead of thinking bridge I was thinking Wall Street.

I had been skeptical of the market for quite some time and I had lightened up considerably. Although my portfolio totaled $461,768 I still had some $64,000 in two stocks. I had 600 shares of Mobil Corp. and 1980 shares of Utilicorp United (a utility).

My clients were in good shape since I had cautioned them to limit their stock investments to these two issues.

But what was happening on Wall Street???

What was the Wall Street Timetable???

Pushing the stock market out of my mind I turned away from the serenity of the ocean waves and entered my hotel room . . . and discussed bridge with my wife! With bridge there is always something to talk about.

The next night, Saturday night, I suddenly awakened in a slight sweat. It was only 2:55 A.M. and very dark outside. Through my patio door I heard the waves as they continued to wash up on the beach. I was thinking Wall Street! For the first time in months I was nervous.

What's the Wall Street Timetable?

I knew what was happening on Wall Street. I have to. I wouldn't be successful otherwise. I only asked that question rhetorically. There are three keys to successful investing and this book will fully explain them in due time.

Understanding what's happening on Wall Street is the FIRST KEY to successful investing.

Utilizing a few simple technical factors is the SECOND KEY. Is it time to sell out? Is it time to turn the second key?

Or is the THIRD KEY which is to apply a few elementary principles called for at this time?

After tossing a few minutes in bed I restlessly tried pacing the room several times. The stock market, in spite of what investors think, is a rational forum that not so quietly but efficiently does its job. It goes up and down . . . up and down . . . up and down. It tells a story in its agitations. It has a timetable!

A time to go up!

A time to go down!

The thought crossed my mind that perhaps I should cut my vacation short. Perhaps I should be back in my office Monday morning to closely monitor the market action.

Perhaps it's time to sell out??? Forget it! I would give

the market another two, three, days to tell its story. I'd be home Tuesday so why not stay and enjoy a few more days? I stayed! I forgot all about stocks until I got back home on Tuesday. That day the market closed up $36.72 at 2508.16. That day was October 13, 1987.

AND THEN THE MARKET TOLD ITS STORY!

Did I say told its story? It BLASTED its story!!! But—It blasted its story only to those who used the SECOND KEY, the utilization of a handful of elementary technical indicators!

ON WEDNESDAY THE STOCK MARKET CLOSED DOWN AT 2412 . . . THURSDAY IT CLOSED DOWN AT 2355 . . . FRIDAY IT CLOSED DOWN AT 2246!

BOOM! BOOM! BOOM! 2500! 2400! 2300! 2200!

BLAST! BLAST! BLAST!

The next day, Saturday, October 17 and Sunday, October 18, I cogitated! I knew what was happening on Wall Street. The question was: "What time was it on Wall Street?"

Buy??? Sell???

What's happening on Wall Street?

THE STOCK MARKET IS GOING DOWN!!!

"What time is it on Wall Street!" I asked, and answered, "IT'S TIME TO LIQUIDATE! It's time to get out!"

I don't have to tell investors how difficult it is to sell. They know! So what's my secret? THE THIRD KEY TO SUCCESS: Apply a few basic investment principles: Don't fight the tape . . . cut your losses . . . control your emotions, greed . . .

Monday morning, October 19, 1987, I called my clients

and said, "sell at the market . . . make sure that you place your orders before trading begins for the day!"

THAT DAY THE STOCK MARKET WENT THROUGH PURGATORY!!!

DOWN A RECORD SMASHING $508!

For the next several weeks all news media carried stories and interviews of the Crash. The stock market made the front pages daily for many days. President Reagan addressed the nation and promised that his representatives would immediately meet with Congressional leaders to agree to a budget. They would work together to reduce the huge budget deficit.

The Federal Reserve Board quickly opened the doors wide to the money supply. The rising trend of interest rates stopped at once and started a quick descent.

Brokerage houses lost millions and liquidated complete departments. Thousands of Wall Street employees were fired. One large and prestigious brokerage firm lost so much money that they immediately sought to be taken over. Other smaller firms simply liquidated. Wall Street was in a turmoil. None of the pundits I heard had a satisfactory reason as to what had happened . . . why it happened . . . or what to do!

Buy? Sell?

I could see it in their faces. They didn't know. All you heard was "don't panic". I would like to ask investors how they would translate that into action. I don't ever recall in my forty-two years of experience when the "street" was so leaderless. I hardly heard a single leader speak with decision!

Against that background I decided that it was time to write a market letter to my clients which I did on November 14, 1987. Maybe the leaders of Wall Street didn't know what to tell investors what to do but I did. The letter follows:

* * *

On October 19, 1987
The DJ Collapsed $508!

WOW! WHAT HAPPENED?
"Elementary! BULL MARKET IS OVER! THE BEAR MARKET IS HERE!
HOW FAR DOWN
"Probably around 1000 on the Dow Jones Average!"
WHEN?
"I don't know!"
DO YOU KNOW WHAT TO DO?
"Sure! Simply apply Investment Principles!"

What Are Some Investment Principles?

1. My very first one is to control the emotions of FEAR, PATIENCE and GREED!
2. Don't fall in love with or ever marry your stocks!
3. Cut your losses!
4. Never let your losses mount until they become disasters!
5. Never wait for a rally to "recoup" some of your money!
6. Never lose a night's sleep!
7. Don't fight the tape!
8. Never get locked in!
9. DON'TS . . . don't be stubborn . . . don't get even . . . don't prove anything!
10. Buy a rising market . . . not a falling star!
11. Don't lead the market . . . follow it!

12. Turn your portfolio over . . . just like a lawn . . . just get out and make a fresh start!

Do You Have a Handle on the Market?

Yes! I expect that the stock market will be very volatile for the ensuing weeks. The pundits say, "If you hold good stocks, don't panic. Hold them for the long term."

One authority says that he was very successful for the past thirty years holding good stocks and expects to be successful for the next thirty years or so buying good stocks now and holding them for the long pull.

I have two questions for Wall Street professionals advocating that doctrine!

1. What's a good stock?
2. What's the long pull or long term?

If they are referring to stocks based on valuation, I say "NUTS". Investors are losing their shirts buying and holding stocks based purely on value.

If long term is twenty or thirty years, again I say "NUTS". I'll be dead by then. Many, many years ago I coined a phrase that reads . . .
"IN A BAD MARKET THERE IS NO SUCH THING AS A GOOD STOCK!"

From the 1946 bust through the 1987 bust I sold them all! I went into a 100% cash position and never had any regrets! When clients and investors speak of "good" stocks they mean stocks that were profitable for them. Stocks in which they suffered losses were just "rotten" stocks!

That's a definition I understand and work

with! Don't ever tell me that the ATT stock that investors bought way back when and paid $60 and $70 for and which I then later bought at about $42 was a "good" stock for them. They bought a *"good" company but a rotten stock.* I bought a *"good" company and an "excellent" stock.*

If you grasp the concept that I am elucidating, then you are at the beginning of your enlightenment, the first step to understanding Wall Street! Wall Street should not be difficult to fathom but you must have an *open mind . . . a "loose" approach . . . a Socratic attitude . . . a realization* that *you are* human. . . . that *you will make mistakes . . . that if you* expect to make right decisions then you must make *many wrong ones . . .* but your decisions must be *based upon study . . . upon analysis . . . upon reason!! T H I N K ! !*

How Am I Going to Manage My Money?

I'm going to forget about stocks for a while. I sold out all my stocks! At this time I don't have ten cents in the stock market. I'm going to try for capital gains in the bond market. I zeroed in on the bonds of Long Island Lighting Co. I have a campaign going on right now.

Lilco bonds are "junk" bonds and "junk" bonds are considered very high risk speculations. They should be purchased only after much consideration and study. Companies could go bankrupt and the purchaser could lose substantial sums of money or all of it.

Consequently not only must the company be researched and studied but the investor should first consider investment goals and objectives. Also deep thought should be given to the strategy and tactics employed.

I started with the purchase of $10,000 par value Lilco bonds on November 20, 1986. You see, while I don't predict the stock market, I understand it very well. I decided it was time to prepare for the ending of the Bull Market so that when I decided it was time to pull completely out of the stock market I could swing right into a campaign in Lilco bonds.

By the end of 1986 I had accumulated $30,000 par value of the bonds. Then I turned my attention back to stocks. It wasn't until June, 1987 that I decided to actively build my position in Lilco. Today I have $90,000 par value of Lilco bonds. The yield on my purchases range from 11.39% to 13.36%. If I could add 3% to 10% capital gains, then with a possible 22% total gain, I wonder why I should risk the stock market in 1988?

What Should Investors Do?

Investors should immediately put investment principles to work! First list your portfolio and get its market value. Next deduct 10% for possible further losses. If the resultant figure is a disaster, then I feel sorry for you. I can only say that should you want me to try to straighten out your mess, I will gladly endeavor to do so.

If your position is not a disaster, then it's not too late to recoup your losses and then go on to increasing your wealth. Start selling immediately . . . not necessarily all your stocks but make a good dent in the total.

Certainly sell not less than 15% the first day. If I were doing it for you, I would sell much more. However I don't know what you are holding or how much of which. Keep selling every day. Sell especially on rallies. Don't wait for rallies but do take advantage of them if one should develop. Within a reasonable time you should be in a 100% cash position.

Don't tell me you *can't sell* a particular stock *because* it is a good company. I already kicked that crutch out from under your feet.

Don't tell me that you *can't sell* a particular stock *because* it has a good dividend or a good yield. If it's so good, why isn't it selling on its high? There is so much money lost on this excuse that when I hear it my heart cries with sympathy. I would just want to take the investor by the hand and say, "My dear friend, why don't you keep all your money in the bank? The stock market is not for you."

"Can't sell because of good yield" is just another excuse used by professionals and neophytes who don't know what to do or say. So I am kicking yet another crutch from under your feet.

Don't think stocks! Don't think yield or dividends! Don't think profits, losses or taxes! *Think only investment principles!* With investment principles you can't go broke . . . you can only get rich!!!

INVESTMENT PRINCIPLES dictate that you cut your losses . . . don't get emotional . . . don't get locked in . . . don't wait for rallies to recoup . . . etc . . . etc. So, in case you are emotional and "afraid", I am applying investment principles for you.

Sell something immediately. Sell every day. The sooner that you are in a 100% cash position, the sooner you'll get a night's sleep!

Last week I went to a bridge tournament . . . had a whale of a good time . . . and slept every night! I used Investment Principles!

* * *

The excitement in Wall street continued. News stories abounded about the many millions that were lost by yet another well-known investor, yet another broker, yet another takeover financier. In the meantime the stock market kept doing its job . . . up . . . down . . . up . . . down . . . up . . . down . . . and through it all, the investment leaders stayed frozen in their "don't panic" state.

I just had to get another market letter out to my clients. Three days after the one you just read I wrote the following. I just had to shake people. Individual investors have good minds . . . just as good as the professionals . . . just as good as the leaders. If only investors would think for themselves they would be so much better off.

* * *

THE K FACTOR NOV. 17, 1987. . .DJ 1922.25

THINK!!

"ALL THINGS have two handles . . . BEWARE of the wrong one"

—Ralph Waldo Emerson, 1837

"THE STOCK MARKET has two handles . . . BEWARE of the wrong one"

—Jerome Krumholz, 1987

You have a choice . . . grab the UP handle of the stock market and buy and hold . . . or grab the DOWN handle and get out of the stock market!!

Ralph Waldo Emerson's message was . . . T H I N K !

My message to you is . . . T H I N K !

THINK! Boeing employs 24 money managers for its pension fund. Throughout a meeting they were asked what had caused the October Crash and *why they had not seen it coming*. Many of the money managers attributed the Crash to portfolio insurance and program trading. WRONG!

THINK! Many brokerage firms, many wealthy investors, many takeover financiers employ experienced and noted professionals . . . and still lost millions and millions and millions!

THINK! The October, 1987 collapse leaves me totally unscathed and "richer" because the purchasing power of my cash as far as stocks are concerned suddenly increased tremendously.

THINK! Think of how well I succeeded and made out in this five year period . . . that I knew when to get in, 1982, and get out, 1987. This doesn't say that I'll be successful in the future but certainly the past is eloquent!

THINK! The most frequent piece of advice that I've been hearing during these trying times is "Don't panic". Just exactly what are you supposed to do with that kind of advice? Exactly what does don't panic mean? To me? It's just another Wall Street crutch! It means "I don't know what to do so don't panic". I told my clients what to do! Buy what I buy! Sell what I sell! Cash in when I cash in!

THINK! JUST THINK!
THINK! JUST THINK!
THINK . . . AND CALL ME!!!

* * *

The financial news kept centering around the recent stock market crash. There were reports that investigative committees were being formed to ascertain the causes of the debacle. Prominent people of the financial and business industries offered their versions of what went wrong. I disagreed with *all* of them.

So once again, this time four days later, I wrote and mailed a market letter explaining why the market crashed and why I and others using the THREE KEYS TO WALL STREET liquidated! The letter follows:

* * *

THE K FACTOR — **NOV. 21, 1987. . .DJ 1913.63**

Why? Why? Why?

HEARD . . . from Wall Street . . . from Washington . . . from Tokyo . . . from financial centers around the world . . .

"WHY DID THE STOCK MARKET COLLAPSE MONDAY, OCTOBER 19, 1987?"

"WHY DIDN'T YOU SEE IT COMING?"

1. I saw it coming! I was out! I took my clients with me!

2. The "trigger" that dynamited Wall Street on October 19th was the apparent ease and quickness with which the 10% level of long term treasuries was penetrated leading me and others to anticipate 11% . . . then 12% . . . then . . .

With stocks yielding some 5% . . . even utilities yielding 5–5½% . . . why should I continue to run a high risk of an imminent stock market crash? Evidently there were proficient professionals who came to the same conclusion at the same time!

In September I bought no stocks. I sold no stocks. I keenly observed . . . and waited!

Tuesday, October 6th the stock market plunged some $92! The dollar was falling! Interest rates were steadily climbing! The U.S. wasn't talking to Germany! Japan was feuding with the U.S.!

That week and all the following week the dollar kept falling . . . interest rates kept ascending . . . nobody was talking . . . and the overvalued stock market kept deteriorating!

A MORIBUND STATE OF AFFAIRS EXISTED!!

Studying this condition over the October 17–18 weekend and reviewing my technical analysis of the market, one solitary technical factor stood illuminated against a thundering black sky . . . the market had sold off sharply towards the end of the week and culminated in a bone crushing plunge of $108.

THAT DID IT! I wasn't going to "FIGHT THE TAPE"! I WANTED OUT! I could hardly wait for Monday morning, October 19, 1987 to call my clients to say: "SELL AT THE MARKET!! *MAKE SURE* YOU PLACE YOUR ORDER *BEFORE* IT OPENS!!!"

That's why the stock market crashed $508 Monday . . . because it became apparent during the 17th and 18th weekend *THAT STOCK PRICES WERE IN A FREE FALL* and would continue to fall until and unless "Somebody said something" that would halt the rise in interest rates!

* * *

Yes, I sold on Monday, October 19, but my clients and I placed market orders before trading started so we got out at the top of the day before the market crashed. Also we had only a very small part of our investment capital at stake that day.

Did my clients and I cause the crash? Certainly not—but there was a record-shattering volume of 604,000,000 shares. Why did we of the 604,000,000 shares act in concert? I think it's because we all knew how to use the SECOND KEY, the technical key that tells about volume and trend and prices. Then we didn't hesitate to use the THIRD KEY that says . . . Don't fight the tape.

Finally when this historic day defied reason, we just used plain old fashioned common sense.

We sold to protect ourselves!

2

Understanding Wall Street: The First Key!

DANGER! DANGER AHEAD!
BEWARE! I am about to hand you the FIRST KEY TO WALL STREET. Before you reach out to accept it, I caution you that the path to success is through a quagmire . . . quicksand that has swallowed millions of investors who tried the journey . . . a morass that could easily engulf your hopes to accumulate a pension.

Your best hope for survival is to THINK for yourself. I'll provide you with the THREE KEYS to success but you must do the thinking . . . or else retain a professional who has himself made the trip successfully several times. I am truly such a professional. I made it, many times. Always unscathed and three times very successfully.

Ready! Let's Go!

I said that you have to think for yourself. Therefore let's prepare your mind to think "Wall Street". Before you buy your first stock, you must prepare your mind for what's ahead. The reason is that Wall Street should hold no surprise for you. You don't have to predict Wall Street. You just must understand it!

Before we invest money let's first explore what it is that we are letting ourselves into. What is it we want? How do we get it? EXACTLY HOW? PRECISELY HOW?

"JUST WHAT IS WALL STREET?"

"WHAT'S IT ALL ABOUT?"

Let's explore different thoughts and then see if we can't tie them together so that we get a concept . . . an insight . . . into our subject. Let's see if this examination won't lead us to the FIRST KEY TO WALL STREET . . . TO THE UNDERSTANDING OF WALL STREET!!!

Shock Treatment!

In order to get you to think every time the subject is investing, I must shock you! Suppose I said that in order to succeed in investing it is necessary that you convert from your religion.

Shocking? Is that a shocking thought? Are you startled? Quickly I withdraw that thought. No I did not make that statement. No you do not have to convert from your religion. But while you are in a shocked state and entering a thinking state let me throw other shocking and blasphemous ideas at you to think about!

"Most people who buy stocks are investors." . . .
THAT'S A FALLACY!

"Buy stocks for the long term." . . .
THAT'S A FALLACY!

"Buy stocks for the dividend." . . .
THAT'S A FALLACY!

"Buy stock of good companies." . . .
AND THAT'S A FALLACY!

And I do make the above four quotes as statements. YOU CAN QUOTE ME FOR THE RECORD!

But aren't these the principles advocated by all Wall Street people? Doesn't everybody espouse them? Yes they are! Yes to both questions. But THINK! They don't work do they? Which neighbor of yours has used them successfully?

They are investment factors used by Wall Street people to entice the public to get interested in the stock market. I referred to them as principles. Actually I consider them not as principles but as factors in the decision making process.

Therefore let's start to understand Wall Street. *LET'S THINK . . . TOGETHER!*

What precisely is conventional investing? (It has a sort of safe sound, doesn't it?) However, by definition from *Webster's New Collegiate Dictionary*

Invest: to commit (money) in order to earn a financial return.

Conventional: 1. formed by agreement or compact
2. lacking originality or individuality: TRITE
syn see CEREMONIAL

Trite: hackneyed from much use: STALE

We see by definition that the entire approach to investing taken by millions of investors is fundamentally wrong from the very start. Trite means stale and conventional means trite. Conventional also means lacking originality. It also means formed by agreement or compact.

Therefore those four investment factors, namely, most people who buy stocks are investors, buy stocks for the long term, buy stocks for the dividend, buy stocks of good companies, that I call crutches are stale and trite and yet Wall Street agrees that they are conventional. THINK! . . . for yourself.

To Invest . . . to commit money in order to earn a financial return! Where did it say to invest is to buy stocks for the long term? Where did it say to invest is to buy stocks for dividend income? Where did it say to invest is to buy stocks of good companies? THINK!

In this bull market let's say you bought stocks for the long term. You bought stocks for income. That was wrong. I bought stocks for financial return. You are left holding stocks. You let a good part of your profit disappear. I sold out with all my profit. I have the cash. I don't hold ten cents in stocks!

WHO IS THE INVESTOR???

YOU OR ME???

Conventional Wall Street

You now know that I don't hold with the people who make up conventional Wall Street. I respect them as people but I find they are of little help to investors. By definition they seem to have an agreement, a compact (unwritten) to issue slogans which entice people into investing hard-earned money while the people on the "Street" keep earning tremendous fees and commissions.

The investor, meanwhile, has nothing to show for years of endeavor but a basketful of paper. The slogans, while at one time original, are now ceremonial. They are trite and hackneyed from overuse . . . stale!

The word, investor, is nothing but a sugar-coated crutch which in turn is covered by molasses and honey, sugar and candy. It is handed to you after they knock you flat on your back, trample you, turn your pockets inside out and take your money.

When you get to your staggering feet you are so bewildered, so exhausted from the vicissitudes of the stock market that you are grateful for the crutch they extend to you. As you get to your feet they give you a lot of paper certificates and say,

"Welcome, you are an INVESTOR!"

THINK! To become an investor is to become a business person! To become an investor is to invest money for profit! It's a speculation . . . it's a risk . . . just as business is a risk . . . The retailer doesn't buy suits to hold . . . the retailer doesn't buy merchandise to store away . . . the retailer buys inventory to sell at a profit! That's the only concept I accept in Wall Street.

When I buy stocks . . . I buy to SELL at a profit . . . I buy for inventory . . . For a year or two I used to assign lot numbers to every purchase I made. When I sold, I thought of it as taking that lot number off the shelf and matching up my buy and sell orders for tax purposes.

Imagine if a stamp or coin dealer never sold any of the merchandise. The dealer would no longer be a dealer but would then be a collector!

IS THAT WHAT YOU WANT TO BE? A COLLECTOR OF STOCKS??

NO!! That was not your intention when you first started investing money. You wanted to make money! Of course, if you wanted just income why not invest in high yielding treasuries just as I do. When I want income I buy Treasuries. When I'm looking for profits I buy stocks!

THINK! This is the beginning of understanding the stock market.

Don't think of yourself as an investor if you are going to collect stocks. Don't use that as a crutch. An investor buys stocks only to sell at a profit . . . frequently it is necessary to sell at a loss . . . just as other successful business people do. The most successful business people and financiers take losses. It's part of doing business!

In my November 14, 1987 market letter which is in the previous chapter, I said, "Don't tell me that you can't sell a particular stock because it has a good dividend."

Now do you know where I'm coming from?

Are you thinking with me?

A STOCK IS BOUGHT TO SELL AT A PROFIT!

The selling is not determined by its yield or dividend but only by the PROFIT MOTIVE! The yield is only a small factor. Yield is only a fundamental factor. The determination to sell is a technical factor. More about this later.

The difference between success and failure in the stock market is not in your thinking ability but what you are thinking about.

The successful investor when confronted with declining prices will think whether the decline is normal and to be expected or whether the investor should sell and take a small loss at this time. If the loss is reasonable and if the investor recognizes that the market is simply doing its thing of moving up and down, then the investor will patiently wait until prices reverse until such time as it is time to sell at a profit. The INVESTOR IS THINKING!!

The investor is alert! The investor is closely monitoring the investments. The investor is thinking only profits and losses.

The unsuccessful person doesn't think of the above at all. Such a person goes into the stock market totally unprepared to cope with such situations. Such a person when confronted with declining prices thinks, "If the market goes down, I'll hold for the long term." Thus "the long term" becomes an excuse . . . it becomes a crutch . . . it's a cop out . . . it's an excuse for not knowing what to think about. That's the quicksand that will soon swallow you whole! That's what will make you a COLLECTOR OF STOCKS and not an INVESTOR IN STOCKS.

So now you UNDERSTAND and THINK of an investor as one who enters Wall Street as a business whose objective is to buy stocks with the intention of reselling them at a profit within a reasonable time or else take a reasonable loss.

NOW YOU ARE BEGINNING TO KNOW "WHAT IT'S ALL ABOUT!"

Just What is Wall Street?

Did you ever notice that sometimes a company will publish a fine earnings report only to have its stock drop on the news?

Were you aware that for years ATT grew in earnings, sales and dividends, yet for years the price of its stock dropped?

Did you ever stop to wonder why the stocks of so many good companies dropped in unison for a period of years?

Did you ever stop to think why the yield on treasury bills sold some years for 12% and some years for 6%?

Did you ever stop to think and to wonder why the stock price of a utility could drop one year, go up another year and then down again . . . and during all this time never miss its dividend . . . never cut its dividend . . . keep increasing its dividend??

Let's stop now! Let's think . . . again, together!!

THINK! When I first heard of program trading and future trading and option trading using stocks as a base, I felt it was bad for the investing public. Then insurance programs were introduced.

I now realized that the nature of investing has reverted back to the days of the robber barons. The days of the corners are back. Corners were outlawed before my time and now I am witness to them.

Today, a group of a few people can cause a crash of the whole market. Today one man can muster billions of dollars and "corner" a stock. He can buy the whole company!

Try to take refuge by buying stocks of big companies? What company is big enough or safe enough? It isn't even safe to buy into companies that are expected to be taken over. You never know when the big buyer is going to settle for "greenmail" and you'll be left holding the bag.

When the stock market came into being it was to help raise capital for business. Today that idea is buried deep beneath the gambling and (inside) information that passes quickly from one professional to another . . . from one place to another place around the world.

That's the broad picture of Wall Street. Let's look at it in detail.

THINK! How do you account for the fact that most stocks have highs and lows every single day? Look at today's paper. Glance up and down the stock tables. All you see is that almost every stock has a price difference between its high and its low. Why is it that the high and the low are almost always different?

What happened to the company during the day to warrant different prices? The yield is the same . . . the earnings haven't changed during the day . . . there is no news out on the stock . . . so why the change?

SOMETHING HAD TO HAVE HAPPENED. What mystery took place? What caused the fluctuation in so many stocks? Thinking?

If the fundamentals of a stock have not changed during the day, then it follows that something else moved the price of the stock! That something else is the *V O L U M E* of buying or selling!

VOLUME IS A TECHNICAL FACTOR.

Consequently how can an investor determine whether to "commit thousands" to the stock of a company only by studying the company itself? How can an investor ignore the technical factors? How DARE the investor pay attention to the stock of a company and IGNORE THE STOCK MARKET? Don't you see how sophisticated the stock market is? Won't you please think about all this? Are you grasping the idea that no one can give you rules to follow? You must think about investing. Even the richest and the biggest sometimes don't know from day to day what's going to happen or what they are going to do.

Let's talk about some market phenomena. From the top of one bull market to the top of another bull market is a cycle. You could also measure the cycle from the bottom of one bear market to the bottom of another bear market. A bull market is when prices rise continually for a protracted period of time. A bear market is when stock prices decline for a protracted period of time.

A cycle has four stages or four parts of which the first stage is the "accumulation" period. This first part takes place when the public has no interest in the stock market. Stock prices move in a narrow range and volume is low. News whether good or bad tends to be ignored. Since prices tend to move in a narrow range, it is difficult for an investor to buy for a profit.

Consequently in many instances the investor would get a bigger return with money lying idle in a bank than subjecting it to the risks of the stock market.

It is during this period of accumulation that investors tend to buy and hold stocks. Since these investors expect to hold the stock for the second stage of the cycle, the bull market itself, these investors have what is called "strong hands". Thus we say in Wall Street that stock is passing into strong hands. We don't expect to see that stock back on the market for a long time.

The First Stage

The first stage, "accumulation", takes from months to years. When stocks start to move up at the start of a bull market, it's said to "break-out". Once a break-out occurs the daily, weekly and monthly range of stocks start to widen. Opportunities develop more and more often. Soon it gets easy to make a profit. The higher prices move, the more rapid are the succeeding highs.

The Second Stage

This succession of constant new highs soon develops into the second stage of the market cycle, the "rise" in stock prices. It is during this part of the cycle that the investor should get rich! Investing is really very seasonal. It's as seasonal as any other business.

An employee expects a salary each week. A business man expects to make money during the season which usually is at least once each year. But the investor is in a unique business. It is difficult for an investor to make money each week or even each year.

True there is always a chance for profit in the stock market but my experience convinces me that the average investor won't make money each week or each month.

Consequently the investor should UNDERSTAND WALL STREET. The investor should know what part or stage the stock market is in and invest accordingly. Therefore since it is lots easier to profit during the rising stage of the cycle than at any other stage, it behooves the investor to take the 200%–400% that is frequently available during this "rising" market!

Third Stage

When stocks approach the top of a bull market, many proficient investors start to liquidate their inventory. Volume will increase dramatically. Prices swing widely. The stock market will be very volatile.

This trading volatility will take months and sometimes years. Smart investors will be liquidating all this time and will be in and out quite often. They will be selling on balance right into and past the crash that seems to mark the end of each bull market.

This third stage is called the "distribution" part of the cycle. It's called that because successful investors are distributing stock to the public. Since it is so very difficult to determine the top of a bull market, distribution doesn't take place in any one day. Investors have many stocks and sell off one at a time. There are factors which determine which and when to sell. We'll take them up shortly.

Fourth Stage

The fourth and final stage is called the "fall". The time of the fall is not the one day of the crash but starts about that time and continues for months or years. It continues until it runs into the first stage of the new cycle. Both the fourth stage and the new first stage will be going on during an overlapping period of time.

Well we have discussed the stock market and noted how stock prices can easily be put up and down by a handful of influential and wealthy people. We have noted that stocks have daily highs and lows. Let us now *THINK* about the input that goes into the stock market.

There are two inputs that go into the stock market. These inputs make the market go up and down. These inputs are the *fundamental* factors and the *technical* factors.

Fundamental Factors

Some professionals study a company's history, sales, management, balance sheet, income statement, product or service, size, dividend policy, capitalization, cash flow, accounting ratios etc. to make a determination which stock to buy and when to buy it.

Some will study all or part of the same but place much emphasis upon its P/E ratio. This stands for the market price of its stock divided by its earnings per share for the year.

Example: A company's stock sells for $20. The company's earning is $5 per share for the year. Dividing 20 by 5 we obtain the figure 4 as the P/E. Since over a period of time a 10 P/E or 13 P/E may be average, a 4 might represent the decisive factor in the buying decision. Some investors even determine at that time that the time to sell and take profits would be when the P/E rose to 20 or any other arbitrary ratio.

Some investors may emphasize yield as more decisive than P/E. Some look for book value or some other fundamental of the company. Some prefer industry leaders.

There are many schools of thought but they all have one thing in common. They use the "fundamentals" that exist within the company. For example the company controls its dividend policy. It is responsible for its sales, earnings, cash flow, debt etc. These are all internal factors. These are all fundamental factors. These factors can influence the price of the stock. At times they don't! THINK about that!

Professionals who make a study of these various factors and use these factors as a basis for buy and sell decisions take what is known as a FUNDAMENTAL approach to investing!

NOW STAY WITH ME ON WHAT FOLLOWS!

There are EXTERNAL factors that influence prices on the stock market which have nothing directly to do with the company under study. For instance the exchange rate of the dollar falling or rising could influence the stock market . . . interest rates rising or falling could influence the stock market . . . the budget deficit . . . an assassination . . . war . . . a catastrophe . . . etc. . . These are all external factors that would influence the rise and fall of stock prices.

While investors are influenced by fundamentals, they are also influenced by these external factors. It's the resultant action that investors take after studying this potpourri of factors that moves the market either up or down. The factor, itself, does not move the market. The yield, the P/E, the book value, the good or bad news is not what moves the market. It's whether or not the investor acts that moves the market.

In the final analysis it's the buying and selling. It's the

orders that come into the stock market that moves stock prices up and down.

DO YOU UNDERSTAND ME? DO YOU UNDERSTAND WALL STREET?

Technical Factors

Now the buying and selling that is constantly taking place in the stock market is the technical part of Wall Street. It's the action that investors have taken. We are not talking about any given stock. We are talking about the stock market itself.

A stock trades on the stock market but it is not the "stock market". The stock is still a stock. You and I are not really interested in stocks. WE ARE INTENSELY INTERESTED IN THE STOCK MARKET. WE DON'T MAKE MONEY *OWNING STOCKS*. WE MAKE MONEY INVESTING IN THE STOCK MARKET! WE MAKE MONEY *SELLING* STOCKS!

Do you have trouble following me? You don't want to trade every day? I don't trade every day! I wouldn't succeed if I did. THINK WITH ME! STAY WITH ME! I am trying to get you to UNDERSTAND WALL STREET. Understanding Wall Street is the FIRST of THREE KEYS to success. I'll tell you how and when to invest successfully with the SECOND AND THIRD KEYS.

Oh! I study stocks. I call management and ask questions. I need to know earnings and book value and price/earnings and sales. I just love to collect dividends. . . . Yes and interest too. I love to get a check every month. Many times I can't wait from month to month so I buy treasury notes to get checks twice a month. I love that. Don't you? Of course!

I know what you want. Do you know why? Because I want that too! I am very afraid to lose money! I want to get regular dividends and interest. I want large capital gains . . . and I want it now . . . I'll wait until tomorrow if I have to!

Don't we all think the same?

We do! Now if only you will think with me, I'll explain how I achieved that dream and how you can as well. Not today and I'm sorry to say not tomorrow, but you can collect steady income and achieve large capital gains. I did it. I went successfully through three bull markets.

You can too!!!

T H I N K !

The Technical Side of the Street!

There are times the price of a stock will decline say for some three weeks . . . then go up some three weeks . . . only to decline for some weeks. While the stock and the stock market were doing their job of down . . . up . . . down . . . there was no news on the company.

The dividend was not changed or declared. There was not an earnings report. There was just no news. Yet the price of the stock fluctuated. No, not fluctuated. I should say it moved up . . . down . . . up . . . down . . . up . . . down. I want you to think of the stock market and the movement of stocks as up . . . down . . .up . . . down . . . rather than fluctuating.

That's how I think of the stock market . . . up . . . down . . . up . . . down. Fluctuate is a disarming word to use here. It implies a desultory condition. I only think of the stock market as a live, vibrant, dangerous business venture. I must stay alert constantly or I'll lose a substantial sum of money.

It's evident that it wasn't the fundamentals of the company that had moved the stock up . . . down . . . up . . . down. It therefore had to be something outside the company. It had to be some TECHNICAL factor at work. The stock moved up and down because people were buying and people were selling . . . not because it was paying a good dividend.

We are going to be concerned with individual stocks. We are going to study their dividend records, earnings, p/e ratio, book value, its management etc. Yes I do consider it all before I buy a stock.

But my *purpose and approach* to making this FUNDAMENTAL ANALYSIS of a particular stock is different from that of Conventional Wall Street. I make a fundamental analysis AFTER I have decided via TECHNICAL ANALYSIS that the stock has the potential for large profits. Then I make a fundamental analysis to CONFIRM my TECHNICAL conclusion.

Most money managers and professional investors FIRST MAKE AND USE FUNDAMENTAL ANALYSIS as a basis for investment decisions and either never pay attention to TECHNICAL data or else give scant attention to it. I buy a stock because I want to make a lot of money within a limited time frame. Conventional Wall Street would have you buy a stock for its yield or for your lifetime. They'll make you a COLLECTOR. I'll make you an INVESTOR!

T H I N K ! I haven't been successful buying and holding stocks for the long pull. Have you?

T H I N K ! I haven't been successful buying stocks for the dividend. Have you?

T H I N K ! If I haven't been successful with Wall Street's advice in the past, am I going to continue taking it?

ABSOLUTELY NOT!

ARE YOU?

THINK IT THROUGH!

THINK! A company reports an increase in earnings. That *fundamental* fact should influence people to want to buy the stock. Buying the stock is a *technical* fact. It depends upon how Wall Street will react to the news that will determine any change in the price of the company's stock.

Surprise! The stock drops two dollars!

Have you ever had that happen to you? Those things do happen.

THINK! Therefore won't you agree that in the final analysis it's the technical factor that moved the price of the stock and not the FUNDAMENTAL factor?

Won't you further agree that we should research and study the fundamentals of a company but it's the TECHNICAL factors that we should concentrate on?

Finally shouldn't it be the technical factors and not the fundamental factors that should determine what and when to buy and sell?

One last point in technical vs fundamental usage. When I avoided the October, 1987 crash I did so as I explained in my market letter because I saw the technical factors of volume plus price decline.

How could anybody using fundamental analysis ever avoid the crash? They can't. Earnings are published only quarterly. Dividends are declared quarterly. In the final analysis you have to rely on some kind of technical data!

To Sum Up

We understand that the stock market moves in a four part cycle.

We understand that in a bear market most all stocks fall.

We understand that as your heart beats every day, every minute, irrespective of our ups and downs so does the market move . . . up . . . down . . . up . . . down . . . irrespective of what stage it's in.

We understand that for periods stocks move in narrow ranges and at other times they swing widely.

We understand that stocks make record highs and record lows and record volume.

Since we know all this . . . since we now understand what Wall Street is all about and what Wall Street does, why should anything surprise us?

Why should anyone who invests in Wall Street be surprised when the stock market crashed on that fateful day on Monday, October 19, 1987 . . . IF . . . they UNDERSTOOD the stock market? I can understand being caught in it. But I can't believe surprised.

I wasn't a bit surprised! NO I didn't predict it. So how do you suppose I avoided it? Not just this one time but many other crashes in the past. The Crash wasn't new! It's "old hat". I have seen it before.

Haven't conventional Wall Street people seen it before? So why are they so surprised? It happened before and it will happen again!

I don't believe in taking stocks up and down. That I leave to the stock market. Let the stock market go up and down. You don't have to predict the market. If you understand it, you'll always avoid the crashes and when you don't, you'll still manage to make large profits.

You will always get in on the bull markets and usually at the start of the rise. In fact you will most likely get in during the accumulation stage before the bull market really starts.

Have you been thinking with me all this time? Shall I shock you with religion again? Or is my disagreement with conventional Wall Street and my understanding of the stock market heretic enough to keep you thinking?

In the first chapter is a market letter which I wrote on November 17, 1987 entitled, THINK!. It was written after the market had crashed. Investors were uncertain whether to buy, sell or hold. I said sell. I gave some thoughts based upon my understanding of what Wall Street and the stock market is all about.

Interestingly enough I find in my files a market letter that I had written just ten years earlier dated August 30, 1977 that is really identical with my thinking of today! My thinking came "full cycle".

Read it carefully as it demonstrates how the stock market repeats itself. It also shows how my thinking coincides with that of the market. In fact I could have just changed the date of that letter and mailed it in lieu of the one I wrote in 1987.

* * *

THE K FACTOR AUGUST 30, 1977

A Private Letter on Wall Street Investments

What Time Is It On Wall Street?

It's time to protect your money! It's time to ignore profits and losses, income and yields, taxes, earning ratios and other *rational* factors and once again call upon one of the investment principles.

"I'D RATHER BE PRUDENT THAN RIGHT!!!"

This means concern yourself only with the preservation of capital. I don't predict the stock market but I do know when it is falling . . . and it's falling right now. Whether it will continue to decline or whether stock prices will embark upon a new rise, I can't predict or determine at this time. Therefore I am selling to protect a substantial part of my capital.

In this type market I cannot afford to risk losses for possible gains. I may be wrong in selling but at least I am safe and as long as I don't suffer devastating losses I will return with the opportunity to make profits once again. The Nature Of Investing!

While it is necessary to be involved with the investment market on a continuous basis, still investment profits are not made on a continuous basis or on any regular basis. Rather investing is a highly seasonal business. You don't know when the season begins or when it will end. You don't know if it will last for months or for years.

Investing is an art that is highly dependent upon "market timing" as well as investment principles. "I'd rather be prudent than right" is one of those principles. "Market timing" tells me that now is the time to apply that principle.

With the stock market lower now than where it was twenty months ago and increasing its rate of decline, I'll get out and wait however long is necessary until the "new season" begins. Patience may be a virtue but in investing it is life itself.

* * *

This concludes my understanding of the stock market and just what it does and what it is supposed to do. I hope that you will think about it just as I do and see it for just what it is . . . an investment opportunity for making money.

Now that I trust that you understand it, I want you to know that you have the *FIRST KEY to Wall Street Riches!* I feel comfortable with that thought. I feel that we have something in common. We have the same keys. We have become colleagues.

3

Money and the Stock Market: The Second Key!

The mecca Wall Street has two kinds of people. One kind is those who work for Wall Street . . . the sellers . . . the writers . . . the mutual fund people . . . the salaried employees . . . the advisers . . . the executives . . . and the owners and financiers.

These people are business people. They are not investors! They tell YOU how to invest. They make their money as business people. Consequently I wonder if they aren't adverse parties to you.

The other kind of people are people like you . . . like me! I am an investor. I AM YOUR KIND! Yes I am writing this book but only because I am a proven successful investor. I made my money investing in the stock market. To date this book is an expense. I have no idea whether I will ever get one penny back . . . nor do I care.

When I tell you or a client what to buy it's only when I have lots of my own money at risk as well! And when I tell somebody to sell it's only because that's what I am doing!

Anybody can publish a list of stocks and say buy. They make it appealing by heading the list with titles such as "For the business man" . . . For Income" . . . Defensive Stocks" etc. If the list prospers, a new guru is hailed!

Comes the day of reckoning and stocks decline. The guru is a rich man from his commissions. You lost your money.

Out comes the "crutch". Out comes the excuse. Out comes the fallacy, "Hold for the long term". The guru has spoken and all the COLLECTORS run to the bank to withdraw more money for the guru.

What can the COLLECTOR do??

Become an INVESTOR!

THINK! THINK! When you become successful you will just love to THINK! . . . you will just adore Wall Street!

Yes. It's difficult to make money by investing. It is not easy. You will be tested . . . you will be restless . . . but you can do it! How? By understanding that . . .

WALL STREET IS AN ART . . . NOT A SCIENCE! There are few artists in Wall Street . . . just many business people. It is really amazing that we have so many people telling us what to do and yet how few of them know how to invest successfully for themselves.

Since Wall Street investing is an art we must do what all successful artists do. Learn the ART! As painters learn to paint and as they learn the materials that they have to work with . . . as engineers learn their geometry . . . as chemists learn about the atom and about compounds . . . as builders learn their squares and angles and as they work with the plumb . . . so must investors learn about money . . . learn and understand Wall Street . . . and learn the "tools" and the principles and the TECHNICAL and FUNDAMENTAL factors that are available.

THINK! That's all it takes!

Money!

To invest successfully in Wall Street you must know money. You should know how to husband it . . . how to use it . . . how to manage it. You must appreciate its function. Then you will be able to invest it with due diligence!

Money may be considered to have two major functions. One function of money is to provide us with our needs as consumers. This money we may call Consumer Money.

The other function of money is to serve as capital for business and investment or for savings and income. This money we can call Capital Money.

Let's just call Consumer Money, money, and call the Capital Money just capital.

When we talk about spending on food, shelter, vacation, clothes, entertainment, charities, gambling, we are talking about money. Assuming you have enough money and capital, then does it really make a difference how the money is consumed?

Will it really matter next month how you consume your money this month? Does it matter whether you lost $50 or whether you lost $60 in Las Vegas? Does the $10 make any difference? Not more or less than extra dessert when dining out!

The money was earmarked to be consumed one way or the other.

In my house if someone breaks a dish nobody even looks up. What's to get excited about? We'll buy another one. Adopt this attitude. Should you lose a $20 bill in the street, laugh it off. You were not going to have it long anyway. What difference does it make whether you gambled it . . . bought food . . . gave it away . . . or lost it? That money was going to be consumed one way or another. Why get upset over things you can't control. Be happy and appreciate the things you do have.

Capital

Capital on the other hand is another story. If you lost $20 of capital, you have cause to be upset. You have cause for alarm. Now you should worry! Yes! Worry for $20 because CAPITAL is irreplaceable. CAPITAL gives birth to CONSUMER MONEY. BUT CONSUMER money is down the drain!!!

NOW when you CONSIDER INVESTING you MUST THINK of the harm that will be caused by losing CAPITAL!!!

Savings

Several years ago the latest game in town was to keep moving savings from one bank to another. Banks were offering gifts. The objective was to collect gifts and extra small percentage gains in yields.

The time and effort that people put into getting these extra dollars points out just how difficult it is to earn an extra ¼ percent in income. ¼ percent on $10,000 is $25 for one year. How long does $25 stay in your pocket?

THINK of this when you go about investing in the stock market. Are you really RISKING $10,000 in the stock market for ¼ percent or did you have 10% to 100% in mind!!

Income

Many people who are not investors keep all their money in banks. They live on the interest their savings provide them with. This is a mistake. Savings that are set aside solely to provide income should be placed in treasury notes and bonds.

The yield frequently is as good and the money is lots safer. Immediately the question is asked, "Aren't banks safe?" NO! Some banks are not! Some banks went bankrupt! Although depositors managed to get their money, there is some anxiety and frequently you may lose temporary access to your funds.

Again nobody can say whether we'll have a terrible

depression again or whether there may be a time when the government will pay off every single depositor.

Also it is easier to plan for income with treasuries because you can plan and stagger your income as you desire.

There is another positive factor that non-investors should consider. When interest rates decline, treasuries appreciate in value so that it is possible to earn capital gains. It may be a bother to get involved but nevertheless the potential exists.

Banks have useful functions for non-investors. They are places where one can build savings in small sums. They are very useful in parking money for short periods of time. Frequently they offer the best yield available while marking time. Checking and savings offer instant withdrawal.

Think! Stay Alert!

Keep reading every word carefully! Keep reading every word slowly! This is not a book of fiction. This is an instructive text about YOUR money. Look at your pass book. Look at the deposits that you made. Note your largest balance and your present balance.

You have to decide how much money you are going to invest. NOW YOU HAVE TO DECIDE HOW MUCH MONEY YOU ARE WILLING TO LOSE!!

These amounts don't have to be exact figures but close approximate ones.

Now that you know your capital and now that you know its importance, we can look towards Wall Street!!!

How To Approach Wall Street!

We studied Wall Street. We know what it is. We know what it does. We know how much we can lose. We know that we can make a fortune and lose a fortune.

We know that it has a stock market and a bond market. It trades options and futures. The people involved in these activities are BUSINESS people. WE, on the other hand, are the INVESTORS!

We are thinking of "committing money for profit" in the stock market. We want to invest. We are not interested in knowing how the stock market functions. We are not interested in the purpose of the stock market.

We don't want to be a part of the growth of any one company nor share in its success. We don't work for the company and we don't own the company. Who wants to "Buy a piece of America" for patriotic reasons? If we want to be patriotic, we'll get out and vote, pay our taxes, support charities and our community.

We aren't philanthropists. We don't want to be collectors and collect souvenirs and paper certificates. We are investors!! We want to make money!! We want to get our profits so that we can enjoy them. We want to spend them. That's our objective!

WHEN YOU ARE INVESTED NEVER LET IT OUT OF YOUR MIND!

The Stock Market

What we want to know about the stock market are the working Parts!

The working parts of the stock market are the FOUR STAGE CYCLE, the TREND, and the VOLUME. These are the major parts that are in force while the market goes about the business of moving up and down.

Since our success in investing will depend upon our ability to buy a stock when it's down and sell it when it's up, it's incumbent upon us to take a very deep interest in these working parts.

We know that even though we think of the stock market as moving sideways in the first stage of accumulation that it still moves up and down every day. The market moves up and down in all stages of the cycle.

Therefore there are always opportunities to make profits. The risks are greater in certain parts of the cycle. Act accordingly! The percentage gains are greater in some parts of the cycle. Act accordingly!

This study and attention . . . this analysis that we are giving to the working parts of the stock market is termed . . .

Technical Analysis!

When the stock market is in a period of accumulation and prices tend to trade in a relatively narrow range, we tend to say that there is no *"TREND"*. We can't determine if prices are going to move up or move down.

This is a good time to buy stocks because the risk is relatively small and losses are more controllable. In this stage there is seldom an urgency to be invested. The market is not going to run away. You can afford to be more selective and judicious in arriving at your buy decisions.

In this market climate it is best to take some early profits because most times stocks will pull back because of the lack of a follow up in buying.

However even in this "quiet" market a trend may be discernible in the individual stock you are involved with. By drawing a line connecting tops together then drawing a line connecting bottoms together, you will see a trend of prices slanting upwards.

Sometimes the up trend is moderate. At times the up trend may be sharp. It is just a positive technical factor. By itself it is not a call for action. In periods of accumulation there are many up trends and down trends.

Trends are very revealing and crucial at times. Frequently they last for just a short period of time. When they are of longer duration, they take on considerable significance.

For example you may find that a stock has a up trend spanning many years. Within that "major" trend may be many shorter term trends both up and down. However the point to bear in mind is that the "thrust" or the main objective of that stock is to rise.

Consequently any profit trading that you contemplate should be with that ultimate "up thrust" in mind.

I said that some trends are modest while others may slant upward quite sharply. When you see a trend rolling along and then note higher prices breaking out of the trend, you will see a new trend being established that is sharper than the preceding one.

This is of major significance. The stock or the stock market may be "breaking out" of its trend. "Breaking out" or a "break out" is a technical factor. It indicates an unusual sharp move up.

While you don't necessarily have to act when you note either an up trend or a down trend, this working part of the stock market is a major tool.

For example, assume that you own a stock and note it is in an up trend. We are in the accumulation stage. The bottom line of the trend may be slanted upward at say a 15 degree angle. The top line of the trend connecting the two highest prices in that trend may be slanted upward at a 30 degree angle.

Now the price of the stock rises sharply in an unusual fashion penetrating the top trend line. It may continue to rise sharply for several days and then drop back a trifle before resuming a rise to higher prices.

Drawing new trend lines, this second trend may have the bottom trend line slanted at a 25 degree angle while the top trend line may now slant upward at a 60 degree angle.

A study of the phenomena of trends seems to indicate that the transition from the accumulation stage to the bull market stage is accompanied by trends that start out as slightly slanted upward only to be succeeded by two, three or four succeeding ones which in turn are successively sharper in their angle upwards.

Consequently this is an important technical fact to help you to decide whether to sell or whether you should be buying more.

TRENDS ARE OF PRIME IMPORTANCE IN AVOIDING CRASHES!!

Since the last up trend of a bull market is always slanted upwards very sharply, should stock prices start to fall sharply, those prices will quickly be approaching the bottom trend line.

As they do, you can't help but be extremely apprehensive as to whether you are about to be subjected to abruptly falling prices. Should sharply falling prices penetrate the bottom line, you should sell without delay relying only on common sense!

Again you can't take this one TECHNICAL FACTOR by itself. If you did, you would be taking a scientific approach to investing and that's wrong. This is an art form that we are involved with. We have to think our way through each crisis.

However if you have other TECHNICAL indicators to confirm what you reason the trend is disclosing, then by all means exit *without delay.*

There are other phenomena about trends that I employ but which I don't care to discuss here. I don't want to complicate this discussion more than I have already. You have what you need to know to be successful.

BE ALERT! Many times these "break outs" turn out to be false and misleading. Naturally! Many times they turn out to be the top of the move. After these tops, the stock may decline for months. Be careful. *THINK!*

Volume!

How relevant is volume?? Just how important is it in the decision making process?? Without it I don't see how investors can avoid market crashes. Perhaps that is why so many astute and wealthy financiers do get caught in crashes.

Perhaps that is why so many stock brokerage houses disappear from the market scene. They simply don't know the importance that volume plays in the stock market and pay token attention to it.

I tell you that the stock market has only three working parts, the cycle, trend and volume. You see the importance that I attach to volume!

It is interesting to note how excited Wall Street gets when the bull market roars up with new volume. It is interesting, too, to note how many people will tell you that it is necessary to have volume to confirm and also to sustain rising prices.

Still when volume mounts on declining or falling stock prices most everyone gets caught! *THINK!* Why do so many interpret volume correctly on the up side and choose to ignore it on the down side?

The only explanation I can offer is that their whole approach to investing is different from mine!

THEY LOVE TO BUY! THEY HATE TO SELL!

Consider this. Many investors follow a doctrine that advocates that you should investigate a company before buying its stock. Therefore the fundamentals are looked into and, if accepted, the stock is then purchased.

The stock may not fluctuate much for perhaps several years. The stock may not be paying a dividend. We know that stocks won't change price unless buying enters the stock market for that stock.

That buying is a technical factor! That buying is VOLUME!!

THINK! We can see that there will have to be more buyers than sellers to move that stock higher!

Analyzing Volume!!

Every time a trade is made in a stock we know that someone bought it and that someone sold it. Many times I'm asked how I know when a stock is being bought or when it is being sold.

A stock is subject to the basic law of economics, the law of supply and demand. When there are more buyers than sellers then a stock price will rise. Should there be more sellers than buyers the price of a stock will decline.

To determine whether volume in a stock is due to buying or selling, we have to look at the change in the stock price. If the change was up, it was buying. If the price change was down, it was selling.

Therefore after we study the fundamentals of a company, it is important that we examine the volume of trading in that stock for the prior period. For that purpose I save the daily and Sunday New York Times for my research files. From that I record the high, low and closing prices. I also record the volume of trading as well. Since it is easier to study a picture than just figures, I make a chart of the data.

Now any unusual trading activity will stand out in the chart. Then I will look at the high-low and last to determine whether that volume caused the price to rise or fall. Thus I will know whether the stock is being bought or whether it is being sold. If the stock was being sold, I would not buy irrespective of the fundamentals. If the volume was buying, then I would enter a buy order.

More on Volume!!

Frequently during the accumulation years there will be short spurts of buying in a stock after which the stock will fall back to its prior trading range. It's important that you don't get caught during these periods.

Many times those run ups should be when you should be selling for profits. It's not easy and many times you will be wrong. But don't ever let that bother you. If you tie in those run ups with the stage of the cycle, you will usually come out OK.

Now, however, when you get larger volume coupled with a break out of a trend, then you want to be buying and not selling. However what you should find in those cases is that volume on the buy side was coming into the stock on a more frequent basis.

As the accumulation stage turns into the bull market, you will see the sharper up trends but now you will find GREATER AND GREATER VOLUME.

Now you have a combination of the three working parts of the stock market!

Volume will now come in waves of buying. Buying and volume will be sustained for longer and longer periods of time. This will continue right to the top of the new bull market!

Then right at the top just when volume reaches a maximum, stock prices will tumble quickly. If stocks fall for a few days with a continued maximum volume, then study your trend line. If the down trend line is broken, sell every stock you own at the market!!

THE BULL MARKET IS OVER!!!

I have often wondered how investors with many stocks in their portfolio expect to avoid heavy losses if they rely only on fundamentals. If the whole nature of the stock market is technical, how can they ignore technical factors?

Have these investors ever considered that precious capital is tied up in stocks that may have been employed successfully elsewhere? Aren't they losing money?

Assume their long term holding in a stock appreciated 18%. Isn't it possible they may have invested in a stock that appreciated 100% in that time frame?

Suppose a good utility is yielding 7% and appreciates 19%. Isn't it possible the capital may have profited 200% in the same bull market?

Suppose an investor ties up capital in a stock not paying a dividend for several years. Wouldn't net worth increase more with capital earning interest until technical indications favor a stock investment?

Their defense is that they are afraid that the stock will get away from them. They are afraid that they'll miss a once in a life time opportunity.

I say, *"N U T S"!!* In over forty years of investing I never missed out. You have just received the SECOND KEY to success . . . the basic TECHNICAL FACTORS.

4

The Art of the Investor: The Third Key!

INVESTMENT PRINCIPLES! THINK! The doctrine and procedures that doctors use . . . lawyers . . . chemists . . . engineers . . . mathematicians . . . astronomers . . . did not come into being to confuse lay people. They are valid. They have been tested. They have been tried and found to be reliable. They have been developed by considerable empirical and other observations and experiments.

THINK! Why is it then that so many investors . . . so many professionals . . . so many analysts disdain and ignore many investment principles which, too, are born of empirical observations and use? The principles sprang into being from hard and difficult experiences.

These principles developed so that investors of today and of tomorrow could prosper and succeed. They are handed down to us as history lessons. They are articulated to prevent future generations of investors from suffering huge losses in the stock market.

Books are replete with stories of large fortunes lost by those who thought they were rich enough to make it in the stock market without due consideration of investment principles.

Let those who inhabit Wall Street go their way but you, the investor of today and of tomorrow, heed well the lessons learned through empirical observations. Heed well the lessons learned from history.

THEY ARE THE KEY TO YOUR FORTUNE!

Think of this metaphor. You have a cold so your family urges you to visit a doctor. The doctor gives you a prescription and tells you to take vitamin C.

When you arrive home you find that you have the vitamins in the house. Being somewhat lazy you take the vitamins and decide to fill the prescription the next day.

The following day you go about your business ignoring both the vitamins and the prescription. So ends the saga of the cold.

In a similar vein the investors, the financial writers, the otherwise astute stock market professionals all treat investment principles like so much vitamins and prescriptions. They don't use them! They are well versed in those principles. They acknowledge their importance. But they just don't seem to use them.

Don't you ignore them! If you were the patient with a cold in the doctor's office, your condition wasn't serious. Here in the stock market it's a life and death struggle. Would you ignore your doctor if you were in a life and death struggle?

T H I N K ! Now I'll illustrate how investment principles are born!

It Started in 1946!

I first became acquainted with Wall Street while I was working on a battleship in the Brooklyn Navy Yard in January, 1946. I was in charge of a group of men who were repairing equipment that controlled the gunfire of the ship's guns.

We had just finished and still had some time before our day ended. One of the men placed a magazine in front of me and pointed to a story about a new car that was soon to be introduced. It was the Kaiser-Frazer auto. He asked "What do you think about the idea of buying the stock?"

Well I knew nothing about the stock market. I had exactly $2000 in savings. I read the article and found it impressive. I decided I would discuss it with my wife later that evening.

She had no experience in investing but had no objection to my decision to invest our $2000.

Remembering from reading the New York Times that somewhere in it is a business section, I looked through the advertisements for help in how to proceed. I found that Francis I. DuPont had an office, if I recall, at 26 Court Street, Brooklyn, N. Y. I think the stock market was open on Saturdays from 10 to 12 . . . or was it 9 to 12?

It was the middle of January on a Saturday that I went on my quest with my $2000, my life savings, to buy a stock I knew nothing about. What was my motive? I don't know. I never thought about it. I'll never forget how scared and timid I was. I didn't know how to buy a stock. I just thought I would invest my entire life savings in Kaiser-Frazer stock. Foolish? Of Course!

I was awed when I first entered the lobby of the office building to visit the DuPont office. As I recall the floor was all marble. The lobby was vast with a ceiling so high that it appeared that an airplane would have no trouble being displayed there.

Off to the right was a swirling marble staircase leading up to the first floor. There was a small sign in gold on the marble wall half way up the stairs that read, Francis I. DuPont. Under the name was a golden arrow pointing up the stairs.

As I looked towards the top of the stairway, I saw many lines of people just standing there and talking. The staircase was very wide. It could accommodate many more lines. But it was a large crowd. I couldn't see where the lines ended because there was an open door at the top with people crowding the entrance.

Shyly, slowly, I took my courage in my hands and started walking up the stairs. As I stood on the threshold of the open door peering into a large room, I stopped in amazement.

All you could see was people and more people. All about me people were smoking. The room was so blue with swirling rings of smoke that it was hard to see a ticker tape that was chattering out prices of stocks.

The tape would stop for a second and then seem to jump into life. It would then rapidly clatter along again. Everyone was talking. Some people gesticulated towards the tape.

There were desks around the perimeter of the room and around each desk were groups of people. In the middle of the room, chairs were lined up in rows. Every chair was occupied. This scene you don't see anymore. Yes! It was a beauty of a bull market. Everybody was making money!

I finally tore my eyes away from the moving tape and from the excited crowd and entered the room. To my left and against a wall was a wired partition behind which many people were busy working. It was the cashier's office and the order room.

"Boy," I said to myself, "This is for me!" A world existed which I had never heard of or seen or imagined. Where had I been all these years?

In a low voice I asked a man (all I saw were men) how to go about buying stock. Such innocence! Such naivete! He guided me to the office manager who in turn sent me to a customer's man. The latter asked me to wait until the market closed.

After the market closed he heard my story and said, "Young man take my advice. Save your money. Forget about the stock. You'll lose your money!"

But I had fallen in love with what I saw!

I HAD FALLEN IN LOVE WITH THE STOCK MARKET!!!

I questioned his reasoning. He said "If you insist, it is your mistake. However there are many other stocks that are preferable. Why don't you go through those books on that table and see what you can find?"

In the far corner of the boardroom was a table with large volumes. They were Standard & Poor's books containing the history of the companies whose stocks are public.

On that simple but eloquent word, preferable, I based my strategy for investing. I went to those books that Saturday and the ensuing Saturday. No I didn't buy Kaiser-Frazer but I made the decision to buy National Power and Light, a utility.

I selected that stock simply because it had the narrowest range for the year and so I thought my risk would be minimum. (What a way to invest one's life savings!)

For the next two Saturdays I went to the broker's office and watched the ticker tape. It fascinated me! I did spend most of my time at the table with the books. From my first visit to the broker my only thoughts were of the stock market. I wondered how one makes money by investing? I wondered just what it was all about?

What was the magic to succeed in this business? What secrets did it hold? I had never heard of fundamental analysis. I had never heard of technical analysis. I'd never heard of charts. All I knew about Wall Street was to go to "that table and find something that was preferable to what I had first had in mind." I soon got to know what was in Standard & Poor's.

About the middle of February, after a few sessions at the "table", I learned that I wasn't going to get rich holding my utility while the market was active elsewhere. It seemed to me that the aircraft industry was the thing of the future. Those stocks were active so I decided to study those which were listed on the NYSE.

I believe there was Douglas Aircraft, McDonald Aircraft, Consolidated Vultee, Beech Aircraft and others. It is interesting to think that Consolidated Vultee traded as F then and today F represents a trade in Ford Motor.

I researched those aircraft manufacturers and then conceived the SECOND KEY TO SUCCESS in investing. I dreamed up the idea of going to an art supply store and purchasing large 17 × 22 sheets of drawing paper. I also bought as many different colored crayons as were available. I assigned one color to each of the stocks I had under study.

Every night I charted the trading movements of those stocks. After a few days I bought the one that lagged the others. The first one was Beech Aircraft. To raise capital I sold National Power and Light at a small loss. I learned the lesson that it pays to take small losses . . . a lesson well learned!

In a few days Beech went up and caught up with the others on my chart. I sold it and bought Consolidated Vultee. In a few days that appreciated in price.

You see I was learning from empirical experience.

I was developing investment principles and investment theory and practice from actually doing it! That is the point I was making before I started relating this personal experience.

What might have happened if I had held my utility stock for the long pull? What might have happened if I'd held my utility for the dividend?

THINK! I DID!

Don't hesitate to take small losses! They won't hurt you!! They keep your mind alert to the dangers inherent in this business of investing!!

There are other successful investors who have preceded me and who have left their findings to you to use. Please don't throw those findings away as though they were the doctor's vitamins and prescription we discussed earlier. Those findings of yesteryear are the. . . .

INVESTMENT PRINCIPLES . . . OF TODAY!

It was in March that I met a schoolteacher from Boys' High School in the broker's office. I told him of my limited experience and how I was charting with crayons and drawing paper. He said, "Here are some books on investing. I've studied them for years. They don't help me. Perhaps they will help you."

Three books were discarded. The fourth is a classic! It was published in 1930. It has many charts and introduced me to technical analysis. Most of what I know today I learned from that one book.

To me Wall Street hasn't changed from the time that book was written in 1930 to today. The reason that investors and Wall Street professionals lose so much money is because they are caught up in gimmicks and slogans. They "think" they've made new discoveries so they throw their doctor's pills away.

The only thing new that bothers me is program trading and futures as well as insurance trading. There is too much power in too few hands. The market is being manipulated. Stocks are no longer the investment medium they were supposed to be and they no longer lend themselves to study and analysis. Not while markets are high and subject to these few powerful people are they "safe"!

The war being over, the Navy Yard dispensed with my services in March. Instead of looking for work I went to the broker every day and charted stocks after dinner until 6 A.M. I bought books containing the daily trading of the Dow Jones industrial average going back to 1927. I plotted a chart of that average from then to 1946. It took weeks.

I studied those ups and downs intently as I charted. I reviewed and memorized sections of unusual movements. It was fascinating to see the years they occurred and the frequency with which they happened.

I noted and learned about trends and break outs and gaps and closing prices. Do you think that you can give me a flippant, “Yes, I know that the stock market goes up and down.”

My very dear reader “you don’t know nuttin” about ups and downs unless you sit for weeks, days and nights, and chart the averages covering years of ups and downs . . . up the bull market, down the bear market . . . the ups and downs within the ups and downs . . . the false moves . . . the major trends . . . the secondary trends . . . the in between trends.

That’s why I repeat and repeat that the market goes up and down. That’s where I learned that the secret to making money in the stock market is to buy stocks to sell. That’s where I learned that if you hold stocks long enough, you *WILL take them down as sure as you are born!!*

Yes! Buy stocks for the long pull. You will take them up. You will also take them down. Almost always will you take them down faster than you took them up!

By the summer of 1946 I had six month’s experience in buying and selling stocks. By then I was one of a group of a half dozen investors who sat and talked together. The leader was a wealthy investor who described October 29, 1929 to me several times. He sat and watched the ticker tape long past the market close that fateful day.

He did a thorough fundamental analysis. He knew many of the presidents of the companies whose stocks he owned. He was a very experienced investor.

The stock market had been weak all summer and sometime in September our group was sitting together when this investor said that he would give $100 to anyone who would tell him what to do in the stock market.

I stood up and said, “I’ll take the $100. The bull market is over. Sell!!”

Everyone laughed. What did I know with only six months’ experience? I didn’t predict the crash that followed. I avoided it. I sold out before it happened. The weeks and months studying the working parts of the stock market had paid off!

Yes 1946 was a learning year for me. I learned the THREE KEYS TO SUCCESS! I learned the working parts of the stock market which is the technical part and the SECOND KEY. It taught me the importance of trends and volume.

And I learned to cut losses. I learned to take losses. There were other principles of investment which I learned. This is the THIRD KEY.

I learned to understand the stock market. What it does. I learned that it always goes up but sure as heck, it doesn't take long to fall down. That's the FIRST KEY.

My First Investment Principle!

1. CONTROL YOUR EMOTIONS! . . . FEAR . . . PATIENCE . . . GREED . . .

We all have fear. I don't see how anyone who understands the stock market can invest without fear. To succeed you must learn to control it. Fear should not play a part in the decision making process.

Patience proves more troublesome. You must have patience with your mistakes. You must come to grips with the knowledge that you are human and since investment decisions are calculated guesses, you may "guess" wrong many times. So why lose patience for being human?

Again you need lots of patience to sit with a stock. It may take months or a few years for a stock to establish its value. Usually it should take only a few months. But don't use patience as a crutch for sitting on a stock and letting capital rot away.

The Emotion . . . Greed . . .

GREED IS A CRUEL TASKMASTER. It rates a headline all by itself. If I had to select the one investment principle that will bring you to your knees, it is . . . *GREED!!*

Why won't investors sell at excellent profits? GREED. Why won't investors take small losses? GREED. Why won't investors sell out when the market drops? GREED. Why will taxes prevent investors from selling at a profit when they should? GREED.

Investors are so caught up in the immediate dollars that they fail to control that most human of emotions, GREED. You may have $2000 or $200,000 but to take a loss of $200 or $1000 is anathema to investors.

They lose sight of the goal of investing. They lose sight of the investment principles of investing. They grit their teeth and say, "NEVER WILL I SELL!" as they surely plunge into the abyss!

Frankly I don't know who gives a care. I'm counting my money all the way to the bank!

I found it difficult to sell stocks in 1984 and take capital gains of $234,723. The bull market was only some two years old and still full of life. I had started 1982 with $127,320. In 1984 interest and dividends were $39,739. I just loved my portfolio.

My stocks, however, were no longer undervalued in relation to the stock market. I learned from the legacy left me by those who travailed in the stock market before me that if you don't take profits when you should . . . deja vu . . . you will take them down and wind up with paper and regrets. Oh yes . . . and excuses too.

It repeats and repeats and repeats. I didn't make it that way. I found it that way. How findeth you?

Back to October, 1987

When we entered October, 1987 I had two stocks and both had losses. The market plunged one day then another day and still another day. Did I find it easy to sell at a loss? My clients, too, had losses in those issues.

Do you think for a moment that I simply said sell? Don't you think I tried to convince myself that after the blow up I would recoup my losses?

GREED. Pure and simple. I just didn't want to take any losses. Well who does?? But in a time of crisis I always let common sense overrule reason and logic. Common sense overruled Greed. Just plain common sense born of investment principles said, "Run. Don't look back!"

I RAN!!!

My Second Investment Principle

2. CUT YOUR LOSSES!!

I learned this investment principle from others. This investment principle is mentioned in every book on investing. Fail this principle and you are dead. No matter how much you know or what else you know, if you falter on these two principles, I'll pass you on the way to the bank every time.

If GREED is number one on the killer's list, then CUTTING YOUR LOSSES is number two!

Let me emphasize it this way. If you can't LEARN to get past these two first principles, don't ever go near the stock market!!

If you can't overcome being afraid that if you sell, you are going to miss something . . . DON'T EVER BUY STOCKS! The whole premise of this book is that you have average or better intelligence . . . that you are willing to think within reason . . . that you are intelligent enough to know that you will be wrong frequently. Therefore it's imperative that when you think that you may be going wrong, CUT YOUR LOSSES!!

Therefore I expect you to make many decisions and take many small losses. Since you are going to make many decisions, SOME HAVE TO BE RIGHT. They can't all be wrong. Since most of your capital is still intact when you are right, you are really going to accumulate that MR. RIGHT and then you are going to TAKE PROFITS on MR. RIGHT and meet me in the bank.

The interesting thing about making many decisions is that many of them will be right. Soon you will learn to have confidence in yourself. Therefore when you have a profit you won't be so reluctant to sell knowing that you have the ability to find something better to replace what you sold.

Again having the confidence to always find an investment that will be profitable, you won't want to be wasting your capital on utilities because of the dividend.

Finally you will find that you won't hesitate to sell off stocks and take small losses because you will be anxious to have the capital available to seek out stocks where you can double your money.

I can't let this point go by. You'll throw out all your crutches. You will be a free person. An investor!

My Third Investment Principle

3. DON'T FIGHT THE TAPE!

This is another major principle I learned from my predecessors. I really should rank it with the first two in importance. It really should appeal to investors if they stopped to think about it.

What it means is that you shouldn't persist in your belief or in your conviction as to the direction your stock or the stock market is going to take.

For example assuming you bought a stock at 40. The stock starts to decline. As the stock declines you keep buying. The stock declines further and you buy some more. Three years later the stock is still down and you still have it. You just won't give up the idea that you have a good stock.

Another example. . . . The stock market rallied and then declined. You buy stock. The market declines still further. You buy again. If the tape, which records the trading that takes place in the stock market, is going down, DON'T FIGHT THE TAPE.

If your stocks aren't going in the same direction as that of the TAPE, at least don't buy more.

Again I recognize that there are many times when it is proper to buy on sell offs etc. but you have to *THINK* using the FIRST, SECOND and THIRD KEYS to know when *NOT TO FIGHT THE TAPE!*

Basically this principle alerts you that you will be severely punished should you persist in investing either against a trend that has been established or one that is gaining momentum.

This principle is one of the first alerts that will help you to avoid stock market crashes. In October, 1987 I wasn't expecting a crash. In fact I bought one stock in early October. Obviously if I bought a stock, I expected that it would go up.

But when the market started to decline as many days as it did, I decided that I WASN'T GOING TO FIGHT THE TAPE. I reversed myself and took a loss on that recent purchase as well as small losses on the rest of what I was invested in. That principle of not fighting the tape made me take another look at other factors that made me decide that the market was headed for a huge plunge.

Investment Principle!!

4. DON'T EVER MARRY OR FALL IN LOVE WITH STOCKS!!

I am listing this principle at this time because it helps make decisions involving the prior principles. It is imperative to remember that you are buying stocks to sell at a profit. Frequently when the profit does avail itself, many investors are so pleased with the performance of the stock price that they just can't put the sell orders through.

It is easy to get greedy and stay married to these stocks. This principle stood me in good stead when it was time to take profits in 1984. It's human to love something that you do well with.

Knowing this principle and repeating it to yourself will help you overcome the emotional part of investing when the need for it arises. When your stocks are on target, sell. Don't marry them.

Another situation that will arise is when you have a stock in a falling market. You may have a small loss but you really do like the fundamentals of the company. It is difficult to sell because it's a "good" stock. You "like" it so you'll hold it for the long term.

Caveat Emptor!!

Buyer Beware!!

5

A Continuing List of Investment Principles

Investment Principle 5

5. NEVER GET LOCKED IN!

Closely allied with 2. CUT YOUR LOSSES is this fifth principle. If you cut your losses, you won't get locked in. Therefore during the times when you are in such situations where your losses do get a little bigger than you had expected and you are undecided as to the course of action to pursue, this principle will force you to sell!!

I pointed out the difference between investing and collecting. Investing leaves you with a reserve to take advantage of opportunities when they present themselves.

Investing keeps you liquid and alert. If you are locked in, you become a long term paper holder. If all your capital and resources are tied up in long term stocks, you may as well take up knitting or some other interesting hobby while you wait years to get back to investing.

To avoid not getting locked in you are forced to cut your losses. Here again you have a choice between reason and common sense. It's "reason" that got you into the situation in the first place. "Reason" may dictate hold or buy but your "common sense" must take charge. "Common sense" will never permit you to violate investment principles.

NEVER . . . NEVER . . . NEVER!

Investment Principle 6

6. NEVER LET A LOSS BECOME A DISASTER!

Working closely with previous expressed principles is this principle. This is an investment principle of last resort. Assume you have one or more investments that pull back to within a permissible parameter. You aren't alarmed.

However the investment trends lower to the point where you are thinking of cutting your loss. You aren't sure. It looks as though the stock may turn up. However it goes lower. Your common sense says, "Hey, cut your loss or you may get locked in." The stock goes lower.

Now your common sense screams, "NEVER LET A LOSS BECOME A DISASTER!! . . . NEVER . . . NEVER . . . NEVER!!!" If you fail to interpret indicators pointing to a Crash and you are caught in one, then by all means you will be saved by calling on this principle. Sell as soon as the Crash starts. Don't get GREEDY and wait a second to try to salvage some of the loss.

Just don't ever let a loss become a disaster!!

Investment Principle 7

7. NEVER WAIT FOR A RALLY TO RECOUP SOME OF YOUR LOSS OR PROFIT!

I've told you a great deal about the stock market. There are answers I still have not given to you and which I know that you have been impatient to hear. I'll get to them. Here is one answer now.

If you fail to see the market crash coming and you get caught in it, is that the end? No! If you are involved in a big loss, the previous principle (6) will take you out. If you are involved with a small loss or if the market is cutting into your profits, then this principle will help you.

If deep down inside you, you know that you made a

mistake and should have sold sooner, then don't wait for the market to rally. Never wait for a rally to recoup some of your loss or profit.

Investment Principle 8

8. DON'TS: DON'T BE STUBBORN . . . DON'T GET EVEN . . . DON'T PROVE ANYTHING!

Investors will use anything for a crutch to excuse their losses and mistakes. I was in a broker's office in 1946. I had told some investors that the bull market was over and advised them to sell out.

After the market closed an investor approached and asked me if I would sit with him and discuss the market. I acquiesced. He told me that he had 1000 shares of a stock that was selling at $20 per share and wondered what he should do.

I quietly told him to sell. I suggested that the stock could fall to $10. I was familiar with the issue as I had studied it recently. To my utter amazement he vindictively snarled at me, "I'm a doctor and I can afford to carry it down to $10. If it drops to 10, I will buy another 1000 shares. Now what do you think of that?"

Evidently I had upset him. I replied," I'm glad that you can afford the loss. However, consider this. If I owned 1000 shares, I would sell them at 20. That would give me $20,000. When it got to 10, I would buy 2000 shares at $10 plus the 1000 shares at 10 that you say you will add at that time.

When it got back to 20, *you* would have $40,000 less the interest that money could have earned." I would be worth $60,000 plus the interest on the $20,000 that I had in the bank while waiting for the stock to drop to 10!! Who would be better off?

What was it that investor was trying to prove . . . and to whom? I saw him for several weeks but as the market sank lower and lower . . . as it sank all the way into 1949 . . . I never saw him again.

Don't be stubborn in your decisions!

We all make mistakes. But you don't have to magnify them! Don't punish yourself for being a nice and decent human being. Every human making investment decisions makes loads of mistakes!! So you didn't see the crash coming. But then use your *THINKING* . . . use your *COMMON SENSE* . . . Acknowledge it!!

It's here! That's a fact! Don't use the crutches handed out by Wall Street. "Hold for the long term!" They want you to just hang in there. You'll hang all right!

You have a choice either to sell and go to sleep with the money that you still have and investment principles to console and restore your prosperity, or just hold your stocks and go to sleep worrying how much more money you may lose the next day and the next day.

If you sold and were wrong, you will still sleep night after night. If you didn't sell and you were wrong, you'll not sleep night after night.

If you were prudent and sold and stocks went higher, you have the capital to reenter the market . . . not with stock perhaps, but with a brand new choice of many others.

On the other hand if you lost money and became locked in . . . good bye . . . give this book to someone who still has capital left.

Investment Principle 9

9. BUY A RISING MARKET . . . NOT A FALLING STAR!!

When the stock market crashes it makes the front pages and all the nightly news reports. It doesn't take long before a barrage of experts are placating a stunned world that everything is just fine.

The President of the United States, to assuage an

alarmed populace, will face cameras and state that in his opinion the stock market will recover . . . or it will soon go up . . . or words to that effect. I would say that, too, if I were the President. That is his job.

But you and I are not the President. Our job is different. Our objective is different. We can't afford the luxury of words. We know that the market has fallen and will probably continue to decline.

Because the President said the market is okay should not be a signal to us to buy stocks that have just plunged. He is not giving us advice. He is assuring us that he is aware of what is happening and will look into it at once. Many investors will buy these beaten down stocks. They may be well known companies and highly regarded. They may be in many portfolios.

THEY WERE STARS that may have brought handsome profits to multitudes. But we must realize that sometimes big and well known companies can't cut it anymore. Many never recover their former prominence.

How long was the stock at ATT depressed after reaching its zenith? Buying stocks in a falling market is known as "bottom fishing". You are simply guessing where the bottom may be.

There is a time when investors may bottom fish but not in falling markets. When we get to the chapter on how, what and when to buy stocks, I will explain how it should be done. Among the many factors that go into the buy decision, you'll never find: "buy because a stock is well known and falling in price."

I never buy a falling star. I buy a stock that is on the rise!!

A buying program that is started and expected to last several years should be undertaken in the first and second stages of the market cycle. It should not be started in the third stage, the distribution stage, or in the fourth stage when the market is falling.

Investment Principle 10

10. DON'T LEAD THE MARKET . . . FOLLOW IT!!

I smile when people compliment me on predicting the changes in stock prices over these many years. I smile to myself because I know that it's not true. That's my "secret". I don't predict the stock market! I simply follow it.

I don't fight it! I don't argue with it! I don't get even with it!

I'm a good little boy. I obediently follow it. If the market wants to fall down, who am I to stop it? I get out of the way. If the market goes up, I latch onto its coattail. I tell my clients that I can't make the market go up. I have to wait until it does. Therefore my clients have to use principle (1) which is Control Your Emotions . . . in this case, patience.

While waiting for a bull market we try for profits but settle for small ones. We have to have patience for the big profits of a bull market.

THINK!! Doesn't the market have a cycle? Doesn't it move up during that cycle? Doesn't that part usually last for years? The last bull market lasted for five years. Can't we make enough money if we got into stocks in 1983 instead of 1982?

Therefore we can make money without being clairvoyant. We have to know the market. We have to know our technical indicators. We have to know our investment principles. Then if we USE them, WE KNOW OUR BUSINESS. IF WE DON'T USE THEM, WE DON'T KNOW OUR BUSINESS!!!!

Investment Principle 11

11. NEVER LOSE A NIGHT'S SLEEP!

This was another principle that I learned. I found in

my many years of experience that when I overinvested I would lose sleep.

There were times when I bought stocks under pressure and before I could think it through to my satisfaction. They led to sleepless nights and stock losses.

Frequently stocks were in a declining trend and I delayed making decisions while losses were adding up. Those sleepless nights alerted me to the fact that I was violating investment principles.

So I learned over the years that the successful way to make money in Wall Street was to avoid sleepless nights. Avoid sleepless nights and you'll avoid getting emotional. Keep your emotions out of the business of investing and you will be half way home!

Investment Principle 12

12. I'D RATHER BE PRUDENT THAN RIGHT!

I don't know if this isn't my favorite investment principle! I drew on this so many, many times during the countless times that I was faced with indecisions.

I didn't learn it from others. I added it to those I did learn and read about. I call it "My Best Friend!" When I had to make decisions to cut losses and I wasn't sure it was time . . . I'd Rather Be Prudent Than Right . . . was my support! I sold!

When it was time to sell at huge profits, and I would be reluctant to do so . . . I'd rather be prudent-than-right made it easier to follow through.

During the many stock market crashes that I avoided, I would see the mounting evidence of impending disaster pile up . . . I would see the skies darkening and slowly approaching . . . I would see dark clouds gather speed and grow larger. I would wonder, "Is this the time?"

I'm never sure when to sell! I'm always reluctant to call the broker for the sell side. When I do place the order it is always with regrets. How strange! Do you feel the same way?

We both have the ability to think but I have trained myself. I have prepared my mind for just such decisions. I have trained my mind that at times I will have to make split second decisions! I have made many mistakes. But the key decisions . . . the "prudent" decisions . . . I never missed!

When I saw the ominous signs in October, 1987, it was child's play for me to avoid that crash and keep my big profit made in the bull market. I told my clients when I said, "Sell", that "I might be wrong but I'd rather be prudent than right!"

I wanted no regrets about losing tremendous percentage gains that I had made in that five year bull market. I wasn't going to take stocks up and down. I didn't want to play anymore. When I want to play again, the stock market will be there.

Over the years I have found this principle so very comforting. Even when I sold too early, I slept well. Even when my sold-out stocks sold higher, I laughed at myself. Yes, I didn't sell out at the top that time but I chortled all the way to the bank.

This investment principle appeals to common sense more than to reason. Consequently this principle, too, may be considered as a safety valve.

THINK! If you never suffer a tremendous loss in the stock market, how can you ever lack capital to get rich? You talk about investing for the long term. Rather than hold stocks for the long term, why not hold CAPITAL for the long term?

THINK! No matter how many mistakes you make, you will eventually come up with a "beauty". That "beauty" will put you onto the track of other "beauties" which will eventually give you "WALL STREET RICHES"!

That's how I did it!
That's how you can do it!

Investment Principle 13

13. TURN YOUR PORTFOLIO OVER . . . JUST LIKE A NEW LAWN!

There are still many investment principles but I'm making this the last one on this list. Let's call it a good baker's dozen. I do want to leave some over so you can have the joy of discovery.

There are times . . . and it has happened countless times when whatever you do is wrong. You take small loss after small loss until you get tired of it. You get annoyed . . . impatient. You can't seem to do anything right. Stocks that you reject go up and those you buy go down.

For these situations I developed the practice of selling everything so that I was back in an all cash position. This practice led me to develop the principle, "TURN YOUR PORTFOLIO OVER . . . JUST LIKE A NEW LAWN."

Just get out and make a fresh start!

Once you get into the habit of taking profits and of not getting attached to any particular stock . . . *without* exceptions . . . you will soon learn that a fresh start will put you into a constructive frame of mind for the business of investing.

You will have no obligations to old friends and stocks. You will have no hindrances. You will know the exact total of your capital. It will be a new ball game. The world, the stock market, will be before you.

You will pick the time. You will choose the stock out of thousands of listed stocks. (I buy only listed issues.)

Start afresh! It's an exhilarating feeling! It's uplifting! It's wonderful! It's a breath of clean, fresh air. Just you and the stock market. Nobody in between !!!

Another time that you should turn your portfolio over is during a bull market after prices have been climbing for a while.

Your technical and fundamental indicators may have alerted you that it was time to take your profits. After taking profits, you try to buy some laggards. As time and the bull market rolls along, you find that you are not making any money. In fact you find that you are losing some of your bull market profits.

In such cases again TURN YOUR PORTFOLIO OVER . . . Just like a new lawn! Make a fresh start!

And thus ends the list of investment principles. THINK! This list of thirteen principles is the THIRD KEY TO WALL STREET RICHES!!! The timely application of this THIRD KEY will determine whether you will be a successful investor. So with this admonition I entrust it into your hands. The THIRD KEY reads, *APPLY A FEW BASIC PRINCIPLES!*

We have just completed a course, "How To Succeed In Investing". We have not discussed how to use what we have learned. The THREE KEYS may be awkward in your hands at first. As you pass through the portals of Wall Street leading to the doors which you must unlock, you may fumble many times while attempting to fit the keys into the locks.

It takes a little thought . . . a little experience . . . a little testing.

To help you get familiar with the keys, read my market letters which tested me and see whether you have developed a new slant . . . a new way of looking at Wall Street. See if you don't feel that you have a good grasp of the stock market and whether this time you have a good chance of investing successfully. After these letters I will tell you what to buy, when to buy and when to sell. Now aren't these the answers that you were seeking on page 1?

If I had told you the answers on page 1, you would

never succeed in applying them because in the final analysis it's your own thinking that will determine your success. I'm only giving you the subject matter. I'm giving you the artist's material. I'm only telling you what to think about! I'm only preparing you for what's ahead!

I am pedantic both in my writing and in my teaching because I know that you are going to violate what I say at the very first opportunity. That is only natural. Thus when you do, by being pedantic, I hope to have impressed you enough to get you back to the ART OF INVESTING.

When you return you will really have to think of the "prudent" decision if not necessarily the "right" decision. If you keep THINKING REASON AND COMMON SENSE, then I do believe that you will succeed!!

The following two market letters were written during the market crash of October, 1978.

* * *

THE K FACTOR — OCTOBER 21, 1978

What The Hell Happened On Wall Street This Week???

One of the ugliest chapters in its history was made last week when the Dow Jones Industrial Average viciously plunged $59.09, the biggest single weekly decline in its history!!!

AND YOU AND I WERE CAUGHT RIGHT SMACK IN THE MIDDLE OF IT! we were heavily invested. Tuesday night, Wednesday night and Thursday night I had practically no sleep . . . especially Wednesday night. That night it was 3:45 AM when I turned my bedroom light off only to awaken with a start and in a sweat at 4:15 AM . . . a scant one and one half hours later.

I had the heavy responsibility not only for my own pension and retirement money but also that of many clients. Other peoples' pension funds, retirement funds, savings!

Yesterday, Friday, October 20th, Wall Street opened for trading as usual at ten o'clock. By 11:30 I felt as though I hadn't slept for weeks and that I had been at my desk and on the telephone making decisions for a whole year!

Making investment decisions that week was like going through a burning fire. Many, many decisions had to be made unexpectedly, quickly and decisively! And through it all one is never sure that one is making a right decision.

Hundreds of thousands of dollars were involved. The decision whether to take losses had to be made. Profits to be taken had to be considered. Taxes were ignored and commission expenses were considered. The needs and objectives of clients flash through the mind. It was a lot of pressure!

But Friday night I slept like a new born infant. My clients and I were home safe. Our investment capital was secure. I sold and I sold. We still held stocks but we had more cash than stocks and when I fell asleep I didn't care if Wall Street sank.

Yes, that night I had the first peaceful sleep of the most disastrous week in Wall Street history!!

MY MONEY WAS SAFE!
YOUR MONEY WAS SAFE!

Dear Client,

I was in the midst of preparing nine month reports when the market dropped so precipitously. Some of you already have received your reports. Other reports are on my desk to be mailed. Other reports I haven't started.

The reports that I have completed all record new record highs but in the light of this sudden and devastating stock market break, the next quarter will undoubtedly reflect declines. Therefore don't be overly enthusiastic about the nine month report.

On the other hand don't be negative about the market break because I always welcome these as new opportunities for making record highs in my net worth. I went through many a vicious break in Wall Street since 1946 and my net worth attained a record high during this past quarter.

So bring on your market breaks and bring on your new challenges. I gladly accept them. I don't predict the market so I don't know what will happen next week. I dread the worst but I hope for the best. But either way I seem to have an uncanny knack of rolling with the market on its roller coaster over the years.

Although I have a very successful past, it does not guarantee that I will be successful in the future. . . .

BUT I'M BETTING MY MONEY THAT I WILL!

Stay cool!

* * *

Notice the different investment principles that letter brings to mind.

It's the single biggest decline in stock market history! Note "Don't lose a night's sleep". So I sold! Note that you never know if it's the right thing to sell! Note that it's best to be "prudent than right." Note that it's important not to suffer large losses. I still made money that year in spite of the historic break!

Note how I welcome breaks as my cash *DOUBLES IN VALUE AS STOCK PRICES LOSE HALF THEIR VALUE!!!*

This was 1978 . . . Ten years later I was far richer and note how history repeated itself. In 1987 I avoided the *NEW HISTORIC CRASH AND AGAIN MY CASH IS DOUBLING IN VALUE AS STOCK PRICES LOSE HALF THEIR VALUE!!!*

I finished the letter by saying that I don't guarantee the future but I'm betting my money that I will prosper . . . And so I did! And I believe I always will! Then. . . .

One week later I wrote a follow up letter. It's a classic! It expresses my deepest fundamental approach to the stock market. Since you have the THREE KEYS in your hands, you should now really appreciate the importance and the timeliness of what I wrote! The letter follows:

* * *

THE K FACTOR OCTOBER 28, 1978 (ONE WEEK LATER)

This Is What Is Happening On Wall Street!

The devastating and historic $59 plunge in the Wall Street Dow Industrial Average that prompted me to write to you last week has been followed by another straight drop of $32 . . . Total for two weeks . . . $91 STRAIGHT DOWN!!!

Abruptly it caused me to switch from a fully invested portfolio to almost complete liquidation! *Why Did Wall Street Plunge?*

Since the volume of trading these last two

weeks has not been that unusual it makes me believe that it wasn't SELLING that caused the market break but *something far more significant*. It was the *lack of buying* that caused the market break and that's what worries me.

I sold because technical analysis indicated that the supply of stocks was overcoming the demand . . . because I lost the last shred of confidence that rising interest rates were proving effectual at this level against inflation . . . that it would take much higher interest rates to dent inflation . . . that no one seemed to know how high interest rates might go . . . that the President at this time would be unable to cope with it!

Apparently my reason for selling may have been the reason that others decided not to buy. Now had the decline been caused by selling, then the technical assumption is that after the "selling dries up" as we say on Wall Street, that it would be followed by a strong upward move which might ultimately lead to a resumption of higher stock prices in 1979 etc.

But the lack of buying indicates technically that stocks may have peaked . . . because should selling volume develop, then all hell could break loose. If there are no buyers and if suddenly an unprecedented volume of selling appears, I shudder to think what might happen on Wall Street, a replay of the infamous . . . (better unsaid).

Consequently, not being able at this time to predict or even reasonably being able to anticipate what may occur in Wall Street, I very prudently decided that we should all take our losses and regroup and get the hell out of stocks . . . way out! (We still have some).

How To Succeed In Wall Street!

The *GREATEST* principle of them all is *NEVER, EVER* permit your *CONTRIBUTED INVESTMENT CAPITAL* to be shattered!!

That means that when you face a crisis that threatens your capital which you put out to risk, you resolve it by throwing out all the books, all the rules, all the newspaper promises of a greater tomorrow and SELL! If you do, you'll always have a second and a third and a fourth and another chance . . . many, many other opportunities to achieve success in investing.

STATISTICS PROVES WHAT HAPPENS IF YOU DON'T!

More Wall Street Theory!

Many, many years ago I coined a phrase,

"In a bad market . . . there is no such thing as a good stock".

Another phrase I coined;

"If a stock is holding up in a bad market, get out . . . because sooner or later they'll get to you too."

I have often said that to succeed in investing, it is imperative that you exercise and train your mind in Wall Street principles. I have given you the theory over the years; now you are going through the practice of it with me.

I have a great deal more to say but will hold it for a later date. I have to get back to work,

* * *

What do you think, colleague? Are we on the same wave length? Doesn't that letter simply repeat what I've said in all these pages?

If you compare the three letters that I wrote in November, 1987 which start on pages 5, 10, 12 of this book, you will note they are almost identical to the letters written in 1978 which you have just completed reading.

In fact if I changed 1978 to 1987 I could have mailed those letters with some slight changes. Note how the facts are almost identical . . . record highs . . . record drops . . . record volume! It's a repeat of history! . . . and history will repeat again with some changes.

My thinking hasn't changed in those two identical stages of the market cycle. I used the same approach . . . the same thinking . . . the same principles . . . the same technical facts . . . the same understanding of the stock market . . . the same profit motive.

THINK! HOW I'M ALWAYS STRESSING AVOIDING LARGE LOSSES!

THINK! HOW MOST INVESTMENT PRINCIPLES ARE TO PROTECT YOU FROM LARGE LOSSES!

6

The Stock Market Indicators

To understand Wall Street so that we can operate safely, calmly and intelligently in an environment that is often bewildering and at other times chaotic, we must learn to understand the stock market and what to expect from it.

We know some of its pertinent intricacies. We know of its movements and its technicalities. Wall Street is an auction market. Money is extremely liquid in that you can sell with a single telephone call. You're in . . . you're out . . . in again . . . out again . . . YOU'RE LIQUID!!

No! Investors don't usually operate that quickly. I don't. *But when you are liquid, it leaves you always in control of your capital!* It leaves you always in control of your "commitment" and that is a most valuable advantage . . . liquidity . . . control!

When you appreciate and operate control of your money . . . of your "commitment", then you are an investor . . . then you will be a successful investor.

To hold stocks for years and years and years is to lose control of a precious commodity . . . control over capital. With capital you call the shots . . . you call the time . . . you call the investment!

Wall Street will always be here. There are always

opportunities. There are many fresh, exciting and better chances to make large profits.

To be in the stock market . . . without capital . . . without reserves . . . without control . . . is to walk around crippled for the rest of your life!

Therefore even though you understand the stock market . . . even though you analyze and recognize the technical position of the market, you won't be successful unless you *APPLY* those basic investment principles outlined in the preceding chapter.

Investing in the stock market is sensitive to emotions. DON'T GIVE AN EMOTIONAL RESPONSE FOR WHAT SHOULD HAVE BEEN AN OBJECTIVE AND CONSIDERED DECISION!

The Emotion Fear

We are all afraid of the stock market. We are all afraid that we'll lose money. In spite of my many successes I approach the market with the utmost humility. I have a deep respect for its towering strength to destroy.

I am afraid of its false moves . . . its ability to incite people to murder . . . to suicide. I know of its voracious appetite for devouring investors' retirement funds . . . investors' savings. I know of its ability to incite people to gamble.

Fear? Yes. I have fear. Then how do you explain how I dared borrow ½ million dollars to buy stocks at the then top of the stock market? Here's the answer:

I feared! I was concerned! I considered!

But I know that *I UNDERSTAND WALL STREET!* I know what is going on! I know the rhythm . . . the cycle. I feel as a lion tamer probably does. He knows the lions. He knows the risks. He knows his job!

I know Wall Street. I know the risks. I know my job! TO THINK investing is to fear investing. But it will be a CONTROLLED fear . . . It'll be a realization that something can go wrong in your calculations . . . in your analysis . . . in your thinking . . . something beyond your control can develop.

War . . . assassination . . . interest change . . . some factor beyond your control or ability to foresee.

AND THAT'S WHY YOU MUST . . . YOU MUST . . . IMMEDIATELY RELY AND APPLY SOUND AND PROVEN INVESTMENT PRINCIPLES . . . not judgment . . . only principles . . . not crutches . . . only common sense!

Consequently with a controlled fear, you will be in control of your emotions and you will be able to function effectively in this highly emotional business.

An anecdote crosses my mind as I write about fear that vividly illustrates this emotion.

When my son was five years of age I knew that he was intelligent and would grow up to be the fine, bright and capable person that he is. He was at that age when we registered him for school.

The day arrived for him to start his first day and lo and behold George couldn't be found. He was hiding. He was afraid to go to school.

When we finally located him we asked why he didn't want to go to school. He replied, "I don't know anything." We had to explain that was why he was going to school. That is how I knew my son was intelligent. He had enough sense to stay away from anything that he didn't know.

Investors should stay away from the stock market if they don't know it . . . if they don't understand it. That is why it is so imperative that you do understand Wall Street thoroughly so you won't be afraid to act. To do so you must know your stock market indicators!

Interest Rates as a Stock Market Indicator

In the preceding chapter I noted the close comparison between the letters I had written right after the 1978 crash and those that I had written right after the 1987 crash. I called attention to the fact that it was a repetition of history and of the same technical and investment principles.

One of the stock market indicators that I used was the interest rate. If you refer to the letter written on October 28, 1978 (page 76) you will see that I mention interest rates and inflation as factors to be concerned with. I wrote "*I LOST THE LAST SHRED OF CONFIDENCE THAT RISING INTEREST RATES WERE PROVING EFFECTUAL AT THIS LEVEL AGAINST INFLATION . . .*

Refer to the letter written on November 21, 1987 (page 12) and there, too, you will find reference to the interest rate. In 1978 I wrote three letters on that crash. Two letters are in the preceding chapter. The third letter follows. Note in this third letter that I again refer to interest rates.

* * *

THE K FACTOR NOVEMBER 3, 1978

The "October Disaster of '78"

THE STOCK MARKET continues to boil and to froth in its wild gyrations. Two weeks ago it made history on the downside. This week just past, it made history on the upside by rising over $35 in a single day. I took that opportunity to sell off the last of the stocks which some clients and I still held. The next day the market dropped over $10!!

I make no pretense at being able to anticipate those rapid changes in direction of stock prices during this period. Consequently to have tried to liquidate on the "highs" would have been to gamble on losing substantially more. I don't gamble. I simply got out as best as I could and as fast as I was able to.

With treasury bills yielding about 8½% and treasury notes 9¼% . . . and trending higher . . . with the talk of the banks' rate going to 13% and 14% and 18% . . . I doubt the wisdom of holding stocks, any stock, in this market!

Change In Investment Policy!

With the abrupt decline in stock values, I suddenly reversed my investment policy and decided to enter the new phase of the investing cycle by liquidating all stocks and buying a money market instrument fund presently yielding 8.14%, and where there were sufficient funds, to start buying treasury bills, now yielding 8.45%.

This I have already done for clients. This starts the process of overcoming our losses and is the first step in the resumption of the excellent upward progress which we have made over the years and which was so severely interrupted by the "October Disaster of '78."

Don't get caught up emotionally in today's stock market debacle. As in life, investing has its ups and downs . . . its jubilation and despair . . . its highs and its lows. See it as I do . . . as a necessary cost for achieving success.

This by no means is the end of the stock market. This setback looms very ugly at the moment but it will fade into the background as we resume our progress. There will be many, many, many other future opportunities for substantial capital gains. As I wrote in 1974 when most despaired and I started to buy stocks . . . THIS IS WHAT I WROTE . . .

Open Your History Books!!

"While I recognize that the scene on Wall Street and economic uncertainties are literally ruining investors and money managers, I am confident of my interpretation of the investment picture which exists . . ."

". . . history will reveal that prudent and patient and thoughtful investors will prosper and flourish. Investments and investment opportunities will not die! . . ."

". . . So to your history books!! TAKE COURAGE AND LEARN FROM THEM!!"

History Lesson!!

"We learn from past stock market behavior that Wall Street never was a one-way street. Stocks go up as well as down! We have a bear market. We have a severe and precipitous decline since March of this year that is sheer breathtaking and murderous, but this can only develop investment opportunities!!!"

END OF 1974 LETTER

AND THEY SURE DID!!!!!

CONCLUSION TO TODAY'S LETTER!

Today we once again had a severe and precipitous decline that was sheer breathtaking and murderous . . . and this decline, too, can only lead to investment opportunities. Stay cool!!!

* * *

That was another good market letter that was prophetic. How right it was! It calls attention to the repetitiveness of the stock market and to the factors that move it up and down. It states that the stock market is history being repeated.

The letter written in 1978 has reference to similar circumstances in 1974 which in turn are almost identical to what happened in 1987!!!

Note the letter opens with "The stock market continues to boil and froth . . . Two weeks ago it made history on the *downside*. This week just past it made history on the *upside* . . ."

Isn't that just what happened in 1987??

Didn't the stock market crash in October, 1987 with record volume and a record drop in share prices?

Didn't stock prices rise for a daily record after the drop only to be followed by a bigger record day rise in stock prices?

MY, HOW HISTORY REPEATS ITSELF IN THE STOCK MARKET!

Read the letter carefully. It is very constructive and informative. Note how many different principles I adhered to. Again I speak about that stock market indicator: INTEREST RATES. In following interest rates watch the FEDERAL FUND Rate. It's the interest rate that one bank pays to another bank to borrow money overnight.

That rate is a key to the direction that interest rates will follow. In the late '70's when most of Wall Street was strongly recommending the purchase of stocks because inflation was on the upswing, it was the FEDERAL

FUND RATE that was the decisive factor that caused me to *THINK* and thus to *REASON* that stocks would go down and not up!!

Stocks just didn't figure to be a hedge against inflation. Not when the yield is fixed and slow to increase and inflation is rapidly on the rise. It figured that physical assets were good hedges . . . not stocks!

This is an excellent example of how *THINKING* proved vastly superior and correct to the erroneous Conventional Wall Street line that was being dispensed all about. At times THINKING about one factor will prevent disastrous losses!

I could go over that letter line by line and point out how it all conforms to my THREE KEYS TO WALL STREET RICHES! I recommend that you go over it line by line and see how much of the THREE KEYS you discern.

How to Use Interest Rates as an Indicator!

The rate of FEDERAL FUNDS does not have a direct relationship to stock prices. If the rate today was 7%, the Dow Jones Industrial Average (referred to as the DJIA or DJ) wouldn't necessarily have to be 1922.06.

The federal funds rate might be 7% one day and the DJ might be 1870.06. The federal funds rate might be 7% one day and the DJ might be 1200.89 or 2243.51.

There is not a direct relationship between the Federal Fund Rate and the stock market but there *is* a *correlation*! What we want to know is the federal fund rate in *COMPARISON* to the percentage rate of return that stocks and bonds are yielding . . . ALSO . . . The *TREND* of FEDERAL FUNDS!

When interest rates TREND UP, stocks TREND DOWN! Therefore, by closely monitoring interest rates, you have a key indicator to guide you. Usually there are many factors to consider in making buy and sell decisions. They don't all have the same weight all the time.

Consequently, interest rates at times will have little weight. Sometimes, as I illustrated previously, this may be the decisive and even sole factor to consider!

THAT'S WHY I REPEAT THAT YOU MUST DO THE THINKING!

The next indicator is VOLUME!

Volume as a Stock Market Indicator

Volume, because it is a working part of the stock market, has to be a major indicator of that market!

It is a TECHNICAL indicator!

Since Wall Street is divided into two camps: those who make investment decisions staunchly relying upon fundamental analysis and those relying upon technical analysis, it is critical at this time to realize the impact that TECHNICAL FACTORS HAVE UPON THE STOCK MARKET AND UPON STOCK PRICES! When we utilize and study and consider technical factors, we are engaging in TECHNICAL ANALYSIS!!

Technical analysts are professionals who use charts in their study of the dynamics of the stock market. They are ridiculed by those who tried it and failed or by those who were so mesmerized by lines and data that they failed to discover the nature of the beast.

I do respect critics' intelligence . . . their wealth . . . their prestige . . . their credentials . . . but to me they just don't understand the stock market.

Frequently there are disagreements among technical analysts on their interpretations of what course to pursue. The disagreements are not caused by the faults of technical analysis but by the faults of the interpreter. The technical factors haven't changed over the years. It's only the people who interpret them that come and go.

Watch the Volume of Trading!

Read the following market letter that I wrote very carefully. Pay particular attention to the conclusion. It consists of only a few lines. But what a few lines! They are so eloquent that they speak volumes on stock market trading!!

IN FACT THEY ARE STOCK MARKET TRADING!

They are the epitome of successful investing!

Take one minute after reading the letter to reflect upon those few lines and to think about the KNOWLEDGE . . . *IDEAS . . . CONFIDENCE* that was behind them!!!

Think how many times they saved me thousands and thousands of dollars.

REALIZE THEY WERE WRITTEN IN September, 1986, ONE YEAR BEFORE THE 1987 CRASH THAT I AVOIDED . . . WHICH SOME SAY I PREDICTED! This is the letter:

* * *

THE K FACTOR **SEPTEMBER 13, 1986**

How to Cope In A Plunging Market

"Buy What I Buy . . . Sell What I Sell . . . Cash In When I Cash In!"

I CASHED IN! During the period from May to August, I sold some $325,000 worth of common stock (some 68% of my stock investments including utilities). So when the market plunged a historic $86.61 on record volume of 237,000,000 shares to be followed the next day by a further decline of $34.17 again on record volume, 240,000,000 shares,

I SLEPT SOUNDLY BOTH NIGHTS . . . and that leaves me calm, cool and calculating. It also leaves me with a profit to date for 1986, a high annual income from stock profits and some $400,000 in buying power to use as investment opportunities develop . . . and they always do!

How To Succeed In The Stock Market!

1. Obey ALL the rules ALL the time! (I compiled a list of some twenty-five rules)

2. Know WHEN to play! (I usually do!)

Some of the rules which I obeyed during this period of selling were to cut my losses (I still have a profit to date for the year), overcome the emotions of fear and greed and to break off love affairs with winning stocks.

It was difficult to sell utilities in the face of rising prices and media hoopla and it was hard to give up my hope of making a million this year. Greed is a tough taskmaster.

Also it was difficult to break my love affair with utilities and Western Airlines and sell them. I also found it tough not to try to get even with losing stocks. But tough as it was, I obeyed ALL the rules as they developed.

When to Play? In my opinion this is not the time to "play the money game". In the best of times this is a very dangerous game to play. But today with many technical weaknesses developing and with today's confusing fundamental picture, I have to adopt a STRATEGY TO MEET THESE CHANGING SITUATIONS! So . . . I DON'T WANT TO PLAY . . . Maybe tomorrow . . . but not today!

Today I want to be an observer. I positioned my pension thusly: About ⅓ federal notes, ⅓ AAA municipal bonds, ⅓ in just one stock. (With some $15-20M in two other stocks).

What's Happening on Wall Street?

As a Wall Street technical analyst this is how I see things: We are in a bull market. We are in a trading range of some 220 points between 1720 and 1940. The bears have mounted tremendous pressure and have engaged the bulls in a battle that is now in a crisis stage.

The results of this critical struggle will determine whether we have left the top of this bull market behind us or whether there can be a tremendous break-out from this large trading range to 2500 etc. on the Dow.

If we have a decisive further decline, my technical interpretation would be that we have seen the top of this bull market. There would then be a very, very strong move up that would last from three weeks to six months. I would change my strategy from buying on weakness to holding on weakness. I would look to liquidate every single stock (almost) on the rally. I would start selling early into the rally and continue all the way up. In the past I always wound up in 100% cash.

If the market holds and moves up, there should be several months of backing and filling in the 220 point trading range. After this I would expect a struggle to develop between the bulls and the bears for a break-out above the trading range.

THAT'S THE TECHNICAL PICTURE AS I SEE IT!

Now The Fundamentals

I doubt high inflation. I doubt high interest rates. I don't believe it was the fear of higher interest rates that just dropped the market. I think it was "smart money" afraid that the economy wouldn't make it and so I think it was really smart money cashing in their stock market chips.

I don't think that they want to play either! I don't like the unmanaged deficit. I think that the new tax law will hurt the economy in the short run, although I favor the change. I don't like the federal deregulation taking place in the banking and security industries. I don't like the SEC permitting future trading. I think future trading will be a major contributing factor in the break of the stock market.

Conclusion

Early in the year a friend of mine asked me to give him just one indication of when he should get out of the market. My answer, **"When you see several 200,000,000 share days on the downside".**

SO NOW YOU KNOW . . . THAT'S WHY I DON'T WANT TO PLAY TODAY . . . MAYBE TOMORROW . . . BUT NOT TODAY!

* * *

THINKING? THINKING? WHAT DO YOU THINK?? Hopefully, you've had quite an education by now. You should have no trouble following my thinking in that letter. You also know the reasons for my actions.

I obeyed the rules. I played the game on my terms. I

didn't hesitate to step out of stocks when I was in doubt. I didn't marry stocks. Again interest rates were considered. Note the other economic and current news that I watched.

NOW FOR THAT CONCLUSION . . . THOSE FEW LINES!!

"WHEN YOU SEE SEVERAL 200,000,000 SHARE DAYS ON THE DOWNSIDE"

What was there so prophetic in 200,000,000 share days? Simply this!

MAJOR TURNS IN THE STOCK MARKET TAKE PLACE WITH MAJOR VOLUME

The history of past stock market crashes were all accompanied by RECORD VOLUME!

Therefore when it would be time for the bull market that started in 1982 to end . . . (and remember it was the greatest one in history) . . . I knew it would have to end with RECORD VOLUME!!

What that volume would be I didn't know. When the volume approached a record 200,000,000 shares on the *upside*, I knew that it would take several days of over that figure to break the market.

THINK!! That's why volume is such a major indicator! Refer back to the letter on page 12, dated November 21, 1987 and entitled, WHY? WHY? WHY?

On Tuesday, October 6th when the DJ plunged $92, the volume was 175,000,000. Now that was very high for volume at that time while the $92 plunge was large for stocks to fall.

On Wednesday, although the market held steady, up less than $3, the volume increased to 186,000,000 shares.

On Thursday the market dropped $34.44 and the volume INCREASED TO *198,000,000* shares!—(approaching 200,000,000)!

That Saturday night, October 10th, I reviewed the previous week's volume and stock prices. Noting that on Wednesday, the 7th, the volume was 186,000,000 and that on Thursday it was 198,000,000 shares, I decided to stay on my vacation as I explained in the letter.

I wanted to give the market a few more days while I monitored the volume indicator. I had to see larger volume. Is that predicting the stock market? Is that being psychic? Do I know more than other technical analysts?

No. I didn't tell you anything they don't already know. Why I use that knowledge and they don't, I don't quite understand. Perhaps it is because as I said, "THE STOCK MARKET IS AN ART!!

The Following Week!

Monday the market was quiet but on

Tuesday, the volume was 172,000,000 shares.

Wednesday, the Dow Jones was whacked for $95.46 and BINGO! *THE VOLUME WAS 207,000,000 SHARES of stock traded.*

Thursday, stocks plunged $57.61 and the *VOLUME WAS A SMASHING 263,000,000 SHARES!!*

Friday, October 16, 1987 the stock market tumbled 108.36!!

And the volume, *THE MAGIC NUMBER*, that "predicted" the *greatest stock market crash in history* . . . the number of shares that was traded that day . . . was . . . *3 3 8 , 0 0 0 , 0 0 0.*

THINK! Did you have several days of 200,000,000 shares of stock traded on the *DOWN SIDE*? What would follow that?

The next night, Saturday, I reviewed the record volume and the falling prices and the other factors that I spoke about in that letter. I noted that the Wednesday volume was 207,000,000 shares . . . Thursday it was 263,000,000 shares . . . Friday it was the decisive 338,000,000 shares!

I had plunging prices which indicated a *DOWN TREND* and *SEVERAL DAYS OF OVER 200,000,000 shares traded!*

I RAN TO THE HILLS!!! I NEVER LOOKED BACK!

It's over three months since the October 19, 1987 Stock Market Crash and I still haven't looked at the stock page!

WHY?? Do you have to ask? Because the stock market cycle is at the beginning of the fourth stage, the stage where stock prices fall and have the tendency to continue falling. This is the only part of the cycle when it isn't *PRUDENT* to buy or to hold stocks!!

Yes. I know that there are exceptions. I said that investing is an art and as such is subject to judgment. Also many things I say are not absolutes either. There may be occasional exceptions.

However, smarter people than you and I lost money in the stock market. Millions of investors always think they are the exception or that they have the one or two stocks that won't go down while all Wall Street tumbles about their ears!

Remembering that we are investors and that we are seeking only profits and not glory, settle for interest on resting capital and give the market a chance to get its poison out of its system!

IT'S EASIER AND SMARTER TO START REINVESTING FROM INCREASED WEALTH DUE TO ADDED INTEREST THAN FROM WEALTH THAT WAS JUST DECREASED FROM SOME STOCK LOSSES!

Trends as Stock Market Indicators

Utilizing trend analysis is a relatively easy thing to do. It does make investing much more interesting as well. You follow the daily, weekly or monthly movement of the stock market. If you develop greater interest in investing then you will employ charts to help you remember and recall the activity of the market and of individual stocks.

Charts have lines or bars, as they are sometimes referred to, and are used to plot and follow the range, volume and direction of individual stocks and of the stock market itself. By direction I am referring to trends.

Technical analysts, such as myself, also use a chart, called a point and figure chart. It takes less time and less work than line charts but tracks less information.

This latter chart uses x's and o's to track price changes only. It does not reflect volume or time. However it is simple and easy to maintain. Days or weeks may go by before you have to indicate a change. It is really so simple that even if you are timid about something new, you will handle it easily if you approach it with just a little enthusiasm. It could be the catalyst for your success.

This point and figure chart is excellent for keeping up with the TREND!

In this chapter we are thinking of The INDICATORS as macro-indicators. We are discussing them as indicators for the stock market as a whole. We have in mind the averages, particularly the Dow Jones Industrial Average. We will discuss them as micro-indicators in the chapters on How, What and When to Buy Stocks and When to Sell them.

When you are in the second stage of the cycle, you are in a bull market. You are in an UP TREND. Study the volume changes as the market fluctuates within its major up trend. You will note how the stock market will rise to new highs as volume surges higher and higher. Just like ocean waves washing up pebbles on a beach, volume keeps rolling along higher and higher and, with each new surge, stock prices will move higher and higher. After some experience you will be fascinated by the confidence that you will gain and you will soon lose your fear as you begin to UNDERSTAND WHAT IS HAPPENING. You will gain confidence as you correctly anticipate the stock market. Mind you, you won't PREDICT but you will EXPECT!! You will expect that every time higher volume comes into the market that you will see new highs in the bull market. They go together just as ham and eggs.

Therefore if you should now have new high volume without a new bull market high . . . or . . . if you should have a new bull market high without higher volume . . . *THE MARKET IS SUSPECT!!!*

Be alert! The stock market may be entering the third stage, distribution, of the cycle.

BUT IF VOLUME LEAPS AND THE STOCK MARKET STARTS TO FALL . . . AS IT DID IN THE EARLY DAYS OF OCTOBER, 1987. . . BE ALERT . . . YOU ARE PROBABLY IN FOR A CORRECTION OR WORSE.

Characteristics of Trends

As was stated in earlier chapters many trends develop, as stocks and the market keep moving higher and higher or lower and lower. The longer the duration of the trend, the more valid is its implication.

Another characteristic of trends is that when a trend line is broken, (whether the top trend line or the bottom trend line), there is a tendency for the market or the stock to return to the trend line just broken.

This opportunity usually will give you a last chance to buy if the break out was on the upside, or to sell if the break was on the downside. However it is brief and sometimes just a token retracement so don't delay in these quick last minute reprieves to correct mistakes.

Another characteristic is that when a trend line is penetrated, not only will the market or the individual stock return to the trend line pierced, but it will continue to make a larger retracement than usual.

In this situation what is happening is that a new trend line is being substituted for the broken one. Whether it is a last minute opportunity or whether it is a new trend line being established, requires judgment. It will require THINKING. I know that this is not easy to absorb but again investing is an art. Have patience. It will come with a little time.

You can succeed without this last point. So don't let it turn you off. With experience, it will unravel for you. *The trend is one of the three working parts of the stock market.* Of necessity it is a major indicator!

Now you KNOW WHY I AWOKE IN A SWEAT that Saturday night while I was on vacation in Virginia Beach which I described in the first chapter.

Here we were in a great bull market and suddenly volume increased *but stock prices plunged.* THAT'S NOT THE WAY OF BULL MARKETS!!

WHAT'S HAPPENING HERE??

Volume is up and prices are plunging! *IS THE TREND REVERSING?* IS IT NOW DOWN? Volume and Trend . . . just as ham and eggs. . . . *THEY GO TOGETHER!. . . . That's why I sweated.* I couldn't come to grips with the realization that the GREAT BULL MARKET might be coming to its end! The rest is history!! It was said many times, many years ago!

7

The Cycle as a Stock Market Indicator!!

We have discussed the cycle as one of the three working parts of the stock market. It is a long range indicator because each of its four stages covers a long period of time. Consequently you soon know which stage that you are in and know what to expect from the ensuing stage, as well as what you can expect from the current stage.

With the Cycle as an indicator I knew that when the stock market crashed in October, 1968 that the market was entering the fourth stage, the falling stage, and that it would take a good year or more to shake out most stocks.

On June 21, 1969, some eight months later I wrote the following market letter: Read it and see if the timing and the thinking isn't what you would expect after reading the previous chapters.

*   *   *

THE K FACTOR JUNE 21, 1969

What Time is it on Wall Street? Let Me Take you By the Hand

That clock looking down towards Broad and Wall is ticking 2:05 PM but on WALL STREET there's no time for teaching so . . .

If you never bought a stock, don't start now unless you get competent advice.

If, on the other hand, you are fully invested, then you are leading a daredevil's life.

If you own a stock and you are hoping and praying for it to return to what you paid for it, then I suggest you renounce earthly endeavors and retire to a temple for continuous prayer. Perhaps for your sake a miracle may happen.

If you think that I am bearish . . . you are catching on!!

What Time is it on Wall Street?

It's time to stop looking for profits . . . it's time to cut down on the losses piling up . . . it's time to apply severe portfolio techniques and stop security analysis . . . it's time to realize that the market prices of excellent companies can melt or drop away . . .

A long time ago I coined a phrase, "In bad markets there is no such thing as a good stock."

After mailing my last letter, I had occasion to speak to a friend who stated that he wasn't too concerned about the market because I wrote that from the 890 area a rally would ensue.

His conclusions were wrong. If I anticipate the market declining to be followed by a rally and a further decline, then a proper analysis would be to sell in the first instance and then IF the market should rally, to liquidate further on the rally . . . NOT to wait for 890 and the rally before commencing to sell.

What do you expect by waiting? For the market on the rally to make up what it lost on the way down? If you do then you have never studied past markets. There was never a severe down market where stocks made up anything near what they lost.

Let me take you by the hand again. In bad markets stocks go down sharper and deeper than in ordinary dips. On the rally, prices of most stocks just lay there. If you get a few points on the middle price or lower ones, be grateful.

Another phrase I coined long ago, "Wall Street always lets you out." There is always a rally but if you are foolish enough to "wait to get your money back," you will pay in spades. This is the "Money Game". Nobody gets their money back. You either make or pay . . . etc. . . .

For Professionals Only!

As I interpret the technical pattern and its indications unfolding, I am firmly convinced that the market has gone too far, too fast, for the primary trend to be anything but down.

Today, I had prepared a mailing which I held up at the last minute as being too bearish for non-professionals to read. (It was this letter).

At this time I am not so much afraid of a test of the 820 area as I am afraid of the 1966 low of 735 . . . and then it's 50–50 whether the next bull market will start from that level or after that area has been penetrated. DJ 876.16

* * *

This market letter like so many of my others emphasizes that there is no rush to buy stocks nor is there any necessity for holding stocks. The letter takes cognizance that the market is always going up and down . . . that the market moves sharply in either direction . . . that every day there is a doubt . . . that however most times you must take a stand one way or the other . . . and when you do, you must be decisive.

There is no question that my confidence in my *understanding* of what takes place in the stock market is unbounded and shows through in that letter. I sit astride the stock market as though I were riding a bucking bronco.

Notice that even though I am bearish, I am still aware that the market has many, many sharp rallies in a *DOWN* market! That's why I buy stocks in a bear market. I am an investor. I take chances at times in down markets hoping to make a profit on the rally.

But I would never get locked into those stocks. If a rally failed to give me a profit, I would then sell at a loss. I would never get locked in.

I don't want you to buy in falling markets, that is, when stocks are actually falling, but when they stabilize you might try to turn a profit *KNOWING THAT STOCKS ARE IN THE FALLING STAGE!*

I want to make the distinction between falling prices and the falling stage. The latter—falling stage—takes months or years. However, you will find falling prices in any stage of the cycle.

Take particular note of the first sentence under the heading: *FOR PROFESSIONALS ONLY!* Note "I am *firmly* convinced that the market *has gone too far too fast* for the primary trend to be anything but down."

Again I am speaking of the stock market indicator—*TREND*. Here, too, we learn from history what happens when the "the market has gone too far, too fast."

Stock market analysts learn from studying past markets to expect a reaction to most actions. They expect that when the market moves up sharply that there will be a correction . . . a pull back . . . a retracement of at least part of that up move . . . perhaps a short down move . . . or perhaps it may be summed up in the words, profit taking.

And when the market moves down sharply, they expect an upward reaction in a similar vein. We find these up and down moves constantly in the stock market. We find them so often that they are the reason that so many professionals get caught in stock market crashes and the reason it is so difficult to succeed in investing.

It is extremely difficult to interpret when a major sharp thrust either up or down will have the expected reaction or whether it will turn out to be one of no return . . . such as the market crash of 1929 . . . 1946 . . . 1968 . . . and we are still on guess for 1987!!

That's why I am emphasizing this letter and this part at this time. What about the 1987 thrust downward? I say it looks like 1968 all over again. The plunge down in 1987 was *too far too fast* for the primary trend to be anything but down. Yet many argue that it was a major correction in a bull market still going on.

Another timely market letter was written a year later. The falling stage is now two years old. It may be time for the first stage of the new bull market which should eventually materialize.

*　*　*

THE K FACTOR OCT. 4, 1970. . .DJ 766.16

The Back of the Bear is Broken

The vicious plunge of the first part of the bear market is over. Stocks are in the midst of a rally which should enable the DJ Industrials to rise above 800 and which should carry into 1971. Subsequently there will be a decline which will probably mark the completion of this bear market.

While we have had previous rallies, technical factors indicate that this is the first rally of significance. It has carried high enough to establish that stock is now passing into strong hands. This means THAT THE PRICE IS RIGHT!

Stock passing into strong hands means that it is going into the hands of buyers for the longer term pull; that it is going into the hands of buyers for accumulation. Therefore, at this time, I recommend some averaging and accumulating. I am swinging over to the long side of the market and have already made some purchases of stocks and convertibles. (Contact our office for recommendations.)

The Bond Market!

Bonds have been firm all year with many issues strong and in demand. Short term bonds have been difficult to get all year. The bond market is the key to this bear market in stocks while federal funds is the key to this bond market.

Hence, whereas federal funds have been

going at a 10% rate for a period, it is with a great sigh of relief that I now observe them going at 6% plus. Thus, I recommend for the first time buying bonds of quality with a little longer maturity for conservative speculation. etc. etc.

* * *

A short letter. But significant!! Where were we in the stock market cycle? Probably through with the falling stage of the last cycle and into the first stage of the new cycle.

Notice that the letter indicates that during the past two years there were many rallies and pull backs. This time a really long rally developed. Stocks were being accumulated for the long term. If you must buy long time, this was the stage to do it.

Note that once the 1968 crash occurred, I was immediately interested in bonds. Again note the many different indicators at work. Interest rates . . . federal funds . . . and note I recommend some *AVERAGING.*

This time I didn't run from the stock market. This time I didn't sell and take a loss. I want you to take note of that now so that when we get to the chapters on How, What and When to Buy and Sell, you will be familiar with this aspect.

We have covered the major stock market indicators, *INTEREST RATES*, *VOLUME*, *TRENDS*, and the *CYCLE*

There are many, many more indicators that technical and fundamental analysts use. These four I believe are sufficient for most investors. I'm afraid that if I add to the list at this time that it may discourage many readers, and that I don't want to do.

In the market letters that I have introduced so far, you may have noticed that I took cognizance of other indicators and factors. I will expound on those in later chapters.

If you don't understand what I wrote about the cycle, trends, and volume, please review what I wrote. Don't give up. It's new! It's strange! I didn't invent it! I read about it and studied it in books.

I tried it! I succeeded with it! You can do it! I have confidence that you can. Without it, you can't . . . you won't succeed in investing.

You must avoid the crashes! You must accumulate stocks to sell at a profit! *YOU HAVE TO KNOW WHEN TO SELL!*

Buying stock is the easy part of investing. We don't have too much trouble with the buying end. It's the selling of stock that takes the master's touch. It's the selling that distinguishes the investor from the collector.

It's the selling that prevents us from going broke . . . from surrendering our profits . . . and makes us rich! Without these *TECHNICAL INDICATORS* how will you ever know when to sell successfully? I haven't heard of another yard stick that is so successful as what I advocate.

The words, technical indicators, scare away investors. It has been ridiculed by so many for so long that I try to play the "words" down. As for me . . . you couldn't get me to invest one cent in stocks without it! It is the important SECOND KEY TO WALL STREET . . . which is. . . .

TO UTILIZE A FEW ELEMENTARY TECHNICAL INDICATORS!

8

Stocks— How . . . What . . . When . . . To Buy!

Now we come to the fun part of investing, buying stock. Always keep in mind our objective which is to buy stock to sell at a profit.

You are going to choose the time and you are going to choose the stock. Keep an open mind and don't bring any hang-ups or pre-conceived ideas of which companies are "good" and which are "bad".

I never know what stock I'm going to invest in when I start with fresh capital. I don't know what will trigger off which stock to study and research. It may be something I read or perhaps in scanning the stock market pages my eye may catch volume coming into a stock.

Whatever it is, the very first thing that I consider is the "technical" picture. My first consideration is how much can I make! I am interested in making 100% per annum. If the stock has the potential, *technically,* to double, then I am interested. If not, I may continue looking. It depends on the market *cycle* . . . upon the amount of capital I have available.

I have chart books in my home office as ready reference. They depict the trading in stocks for many years. A glance will indicate whether the stock is selling near its high, low or somewhere in between.

Noting the high price for each year and the corresponding low price for each year, will indicate the volatility. Stocks whose annual price ranges are narrow, relatively are not good candidates for doubling your money. Those with relative wide swings are better choices.

If the stock happens to be near the lower range, when it first comes to your attention, then you have one with the potential to double.

It's convenient and much easier and faster to keep chart books at home. However, if you aren't familiar with charts, you can go to the public library and inquire. I'm there all the time doing fundamental research.

There are two major services. Standard & Poor's and Moody's. Both are excellent. Standard & Poor's contains all the listed stocks of the NYSE in four volumes. They then have four different volumes for the ASE issues.

These volumes contain single pages describing each stock listed. The front page has a chart of the stock prices. This is the chart to look at.

My first consideration is how much could I make?

My second consideration is how much could I lose??

When I consider how much I could make, I do so in a very slip-shod manner. Profit is profit! Does it really matter if I double my money? Won't I be happy with 50% for the year? From experience I know in most years I'll settle for 25%.

LOSS? NOW WE START THINKING LIKE INVESTORS! This is where the money game begins. It is at this point that we leave conventional Wall Street and we do our own *THINKING!*

THINK! HOW MUCH AM I READY TO LOSE OF MY CAPITAL? The question is not how much am I ready to *RISK* because I can risk $10,000 and expect to lose $700. How much am I ready to lose?

I know that there are thousands of stocks to select from. I know that all stocks fluctuate and therefore go up at some time. Consequently it isn't really difficult to find a stock to go up as it is to find one that will go up and still not cause me to lose more than I had in mind.

My real search is to uncover a stock where the choice is between making a small profit versus making a big profit. With all other stocks the choice is between making a big profit versus a big loss. Or perhaps just a profit against a loss.

At the race track I don't expect to make money. In the stock market I do! This is the first crucial factor that you must resolve before you waste time on any further research. *You must determine just how much you think that the stock will correct before you are going to take your loss and sell out!*

Let's try an example. You get interested in a stock that is selling at $20. The low for the past year is $12. If you think the stock may correct to $15, you have to ask yourself are you willing to take that loss?

Let's try again. A stock is selling at $4 per share. You think the normal correction will be no greater than $3. That may be okay. It's not the percentage loss in any one issue that matters as it is the loss in TOTAL DOLLARS.

This is what I call the KRUMHOLZ FACTOR! My clients call it

THE K FACTOR

I am tremendously interested and concerned in the *total amount of money that I can lose!*

During the bull market, 1982–87, I had at one time over 25,000 shares of Inter-City Gas at $12.375 per share. The market value on August 31, 1985 amounted to over $313,000. That represented almost ⅓ of my portfolio. I wasn't afraid to have so much money committed in that issue because I didn't expect to lose more than $1 per share. I had a tolerance for a $25,000 to $35,000 loss.

While I had that much money at stake in Inter-City

Gas, I only had 600 shares of Gibralter Financial which was selling at 9⅝ the month before. The market value of the Gibralter stock was $5,775.

Why was so much money invested in one issue and not the other? The answer is the KRUMHOLZ FACTOR. It appeared that the Gibralter stock could decline 50%. I had no tolerance for that kind of loss with a big investment.

By holding my investment to $5,775 I could lose half that or about $3000. I wouldn't lose a night's sleep over that. I wouldn't lose a night's sleep over losing $25,000 in Inter-City either!

Do you know why????

The answer is what I have been trying to communicate to you in all these pages. *IF YOU KNOW WHAT TO EXPECT . . . IF YOU UNDERSTAND WALL STREET, THEN YOU CAN COPE WITH IT!!*

THEN YOU CAN ACT DECISIVELY! YOU CAN ACT WITH THOUGHT! YOU CAN DECIDE WITH REASON!

You won't be ALWAYS REACTING EMOTIONALLY WITH CRUTCHES. You will react INTELLIGENTLY WITH REASON. *YOU WILL BE A THINKING, SUCCESSFUL INVESTOR!!*

Let's go back to examples. Now say goodbye to "Conventional Wall Street" and say hello to Stock Market Technicians. If a stock selling at $20 a share, appears that it's pull back may be limited to $18, then you expect a loss of $2 per share.

To figure how many shares to buy, divide your loss tolerance, (the KRUMHOLZ FACTOR), by the $2 loss and you will arrive at the total number of shares that you intend to buy!

By doing this you will know how much your loss may be. It will be a controlled loss. You will still have your capital unimpaired. You will be able to function without fear.

Now let's try it. If you look at the chart on the stock, International Aluminum, it appears as a "blackout". That is a glance at the chart seems to indicate that the stock has been trading in a very narrow range for a number of years.

Looking at the high and low for the years 1983 to 1987, it appears that the high is about 24–25 while the low is about 15–16.

Therefore if you had an interest in buying that stock at 18½ in January, 1988, just after the market crash of October, 1987, it is reasonable to expect that the stock could drop back to the 15 level.

Thus you should make your investment based upon a tolerance of a $3 loss per share. Divide the $3 by what you are prepared to lose in that investment and you will have the KRUMHOLZ FACTOR. This will give you the total number of shares that you will intend to buy.

YOUR LOSS IS LIMITED!

What I am asking you to do is to utilize a technical factor. Isn't that my SECOND KEY to Wall Street riches? Please don't let the word technical analysis discourage you. They are only words by which you and I and others can communicate with each other.

They are not the esoteric words of witchcraft. Is it that difficult to go to the library to get rich? If looking at a chart is such "crystal gazing" hoopla . . . if it is such an arcane art. . . , why do much highly respected publishers include charts in their work?

Is it a gimmick to help sell? I like to think that publishers appreciate the significance and aid that technical indicators offer. If most fail to interpret or to use charts successfully, then let those who can do so and those who can't have enough good sense to keep quiet.

You now know two technical factors, the upside potential and the downside risk!

Now let's see how I might proceed with my research. For this example I will consider Genovese Drug Stores which is listed on the American Stock Exchange (ASE). We will refer to it by its symbol on the exchange, GDX.

Let us assume I did the study in the past . . . assume on December 13, 1987. The stock had closed the prior Friday at 11⅜. The high for the prior twelve months was 16⅛ while the low was 6⅞.

I went to the library and turned to the page on GDX. I noticed immediately that the stock appeared to be "blacked out". It was trading in a narrow range. The range appeared to be between 10 to 15 for the years 1983 to 1987.

Looking at the bottom of the page of the Standard & Poor's sheet, I noted that the stock had sold for a low of 1⅝ and $2 for several years from 1978 to 1982. Noting that the blackout range, 10–15, appeared to be a "flag" arising from a low of about $2, I asked myself what part of the four stage cycle GDX might be in at this point?

NOTE: Flag is a word used by technical analysts to describe the price movement of a stock. Genovese Drug had moved from 2 to 15 without too much sideways movement. This was followed by a considerable sideways movement in which the stock traded in a range between 10 and 15. If you look at the chart at arm's length, the price movement from 2 to 15 would take on the appearance of a flag pole. The sideways trading from 10 to 15 would take on a "black out" appearance as a flag attached to the flag pole.

Since the span covered a broad period of time, 4–5 years, the span was long enough to actually be one stage of the cycle. So the question arose: was GDX in the first stage of being accumulated . . . or was it in the third stage of being distributed?

Was it primed for a rise? Or was it primed for a fall?

I really didn't know! I was on guess. I don't predict. I think! I reason!

Right or wrong I was going to make my decisions based either on reason or common sense. I was not in an emergency at that time so I reasoned. My reasoning said, "If we are in a falling stock market after the greatest bull market in history, in order for GDX to rise, it must 'fight the tape'. It must buck the general trend of the stock market." It's difficult enough to select stocks in rising markets so give it thought!

Therefore I reasoned that GDX must be in a state of distribution. Even though I would not buy, I was prepared to see it rise as there were still many committed bulls who might see it otherwise. In fact with the big takeover game in play, perhaps it might be taken over.

Stocks don't all reach their highs at the same time in bull markets. Nor do they bottom out all together in bear markets. Perhaps GDX has not made its top in this past bull market. The averages and many others may have topped out but GDX may still be alive.

But I reasoned this way: I am an investor. I am in this for as much profit as I can make with as little risk as possible. Should I elect to buy the stock, with a trading range of 10–15, I wouldn't expect the stock to sell less than $20 per share.

Therefore if I bought the stock at 11⅜ on Monday, I wouldn't be disturbed if the stock dropped to $10 which is the bottom of the range because I expected that as a possibility. You see what I mean by understanding Wall Street?

That's what I mean by "knowing what's going on". Most people say the stock market is irrational. I think it is very rational. It's rational because it is doing just what it is supposed to be doing . . . moving up and down. Therefore part of understanding Wall Street is to know when to sell.

Since it would be normal for GDX to fluctuate down to 10, it would be unexpected if GDX sold down below. If it did sell below 10, it might then continue to fall to perhaps as low as the $2 that it started its rise from.

Therefore it is imperative to sell as soon as the stock

falls below $10. I would take that small loss to avoid a substantial loss later on.

That is why it is imperative to establish a limit on your loss, the KRUMHOLZ FACTOR . . . *BEFORE* . . . YOU BUY!!

If I did buy the stock, the loss from 11⅜ to about 9½ would be about $2 per share. If I stood ready to lose $5000, I would divide $2 into $5000 and stand ready to buy 2500 shares of Genovese Drugs.

After this brief technical research, I went on to do fundamental analysis. I went to study the company, itself. I looked at earnings per share for the past few years. I looked at the book value per share for the past years. I looked at sales and all the data listed on both sides of the page.

I look for signs of growth. I am interested in the growth of earnings, dividends, book value, sales, net etc. I then make an estimate for the immediate ensuing quarters.

The payout ratio is often interesting. This is the percentage of dividends that some companies pay out of earnings year after year.

Interest and debt are two important and interesting factors to examine. Looking at all this data I try to weigh the momentum of growth and safety of investment.

If I get a positive reaction then I make a copy for my files. Later I read, reread and then reread another ten or twenty times to make sure everything has registered. Often I'll reread something weeks later and find one detail that will make me go out and buy some more.

Think of my prologue . . . there is none so blind as those who will not see. It's not that we don't *want* to see. But to concentrate on every word . . . such as I ask you to keep THINKING as you read this . . . is difficult. I underline in red everything that is a factor to note.

If, after thinking through all the technical and fundamental data, I feel that the stock has merit and may prove to be a profitable investment, I still have some very important research to do before the final buy decision.

Remember that we are in a market place. Remember that our objective is to buy and sell for a profit. Supposing that you were a coin dealer and that you were offered coins for inventory. Wouldn't you shop around to see if you were getting good value? Wouldn't you compare the proposed purchase to other coins for value?

Would you pay full value? Therefore in the stock market I always compare *THE VALUE* of my proposed purchase to the value of other stocks. After comparing the value to other stocks, I would then compare the value to stocks in the same industry.

If I now discovered that my contemplated purchase seemed genuinely undervalued, I would consider it, . . . *A SPECIAL SITUATION!* and I have found many over the years.

CONSIDER THIS . . . THOUGHTFULLY! The objective of an investor should be to make 100%, 200%, 300%, 400% and more on an investment. For example . . . On April 1, 1981 I had bought some Genovese Drug that cost me $1,156.74. I sold it January 5, 1984 for $7,150.72.

That was over 600%! That was not an isolated case—as I have had excellent results many times as my wealth will testify to. However offsetting that 600% result, I have *many, many more cases where I LOST money.*

Therefore from my experience, I have found that while the objective is high, *it is extremely difficult to just earn 100% on your capital!!!* Let's examine this further.

A Basic of Investing

You invest $10,000 in an effort to double your money . . . to make 100% on your investment. That's feasible. It doesn't happen often but it happens. It's a realistic objective . . . difficult . . . but feasible! It could happen.

But again it doesn't happen often enough that you are anxious to invest all your money in that one effort. Although doubling your money is attainable, really, it is very difficult to achieve. So difficult to achieve that in fact most times money is lost.

What if you started with capital of $10,000 and lost half of that? Now you would be left with $5,000. In order to reach your goal of $20,000, you would now have the task of investing $5,000 to make $20,000.

THAT WOULD BE A PROFIT OF 400%! Gracious! It is difficult enough to make 100%. THINK how much more difficult it is to make 400%!! Besides the waste of capital, there would be a *TREMENDOUS WASTE OF TIME!*

Sometimes it takes years to make 100% . . . just think of how many years it would take to make 400%!!

THIS IS A BASIC FACT OF INVESTING THAT YOU SHOULD ALWAYS REMEMBER . . . AND AVOID AT *ALL COSTS!*

This basic fact . . . this 50% loss that we discussed . . . should protect us from taking substantial losses. This is the safety valve . . . the parachute . . . the protection that I employ and urgently recommend that you always bear in mind!

A Second Basic Fact of Investing

The second basic fact of investing is knowing that you are going to make a lot of mistakes . . . that you are going to make sickening mistakes . . . that you are going to lose money frequently.

Here you must exercise the first principle, PATIENCE! Don't be discouraged . . . Don't give up . . . don't be disheartened . . . Be patient!

How Much to Buy?

Referring back to the decision to buy 2500 shares of Genovese Drug at 11⅜, I wouldn't place an order to buy the entire 2500 shares at one time. I would place an order to buy ⅓ to ½ the amount. I would place an order to buy 1000 shares in this illustration.

I would wait a few hours or a day or more and then buy 500 or more. It would depend upon how the general market was acting and how GDX was doing.

The reason for the delay is to avoid large losses. We know how difficult it is to make up losses. I don't want to waste time and money making up losses. It is much preferable to move slowly!

If I buy 1000 shares of GDX at 11⅜ only to have it decline to 10⅞, I am looking at a $500 loss. That's lots easier to sleep with than buying 2500 shares and looking at a $1250 loss. Therefore, I tend to buy in 3–4 lots.

If I buy 1000 shares of GDX and it immediately rises to 11⅞, I am delighted and a little regretful at the same time. I am delighted because NOW I HAVE THEIR MONEY! Now I can invest with a little less pressure. A little regretful? It passes quickly as "I drive to the bank".

If the New Investment Declines . . .

If the 1000 shares of GDX declined to 10⅞, you would have a $500 loss but since the KRUMHOLZ FACTOR provided for a $2500 loss, there would not be excessive pressure because you expected at least that amount of loss.

Now I would buy another 1000 shares!

Perhaps in this case since we are so close to the bottom range of 10, I might buy 1500 shares. If GDX were to continue to decline below $10, as we discussed earlier, and if it appeared that it was going to surpass our loss limitation of $2500, I would sell it all, take my loss and start all over again with some other stock.

Remember that you are an investor. If your analysis and your thinking are wrong, then you want to mark the merchandise down so that you can reinvest the proceeds in a stock or in merchandise that will be in demand and which may prove profitable.

Don't become a collector! Imagine a businessman taking up a hobby while waiting for ten years to resume business because he has old merchandise on the shelf and lacks the capital to replace it!

If the Price of the Investment Rises . . .

Should the price of the 1000 shares of GDX rise, I would then buy another 500 shares or so, after which I would expect the stock to pull back. On the pull back I would buy the balance of the 2500 shares I had in mind!!

The Stock Campaign

Should the price of the stock of GDX continue to rise, I would now consider "accumulating" the stock! This I call a CAMPAIGN in Genovese Drug!.

I would now like to buy as much of the stock as possible . . . within limits and within REASON. Therefore it is necessary to take a fresh approach to this situation.

It is necessary to start at the beginning. Strict attention must now be paid to the technical factors. Just what is the trend? Has a new trend line been established? What was the volume that accompanied the up move?

Is the trend a long term trend or was it formed recently? Just how large was volume in relation to normal days? Was large volume of one or two days, or was there large volume in the stock for one or two weeks or longer?

What was the daily range and the weekly range of the

stock recently compared to the range before the stock started to rise?

Now of course the major question! How much of a pull back can be expected? Just how much will profit-taking depress the stock?

Finally will the pull back be just that, or a topping out of the issue?

THINK! I can't help you with these questions. I can only guide you through them! But don't be afraid of them. Investing is an art. Sometimes you'll profit more, and other times less. I never know the exact answers either!

The Campaign Continues

Unless YOU THINK that your stock has reached a top, or if you suspect that there is a large correction on the horizon, then never think of selling! Just think of buying.

Usually successful investors take lots of small losses. When a "good" stock comes along, the investor must take advantage of the opportunity. Not only must all the many small losses be regained, but the original objective of the doubling of capital must be attained and surpassed.

Investing is a never ending process. The value of the stock you purchased today is different in comparison to the value of the thousands of other stocks tomorrow.

Tomorrow your stock is a "new" company. You must look at it as though it's the first time you ever heard of it. Tomorrow you must ask yourself should you buy more?

If you don't want to spend that much time on investments, then look at it once a week or whatever time you care to invest in meeting your objective.

But as long as the stock rises and shows little signs of a major correction, you should always be trying to . . . . *Continue the Campaign to its Optimum Conclusion.*

We have been concerned with the buying of just one stock. There is more to this aspect of investing which we will cover when we get to managing a portfolio of stocks and bonds.

Volume Indicator for Stocks

We have studied how volume is and was used as an indicator for the stock market. Let's see how it is used as a technical indicator for stocks.

After you have satisfied yourself that the basic technical and fundamental factors warrant an investment in a stock, you must be concerned with the volume of trading.

This is done by going through the back issues of the New York Times. I use seven column accountant's paper for this research. You may use whatever paper or chart that you feel comfortable with.

First I check the daily Times. I usually go back to the end of the previous month. I copy the volume for the day, the high, low and closing prices for each day.

Next I resort to the Sunday Times and extract the same data but now on a weekly basis.

By reviewing the data your eye can scan what the normal amount of trading usually is, and can also pick out any unusual amount of activity in the stock.

Frequently, the data extracted may not quite satisfy me whereupon I go further back until I reach what appears to be the normal trading range and the normal trading activity.

If you buy the stock, you should monitor the range and the volume as long as you are invested in the issue. Accordingly after a period of time, it will get increasingly difficult to handle and to manage that much detail on paper.

When you have more than one stock, it will be almost impossible to cope with. It would be easier if you purchased 17 × 22 graph paper that is ruled with boxes 8 × 8 to the inch. Since stocks trade in ⅛'s, 8 × 8 is convenient.

If the stock has a small number of shares, I would let one square equal 20,000 shares. If the stock has more, I might assign 50,000 shares to one square. With large capitalized stocks, I let one million equal one square on the graph. Again THINK. You'll work it out.

As to price range and changes, I almost always let one square equal ½ point. Thus if the range of a stock was one point for the day, I would make a pencil line two squares deep.

I keep charts for the week and for the month on all stocks. For some stocks I also keep daily charts. Again, you will soon find what suits you.

Investing now takes on more of a business aspect! There is a job to do. The work gets intriguing! You connect tops with straight lines. You join bottoms with straight lines. Trends emerge. They change!

You draw lines each day or each week indicating the volume of trading. Armed with this information . . . and it is priceless information . . . you should now look for unusual changes in volume.

A change represented by one, two or three lines could be meaningless. You could be misled by this change which simply indicates that some institution or large investor is accumulating the stock. However should several lines on the chart appear indicating a concentration of buying (this is a judgment call), then buy!! It may be a "break out".

False Moves

If it turns out that you are misled into buying by these volume changes and the stock turns down, it may be necessary for you to sell and take losses. Don't make a big deal out of it . . . sell . . . you'll get it back in spades the times you will be right!

Now this is where tactics come into play. Remember that you are in an art form . . . you will be mistaken often. Don't change your tactics. You are trying to keep losses down when you are wrong and making large profits when you are right!

Since all of the indicators are just indicators and not scientific instruments, they are frequently wrong. When they are wrong, we will misinterpret them. These misleading indications in technical talk are called "false moves".

But they are the only tools that we have to work with in this business. Without them, I for one, would not invest ten cents in the stock market. With them I suffer many, many losses which are completely overshadowed by the tremendous profits.

The stock market is strictly for professionals! These are the only tools that allow me to compete with them!

When Volume is Not a False Move

When the stock market collapsed October 19, 1987, why did so many professionals and other investors buy and hold stocks? Now that's a very interesting question at this time of our enlightenment!

The question, of course, at that time was whether the fall ended the Great Bull Market or was it a major correction with new highs to be seen in a reasonably short time?

Again I don't predict the stock market but I simply apply what I have successfully experienced. When volume mounts repeatedly, increasingly and continuously in the early stages of the cycle, it presages a bull market.

We may ask what makes us think that the early rise is not another false move?

History recorded that in situations when volume was so large and continuous, that a bull market always arrived. It would be historic to have a market reverse itself from a rising market to a falling market under similar conditions.

The reverse is true on the downside!

With the volume of selling and the steep fall in stock prices that was witnessed October 19 and 20 in 1987, it would be historic if the bull market were not to end!

Volume as an indicator of the stock market works the same as an indicator when applied to individual stocks. It is a very important tool for investors!

How Volume Moves Stock Prices

The importance of volume as a stock market indicator is established by an examination of the theory behind it. We know that for every trade there is a buyer and a seller. No matter what the volume, there is an equal number on both sides of each trade.

However the number on each side is of no importance. What is consequential is the *BUYING AND SELLING POWER* that is exerted which sways the ebb and flow of stock prices.

Assume a stock is trading between $10 and $10½ for several weeks and that the mean average volume of trading is 10,000 shares. Assume further that the stock is at 10¼.

Question: Is the stock being bought, sold or just fluctuating? Let's analyze the volume.

When the volume was 10,000 shares on any given day, that 10,000 shares wasn't a single trade that took place in an instant. That 10,000 shares was traded throughout the day.

When there was a difference between the bid price for the stock and the asking price, no trade took place. Therefore when the stock market opened for trading, we had to wait either for the buyer to raise the bid or the seller to lower the asking price.

If the stock is at 10¼, let us assume that the bid is 10⅛

and the asking price is 10⅜. Unless a buyer met the asking price of 10⅜ or a seller met the bid price of 10⅛ no trade would take place.

At this point the bidder of 10⅛ may raise the bid to 10¼ or the offerer of 10⅜ may lower the asking price to 10¼ or perhaps third parties can bid or ask the 10¼.

Even if there is a new bid or offer at 10¼, a *trade* won't take place at 10¼ until there is a buyer and a seller agreeing on the price.

Supply and Demand Affects Volume

What happens, if after an hour of no trades, a buyer wants to buy 4,000 shares and finds that there is an offer to sell 2,000 at 10⅜??

If the buyer wanted the stock he would bid 10⅜ for the 2000 shares but would have to raise the bid to the next higher offering price.

If the buyer now finds that only 500 shares are being offered at 10½, the buyer would make a judgment call on what to do. The buyer could bid 10½ for the 500 offered and then raise the bid to the next offering price which might be, let's say, 9500 at 10⅝ or simply bid for 1500 at 10½.

After awhile of no further trading, some seller might meet the 1500 share bid at 10½ and the buyer would have the 4000 shares wanted.

Now if a seller decides to sell 1000 shares, that person would find 9500 offered at 10⅝ but now that the 4,000 shares are out of the way, the bid prices might be back to the 10⅛ bid that opened the day.

Now the sellers would compete to sell and the price could drop back to 10 and then up to the 10¼ again.

When Volume = Demand

What would happen if a buyer wanted 50,000 shares of that stock? The buyer might have to pay perhaps $11 for the stock.

What might happen if a buyer wanted 250,000 shares? The buyer would have to buy at a price over 11 or put a bid in at 11 and leave it there for a few days.

What you might find then is several days of the stock selling at a low of 11 and higher volume than normal for several days.

When this happens the news is published to the world that there is a *DEMAND* for the stock! They know because

When a Stock Rises on Volume it = DEMAND!

Volume = Supply!

What would happen if a seller wanted to sell 95,000 shares of that stock. That seller would depress the price and you would see a drop in the price and the larger than normal volume.

Again if the block to be sold was 250,000 shares, the seller would have the choice of forcing the price of the stock to perhaps a new low or just placing the order at a determined price and waiting.

If the order was executed in one day, there would be abnormal volume and a large drop in the price and the news would be published to all the world. You and I would know that there was *SELLING* going on! . . . BECAUSE . . .

When a Stock Drops on Volume it = SUPPLY!!

9

Building a Portfolio: How . . . What . . . When . . . To Buy!

The stocks that you should buy are those stocks which are listed on the New York Stock Exchange and those stocks that are listed on the American Stock Exchange.

There is less chance of fraud in listed stocks and they enjoy a broader market. The trading range and close as well as the volume will be published by the New York Times.

Don't buy new issues! They are not for investors. Venture capitalists buy new issues. That's their function. That's how they expect to profit. That's their business!

You are an investor. You're in a DIFFERENT BUSINESS!

Tend to buy lower price issues. It takes less capital and the chance of doubling, I believe, is greater than high price stocks.

In a bull market you can buy anything! If it's listed, it rises! However in other times, favor stocks with less number of shares outstanding. Because of the thinness of shares outstanding, sometimes it is easier for a stock to move sufficiently to return large capital gains.

Of course with the introduction of program trading and the modern surge in takeovers at phenomenal prices, the size and price of outstanding shares may not be significant anymore.

Avoid stocks in the averages, I almost never buy them! They are so completely analyzed and monitored that it is difficult to find an undervalued situation there.

Here, too, program trading and takeovers may have changed all that. Certainly the mistake that I made in 1986 as well as 1987 was not investing in just those stocks. But though I knew it was the thing to do, I just couldn't. It would only be GAMBLING on what the program traders would want to do. It was a DIFFERENT BUSINESS THAN INVESTING!

Starting the Portfolio

When I first bought Genovese Drug, I considered others in that industry. They appeared to be fairly valued and were selling at higher prices.

However when the bull market erupted and Genovese Drug started to go up, I looked around to build a portfolio. The first stocks I investigated were the drug stocks. Yes. I selected the same industry.

Using Genovese as an indicator, I quickly saw that the laggards in the industry would follow the example set by Genovese and would appreciate.

Later by constantly comparing prices among those stocks in the same industry, exactly as I did the aircraft manufacturing industry when I first started in the stock market in 1946, I was able to build my portfolio rapidly and to make large investments in those stocks.

Therefore the key here is to use *ONE STOCK AS AN INDICATOR!!*

When to Buy

Just suppose that after a few years of accumulation, which is the first stage of the new cycle, stocks break out and stock prices start to rise.

You had been considering many stocks, one of which was selling at $8 per share before the break-out. You failed to buy the stock and soon it is selling at $12. You aren't going to buy it at $12 if you missed buying it at $8.

In due time the stock sells at $25. As happens to all bull markets, this one ends too and the stock falls in price to $2 per share.

You went through an entire cycle . . . an entire bull market . . . and missed an opportunity to profit, after spending time and thought upon the company.

During the entire cycle the stock market went up and down and this stock, too, went up and down. Not straight up to $25 nor straight down to $2, but it went through many, many rises and set-backs in its struggle to the top and in its struggle to survive.

It's true. It isn't easy to make investment decisions!

Now Consider This

Assuming that you had bought it at $8, would you have sold it at $25?

No!! We know that we usually don't buy at the bottom and sell at the top! The conventional approach for long term holders would be to have carried the stock to $25.

After holding the stock for years while the bull market gets to the top, the holder would then carry it for years until it falls to $2. At $2 the long term holder is still holding the stock.

THINK! If you wouldn't have sold it in our consideration just described, then isn't it true that you might have sold it on its way up to $25? Yes! That's a reasonable assumption.

If you didn't hold the stock for the maximum profit of $17, the difference between $25 and $8, then you profited less. Since we can't determine beforehand what our profit will be, then doesn't it make sense to simply try to obtain and expect to obtain some satisfactory profit?

If we understand Wall Street right, then we understand that we can't make the maximum profit but that it is possible and feasible to make some profit.

THINK! Doesn't that make sense? We are only ordinary human beings. Let's then attempt to accomplish things that ordinary beings can accomplish . . . that is . . . a profit in Wall Street . . . over a period of many years and several bull markets.

Let's make the market a place where we can invest safely. So many people lose money and so few succeed that the market is an ogre to most investors . . . only because they don't understand it!

QUESTION. Suppose you bought the stock at the bottom, $8. Suppose you are an investor, and when the stock reached $12 there was much buying. After the buying the stock pulls back after which it rallies and retreats several times until at last you decide to sell at $12 and take a 50% profit.

With the proceeds you will look around for another investment.

Suppose I first noticed this stock at $12 and bought it at that price. Later I elected to sell at $24.

Who do you think was more successful? You only made 50% on your investment. I made 100%.

The point that I make is that it isn't necessary to buy a stock at the bottom to make a profit! Understanding this should take the pressure off of you. You do not have to be afraid to miss stocks when they are low.

Low is a relative position. Don't think price! Think stock market!

If you understand the stock market, then you are always relaxed no matter what part of the cycle that the stock market is going through. The market always has chances to make profits.

If you missed the low, don't worry. You'll have another and another and another opportunity to buy that stock. Just buy it anywheres on the way up and you'll make money. No! It's not that simple . . . but that's the way it is!

Developing a Portfolio

When a portfolio is started during the accumulation stage of the cycle, several years will probably elapse before a bull market occurs. It is during this part of the cycle that it is most difficult to know when to buy and sell.

In these years should one or more stocks in your portfolio rise for a marked profit, while other stocks in your portfolio fail to do likewise, then I would be prone to take *some* profit. Whether the profit is only 5% or more is of no consequence. What is of consequence is that you don't take stocks "up and down".

I hate to see a profit evaporate and more times than not, profits turn into losses. It's a waste of time and time is what investing is all about. I don't use formulas in selling. I have only one reason for selling. I sell when I think a stock may go down.

Since stocks don't go straight up or down usually, I like to take profits in the accumulation stage. It keeps me in control of my patience. Remember principle 1 . . . it reads: control emotions, patience, greed.

Moving into the second stage of the cycle, the bull market is about to begin. You have several stocks in your portfolio. If you miss the start and you are in 100% cash, it's no big deal. So you won't make a million. You'll have to settle for ½ million!

We discussed this aspect before.

Don't always be afraid of missing an opportunity. *STAY IN CONTROL OF CAPITAL . . . AND THINK.*

Throughout this treatise I'm going to repeat control of capital . . . control of Wall Street and THINK!

When I am in control of the stock market, I feel as though I am a lion tamer locked in a cage with a dozen lions circling me and growling and snarling at me continuously.

I picture myself with a confident smile on my lips daring those animals to challenge my authority. While they are moving at my command, I smile and wave my whip while they jump through hoops.

They jump through fire always growling but always doing my bidding. I am master of my fate. That is how I feel about Wall Street and the stock market.

I risk my life savings! I smile! I dare them to take it all away from me. Smiling, confident, knowing they never will and knowing that they will grudgingly submit to my reason and to my common sense and that they will add to my wealth.

What can the lion tamer expect from lions? How will lions react under certain circumstances??

What can investors expect from the stock market? How will the stock market react under certain circumstances?

We aren't going to tame lions but we are going to invest our money. We should see what we can expect from the stock market.

In the accumulation stage we expect that stocks will behave more "rationally" if they ever do at all. There is less interest in stocks. They are better valued. Their price range is narrower.

Frequently they won't respond to either good news or to bad news. They will be in the doldrums for a long while. During this period gambling and speculating fever will have a minimum input on the direction of stocks.

However as we get into the bull market which follows the stage of accumulation, we run into something very interesting. Speculators, reading about the bull market starting or about a bull market being in place, will start entering the market. Along with speculators there will be many gamblers.

The shade between investing, speculating and gambling is gray. You can argue or debate the semantics. But speaking in colloquial terms, you can picture what starts to take place in the stock market.

The three are so intertwined and mixed together in a

frothing, feverish melting pot, that after the crash, writers will start to compare the mad rush to dizzying heights to the tulip craze of the 1600's and the stock market crash of 1929!!

The point to remember is that we understand what happens in every bull market . . . in every part of the cycle. Isn't that what a cycle means? It comes full cycle! Isn't that a familiar phrase?

If we know that and know how the stock market will react under all circumstances, then we are in control of the lions . . . of the stock market.

Then why don't investors sell when they should? Because they never learned to expect how the stock market will react under certain circumstances!

Now let's move to buying stocks and holding a portfolio of stocks in a bull market. In a bull market stocks move in large price ranges and with great volume. In a bull market when one of your stocks moves up, you buy! The higher the stock moves, the less likely are you to lose money.

For example assume you own 500 shares of stock which you had purchased at $10 per share. Your Krumholz Factor was a loss of $1000. The stock may move to $13 and then pull back to $12.

At that point buy another 300 to 500 shares with the intention of selling the last lot if the stock backs down to $10 again. At that point you will have lost no more than the Krumholz Factor had established.

However at $10 you will have to determine if you are willing to establish a new loss limit and stay with the original investment. You should. But if the stock penetrates the $10 area, then you should get out immediately and start afresh.

I keep repeating that investing is an art and that we must THINK our way through with proper guidelines!

Buy a Rising Market . . . Not a Fallen Star

What we have accomplished is this. Our capital is intact. Although we have bought and sold and bought and sold during which time we have taken frequent losses, there will be times, that things will work in your favor.

You will select stocks, many of which will not be right. But when you do get the "right" stock and the stock market is full of them, you've got yourself $100,000 . . . not once but many times!

The object is not just to acquire a portfolio of stocks but to get one or two or three that will make huge profits.

What I say is just keep using your reason. You have to invest your money to start but it's the profits that you should risk . . . not your capital.

It's the paper profits that you take the large risks with. *PARLAY YOUR PROFITS, NEVER YOUR CAPITAL!* This is the key to success. Perhaps I should make it a principle!

IN A BULL MARKET . . . BUY STOCKS ON THE WAY UP!! THINK!

My experience has been that the only time I made big profits was in bull markets! It seems that there is an opportunity once every ten years. That's why it's important not to buy more of a stock on the way down. Take your small losses on these. When you have a stock that has profits, then buy more as it keeps rising!!

Whether the stock market is simply meandering for several years or is in the bull market stage, you may uncover a stock that appears to offer a minimum risk. The Krumholz Factor may be very low and yet the upside potential may appear to be not too far off. It may be as much as a year or two.

This stock attracts you more than others. The risk is so minimum and the rise appears so imminent and so certain that it keeps drawing you to it. With these stocks I launch what I call a campaign. It's discussed in a previous chapter.

Masters of the Stock Market

Many years ago there was an era in which lived, "the robber barons". In that age lived people with such names as Jesse Liverpool, James Fiske, John D. Rockefeller, Jay Cooke, Daniel Drew, Cornelius Vanderbilt and many, many others. Those were the days of the "corners". Wealthy people would accumulate block after block of stock to drive prices up. At other times they would "short" block after block of stock to drive prices down. In both instances prices were artificially established. And of course those prices were also temporary!

The point is that they made big, big, profits by buying *LARGE QUANTITIES* of just one or two stocks . . . they did not become famous as stock market pundits by sitting around with a basket full of stocks.

THEY WERE MASTERS OF THE STOCK MARKET!

THINK! What can we learn from the way those *STOCK MASTERS WORKED* IN THE STOCK MARKET? Well we learn that they launched campaigns and created artificial and temporary stock prices. The latter should not be a startling revelation.

Yet when I read in the October and November, 1987 newspapers about the many professionals who lost money in that crash, I sometimes think that I was just one of a few who seemed to know that stock prices in 1987 were *temporary.*

In those earlier years when those masters concentrated on a stock, they would keep buying continuously. When the stock of the Erie Railroad was being "cornered", it was said that *"there was a campaign going on to corner Erie".*

Other famous corners of that era . . . and they make fascinating reading . . . was the campaign in Northern Pacific Railroad and a famous story in the campaign to corner "Hudson".

I use that term "campaign" today when I zero in on one particular stock with low risk and good potential! I concentrate my attention and my capital to the exclusion of other stocks.

Managing a Stock Portfolio

History showed us how the stock masters worked with campaigns during the age of the robber barons. It seems only natural that the same approach should be used in managing portfolios. Accordingly, I use an approach that I call *"STREAMLINING!!"* It works like this—

Managing a Portfolio: Streamlining

Conventional Wall Street advocates the theory of diversification. It is predicated upon the theory of safety in numbers. They assume that you are going to lose money. Therefore to protect yourself from loss, they want you to spread your money around.

To diversify you should buy many or several stocks of different companies. How many to buy they leave to your judgment. Usually investors wind up with a basketful.

Don't you do this. You should *STREAMLINE—NOT DIVERSIFY!*

I assume that I am going to MAKE money and not *LOSE* money. If you practice sound investing principles, you have built in protection against losses. It seems all I talk about is taking losses and protection against losses.

It's time that we talk about making profits! Let's do that. Here's how.

When you start building a portfolio, you are going to

find more than one stock to invest in. For example while I was discussing the purchase of Genovese Drug, I had other stocks under consideration.

I am always seeking undervalued investments. I apply the same research approach and the same cautious buying habits to them all.

At this point let us revert to a rising bull market for explanation. It will be easier to understand the explanation.

During the accumulation stage, let us assume that you had a portfolio of six stocks. Since not all six are selling at a loss, some will have small profits. Therefore those profits will lessen the threat of your approaching the protective level established by the Krumholz Factor which established your overall loss.

Now as those stocks with profits continue to rise, you buy more and expose more of your reserved capital to risk. Don't buy more of the laggards or of the losers. Remember that your paper profits act as a safety factor against loss of capital. These are the tactics that you are going to follow.

As this process continues you soon will find that only one or two stocks are making all the money. You will also find that you have used your entire capital.

What to Do

You finally have the vehicle for getting rich. But you have no capital. At this point I always use *MARGIN*. Again Wall Street, with tongue in cheek, says don't use margin.

If you don't acquire the professional knowledge to succeed in the stock market, of course I agree not to use margin. If you watch your losses . . . if you watch your GREED, if you become professional enough to make it . . . I use margin!

Whether you use margin or not will also depend upon

your confidence in interpreting what is happening on Wall Street. At any rate the next step follows:

In order to raise the capital to take advantage of these one or two vehicles which you have uncovered . . . in order to take full advantage of these one or two stocks . . . SELL OFF ALL YOUR OTHER STOCKS AND WITH THE PROCEEDS BUY THESE ONE OR TWO RISING STOCKS!

Now instead of a basket of stocks . . . now instead of a diversified portfolio, you will have one or two or three stocks and a STEAMLINED PORTFOLIO!

Now when your stocks appreciate one dollar, instead of making $300 holding 300 shares, you will make $3000 because you were holding 3000 shares!!

Interpret the market letter that follows which was written in 1986 during the bull market.

* * *

THE K FACTOR DEC. 10, 1986. . .DJ 1932.93

Streamlining A Portfolio

THIS SUCCESSFUL INVESTOR SAYS:

"Don't diversify your portfolio . . . STREAMLINE it!

This is one of my investment principles. It's an idea all my own. Examine your portfolio. What is the market value and how many issues do you own (including penny stocks and those you hold for years?) Now compare it to mine!

October: The market value of my portfolio: $465,445.

November: 1. I added to my "streamlined" stock (the 14,000 share investment I wrote about.) 2. I added bonds yielding about 11½%.

December: I sold one stock.

QUESTION?

How many stocks are now in my portfolio?

ANSWER!

Would you believe two? That's it . . . just . . . only . . . TWO!!

QUESTION?

What is the market value of each stock??

ANSWER!

My "streamlined" stock is fast approaching $200,000.

My other investment is stuck at $5,000. Study very carefully what I am doing and how I am managing my pension fund. I want to impress upon you that this is what I am doing with *MY MONEY.* It's been working for me successfully through bad markets and good markets.

It should work for you! *Now let's consider how "streamlining" works and why!*

Theory Behind Streamlining

Ivan Boesky made millions and millions in Wall Street not by *diversifying* his investments but by *"streamlining!"* True, he owned many, many stocks . . . but each investment was a "streamlined" issue . . . a special situation. He didn't invest $100,000 in each of many issues but instead invested millions in each "special" issue.

Why? Because he knew the *risk was slight!* He had inside information. When he knew the risk was slight, he laid it on!

Wouldn't you lay it on if you knew the "risk was slight?" I'm sure that he wouldn't have invested so much in each issue if the risk was "normal".

Hence "streamlining" means making a heavy

and substantial investment in a stock or issue AFTER GIVING *EXTREME CONSIDERATION* to the *RISK FACTOR!!*

Consequently, if you are satisfied and convinced that the risk factor is what I would say "understood" or to put it another way, if you are convinced of what the risk is, then you would lay it on just as Mr. Boesky did . . . just as I do . . . just as I did!

And that's what I do and that's how I made my big money!!

The Streamlining Process

You start out by examining thousands of stock issues. You search and sift through these looking for a "low risk" situation. Next you examine the relative potential gain. Then you study various research reports and make telephone calls pertaining to the investment and consider the many fundamental factors surrounding it. Finally you research technical data.

Next you make initial purchases in perhaps ten different issues. As time goes by you slowly sell off those you find are not gaining and those that are turning into losses.

The proceeds of these sales are reinvested in those that are working out and into new issues that may arise.

When you finally find one or more stocks that are gaining in price, you then turn the investment into a "campaign" of this now streamlined issue (such as my one issue. I expect a substantial increase in price in 1987. You really should make it a streamlined stock for your portfolio).

So to Succeed in Investing . . .
Don't Diversify . . . Streamline

* * *

Conclusion

If you train your mind to understand what Wall Street is all about . . . If you train your mind to accept losses while you joke over a cup of coffee . . . you've got it made!

Now you will know that you can jump into the market at any time . . . and not just that you have to catch a stock at the bottom. Now you will know that the market goes up and down and that you can't predict what it's going to do day by day or week by week or month by month.

But you will KNOW what time it is on Wall Street. You will know what part of the cycle that you are in. Even though you know these things but because you can't predict the market either daily, weekly, or monthly, you may suffer holding a losing position . . . that perhaps your judgment was wrong in handling some fundamental or technical interpretations and consequently wound up facing a loss.

Don't hesitate to take a small loss. Don't let it become big. Take it once. Take it twice. Take it a hundred times. I take losses many more times than I take profits.

If you learn to breathe with the rhythm of the stock market, . . . if you learn to swim in the ocean with its big waves by jumping in again and again, . . . if you fall off a horse again and again and again, . . . you'll soon understand the horse . . . and what to expect . . . and how to cope . . . and how to ride with your hair in the wind . . . with a smile on your lips . . . and a gleam in your eyes. . . .

That's the way to conquer Wall Street . . . that's the way to succeed in Wall Street! UNDERSTAND IT! THEN PLUNGE IN! . . . AND NOT THE OTHER WAY AROUND!

10

Selling Stock: When . . . and How Much

Selling Principle: If You Don't Sell . . . You Don't Get Rich

I think that you will find that a consensus of experienced investors will agree that while buying isn't exactly child's play, compared to selling, it's a piece of cake!

Somehow it's "natural" to buy! Most people seem to be buying stock. But you don't often hear someone say that they are selling stock.

Most investors are always bullish. They don't like down markets. They don't even like to talk about selling or talk about down markets. Consequently these investors tend to be very, very clannish.

I've had some interesting experiences voicing my opinion when I was bearish. Invariably I stood almost alone defending my position against frustrated challenging bulls. It's not difficult to find reasons to buy. It's the natural, easy way of doing things in Wall Street.

SELLING, on the other hand, GOES AGAINST HUMAN NATURE! It's unnatural! Somehow it's clumsy!

Many times I felt I was betraying my friends.

When I used to spend time in my broker's office during bull markets, people who wanted to place sell orders always did so with low voices and in a quiet manner. They didn't want to call attention to the fact that they were selling. As though ashamed of this act!

The act of buying opens new and exciting vistas. We never know how much that stock is going to jump immediately after we buy it. There is something to look forward to. We anxiously read the papers every day after a purchase.

SELLING IS AN ACT OF FINALITY! It draws down the curtain on an episode of effort and time and watchful waiting. It is difficult to say farewell to a good and rewarding friend. It's almost impossible to take a loss and admit that *YOU* made a mistake!

Therefore it's easier to understand why . . . *SELLING IS THE ART IN INVESTING!*

Bad buying decisions can sometimes be corrected by buying more or sometimes just by waiting. The buyer in the latter case is not required to take any action. The buyer can go to the movies for a while or simply forget about the stock market.

Selling takes positive action! It's a decision that must be made. People hate to be forced to do anything that they don't want to do. And they sure never want to sell. I think we can understand why buying tends to be easy compared to selling!

When to Sell

Sell when you approach the level established by the Krumholz Factor—that is, the approximate loss you decided that you would accept before you bought. That was the maximum predetermined risk that you would subject your capital to.

Note this important point: While it is imperative to set

a selling point below the level of purchase, we never set one above that level.

Now I conform with conventional Wall Street doctrine.

Cut Your Losses! . . . Let Your Profits Run!

We have discussed the several principles used to help us do this "unnatural" thing, selling. Now you know why it is so necessary to spend a great deal of time talking about them. Rather than have you memorize material, I believe that by osmosis you will absorb all you have to know.

If any of these principles fail you, then turn to your common sense and for no other reason . . . get out! In some of my market letters I say: "I don't want to play today . . . maybe tomorrow but not today!"

You do the same thing. You don't have to be in the stock market all the time. In fact, you won't get rich if you do.

Watch the Trend

Another time you should sell is when your stock breaks a trend. Usually they are broken with unusual volume. I'm talking about stocks which are declining or falling in price after being in an up trend. The bottom trend line should be decisively pierced. In a bull market some trends are sometimes broken only to have the stock make new highs and establish a sharper up trend then the one just broken.

Sometimes this indicator is difficult to interpret. Sometimes the stock may be undergoing a correction in an up trend. In a market cycle there are usually several corrections. Using the market cycle, volume and trend all together will give better indications of what may follow.

However I have frequently found that if I don't get out at the beginning of a correction, the correction invariably falls much further than most investors expect.

I know that it costs commissions to get in and out and I know that you will miss points, but I also know that any kind of insurance is expensive and necessary.

Every business has expenses. Don't try to save hundreds only to lose thousands. Here it is far better to be prudent than right. I may be wrong but I have the impression that when I started investing in 1946, I used to hear more about prudence than I do today.

Perhaps the professionals in those years were closer to the 1929 Crash than the professionals of 1987 . . . before the Crash! In the aftermath of the '87 Crippler I heard lots of "Don't Panic" but I don't recall hearing much admonitions of "Be Prudent . . . Sell".

Do you want to know when to sell?

WHEN THE MARKET DROPS FOR SEVERAL DAYS ON HUGE VOLUME . . . S E L L ! BE PRUDENT!

Or if YOUR STOCK declines for several days with unusual volume . . . *SELL! BE PRUDENT!*

How Long to Hold a Stock

Many times I recall buying one day and selling the next day. In fact it was in the early part of 1987 that I bought Texfi in the morning and sold it that afternoon.

I had been dubious about the stock market for a long time. Remembering that investment principle of not fighting the tape, I was going to keep buying something to go along with the bull market trend. Anybody can holler bear market years ahead.

Well, January 30, 1987 was a Friday. The stock, Texfi Industries, had caught my eye for some time and that morning I became aware of *TECHNICAL ACTIVITY* in the issue. The stock was moving higher on bigger volume.

That means I know nothing about the company or its fundamentals but the *forces in the market place were buying the stock!*

You know! The three working parts of the stock market were in harmony: CYCLE, TREND, VOLUME!

Well I did something I seldom do. (This illustrates that I stray, too. I keep repeating it's not a science). I bought 1000 shares at 6⅛ without going to the library to do my homework on the fundamentals of the company.

From the technical analysis that I did, it appeared that the stock could double in a very short time. After I bought the stock I went to the library to research the company's fundamentals.

What I saw embarrassed me. From a fundamental point of view my impression was that the stock wasn't worth much, if anything, let alone $6. I couldn't wait to get back to the office to sell it—(or did I call the order in from the library)?

I sold it for 6⅜. I would have sold it at any price. I just didn't want that thing in my portfolio. The stock did go substantially higher almost immediately. We were in a roaring bull market. Stocks were being taken over. But I had no regrets. I was wrong but "prudent".

This is just another instance of when to sell. When a factor develops that you feel can have a strong negative impact on the price of the stock, then again, be prudent, sell!

This episode should help me find favor with the fundamentalists. They contend that technical analysts give no heed to anything but technical factors. While it is common for many technicians to hold to that opinion, I just don't complete my technical analysis until I am completely satisfied as to the fundamentals.

I rely completely on my *THINKING FOR MY DECI-*

SIONS. Good fundamentals are the cushion that lets me sleep nights!

Sell to Increase Your Potential

We discussed "STREAMLINING". In the management of a portfolio, it is always necessary to keep your capital working at its optimum potential. Every portfolio at times will just idle along.

There may be some utilities mixed with industrials, financial, and conglomerate issues. They may all have small paper profits. Meanwhile the market may be rising faster than the issues in that portfolio.

It is good investment practice to seek to switch one or more of your stocks into something else . . . an industry that may be in favor. Try a stock that has recently moved *higher on volume*

Of course, it may be time to engage in the streamlining process. We discussed that. You may need the capital to *launch or continue a campaign!*

Sell After a Fall

We have discussed how to avoid stock market crashes. However there are times when the market suffers severe drops in stock prices that are corrections to sharp up moves. The declines in corrections are often punishing.

It is almost impossible to avoid all crashes and all corrections. Therefore when you fail to avoid either a crash or a correction, SELL immediately after. Use COMMON SENSE! Be Prudent! *DON'T TAKE A CHANCE ON HEAVY LOSSES MOUNTING! OR . . . DON'T LET PROFITS SLIP AWAY!!*

Sell on Rallies After Falls

We know that the most difficult part of investing is to know when to sell! It is always a judgment call. There are times when in spite of what we know, we will be caught holding stocks.

If we fail to avoid a *crash* and fail to sell immediately thereafter, then when the inevitable rally follows, don't miss your third and last chance to do the proper thing . . . *SELL!* It's proper because it's PRUDENT! Don't let a BEAR MARKET TRAP fool you.

Bear Market Traps

After a bull market crash, historically it is followed by MAJOR BEAR TRAPS! They are called that because most investors refuse to believe that bull markets end.

MOST INVESTORS THINK that when they see prices selling 30% and 50% lower than they did just a few weeks ago, that stocks are bargains and so they rush in to buy the "BARGAINS".

Since we are in the third stage of the cycle, these buyers will be buying the stock that is being "distributed". When buyers find that the supply is greater than the demand, they will step aside and prices will resume the primary major down trend until the lows are established!

Bear Traps are found throughout the falling stage of the cycle. This latter stage may take several years to complete. They are difficult to interpret because many key indicators seem to support a bona fide rise in stock values.

In 1971 I was caught in a beauty of a Bear Trap which caused me to write a market letter on it because it was very instructive.

The stock market had topped out in 1968 after many years of a bull market. In 1971 the market appeared to be getting strong so I started to buy stocks. The letter which follows is self explanatory.

* * *

THE K FACTOR FEB. 28, 1971. . .DJ 878.83

The Wheel of Fortune . . . Caught in a Bear Trap!
(NYSE Occidental Petroleum 18⅝)

On February 15th I wrote that it's "Still time to buy" and recommended the purchase of three stocks and one warrant at the market. Included was Occidental Petroleum.

I had maintained a continuous study of the company for the longest time without holding a position until recently when I started to accumulate the stock.

It appeared to me that there was buying coming into the issue and that the stock could move considerably higher. This technical analysis was bolstered by my interpretation that early reports were indicative of a settlement that could endure for some time between the major oil companies and the countries of the Mid-East.

Consequently I began to accumulate the stock. However on Tuesday and Wednesday, I started to get uneasy about the market generally and commenced to take profits in other securities.

But I kept buying Oxy. I bought some more of the stock on Thursday, even though I was getting apprehensive about the rest of the market. Occidental Petroleum "looked good technically".

Friday at 10:15 the stock had not yet opened and I immediately sensed that something was wrong. Oxy doesn't open late. When it did open, it opened with a gap down. I was tempted to step in and buy, but the late opening raised signals of "danger" for me. Red flags of alert.

Technically it didn't make sense to me. All day I was tempted to buy but I curbed emotion with investment principles. Some of which follow:

INVESTMENT PRINCIPLES:

Don't aggravate a bad situation by jumping in and averaging too early.

Don't sell out under emotional stress.

Don't get locked in.

Don't look for excuses and be immobilized.

But *DO* calmly trade your way out!!!

I have no idea how low the stock will open tomorrow (Monday) or if trading will have to be suspended again. I don't know what I'm going to do at this time but my policy and plan are set:

Buy if the price is right. Sell if a rally develops.

During 1969 and 1970 I nimbly and easily avoided the wrath of the bear market. Now in 1971 I am beautifully ensnared in a BEAR TRAP in one stock!!

That's Wall Street!! The Wheel of Fortune has turned and caught me on this one!!

What Time is it on Wall Street?

It's time to start selling and to build large cash reserves again. I started to sell rather heavily this past week. The market will probably rally but my opinion is that the market will whip-saw, after which it will drop. Hold off buying and concentrate on selling.

My policy is to get out early with plenty of cash. If I should be wrong, I can latch on to enough behind the market stocks to catch up with the stock market later on.

You see, I don't buy stocks because I love them or because they are my favorites. I only buy and hold those stocks that might help my capital grow. I believe in switching stocks and in timing stocks.

The wheel of fortune may be starting to turn down again. Yes? No? My money says yes and I want to see it back in the bank. Do you know where your money will be tonight?

*   *   *

T*HINK!*—Of the many facts that I have already presented to you that are voiced in the letter!!

Let the letter remind you to be careful not to get caught in a bear trap after a BULL MARKET CRASH!!

Sell With a Substantial Profit

We have said that during the first stage of the cycle, we should take small profits. That would help offset many small losses. We said that as the stage develops, we wouldn't take profits but rather buy more of the issue.

This is a critical decision. Do you sell and take a small profit or do you start accumulating? I don't have any formulas or panacea. JUST THINK AND REASON. You know enough now not to worry about mistakes. You'll make up for them!

If you decide that you should accumulate and if that issue should rise until it becomes fairly valued—(it will usually have at least doubled in price), then carefully watch for volume to come into the stock.

You will find resistance to higher prices. There will be

backing and filling. This means that the price of the stock is fluctuating with the increase in volume. THAT'S THE TIME TO SELL!

Sell When the Bull Market IS Roaring!

A phenomenon of a bull market is that not all stocks make their highs at the same time that the stock market does! Some stocks may make their highs one year or more *before* the stock market does.

Other stocks may make theirs *after* the stock market does. It may be during a correction right after a market high that is then followed by a rally. This rally could precede a crash. Most stocks will make their highs about the time that the stock market does.

During a roaring bull market there should be one or more campaigns going on. Since we know of the phenomena that all stocks don't top out with a bull market, it may be necessary to end a campaign at an early sign of distribution to lock in that profit.

Locking in the profits of a long and fruitful campaign removes considerable pressure and thus permits us to be less emotional in evaluating our other campaigns currently in force.

Also, by removing profits and capital, there is less exposure to risk.

Finally don't risk years of effort by taking a fully invested portfolio through a bull market that is known to be of age. Remember . . . *IF YOU DON'T SELL . . . YOU DON'T GET RICH!*

Summary

This chapter doesn't tell it all on "How to Sell". These pages just open the door to your THINKING about

"How to Sell". The real art of selling is explained throughout the pages of this book!

Investing is not easy work. It's not hard work either. It is a continuous stressful effort encompassing a lifetime. You have to like it! You have to want to do it! You have to like the challenge!

11

Bonds— How . . . What . . . When . . . To Buy!

The Start to Wall Street Riches

It was early in October, 1972 that I was sitting slouched low in my big leather office chair with my elbows resting on its arms. My head was tilted forward so that my chin was touching my chest.

My eyes were closed but seeing. My hands were clasped in my lap while my feet were fully extended. I crossed my legs so that one ankle rested on the other.

I was feeling low and dejected as I mentally reviewed my financial status. For years my wife and I had worked and whatever we had managed to save, I kept losing in an effort to establish an investment company.

Suddenly I realized that after thirty-seven years of hard work, many years running two separate and different enterprises, day and night, at times working as much as three days without sleep, that I still had no money!

I WASN'T GOING TO MAKE IT WITHOUT CAPITAL!

I WASN'T GOING TO MAKE IT BY SWEAT ALONE!

All that I had accomplished in those thirty-seven years of struggle was to save some $3,000 in a Keogh plan and a few thousand dollars.

Oh yes! I just remembered 1958. I had not invested in the stock market in much of the fifties because I had no money. I did keep abreast of the stock market.

That year, 1958, I couldn't resist the opportunities that seemed to appear in Wall Street. Not having any capital, I asked a client for an advance on fees that I expected to earn that year. It amounted to $500.

Then I went to the First National City Bank which is now Citibank and borrowed $1500.

I invested that money in 1958 and sold out for well over $8,000, if I remember, in 1959. In 1959 we bought the house that we still live in with a $5,000 down payment. We also had about $1,000 in expenses for closing costs and moving expenses. And we bought some furniture for the new house.

The house needed a $5,000 alteration that we partly financed. And there went my capital . . . it went into consumer money! We were living in a rented apartment at the time we bought the house so we did need to do a bit of furnishing.

(Do you remember the earlier chapter on Money . . . And The Stock Market? Capital must be kept apart from consumer money!)

Thinking about the money that I made in the stock market in 1958–59 gave me an idea. I'd always had success with stocks since I first started in 1946. I only had six months' experience when I called the end to the bull market as it was developing and before it crashed.

That bull market had started in 1941–42. I had called the crash when professionals with years of experience continued buying for months and years while prices kept falling!

I could never really get started in the stock market

because I never had sufficient capital for a sustained effort. How much could I make with $2000 in 1946 and no job? I always needed my earnings for my family.

My idea was this: simply switch! Channel my efforts into the stock market! I had tried to earn money for thirty-seven years without success. The times that I tried to make money in Wall Street met with success. So why not devote myself completely to investing in the stock market??

I raised my knees high and bounced out of the chair landing on my feet with a thud.

"That's it," I said. "I'm going to become an investor in Wall Street!"

From now on I was going to stop my losses and end all other endeavors. It would take time because I still needed income and importantly I had to accumulate savings to build capital for investment only!

It would take years but I had direction. I had a plan! I had an objective! I was going to start building for my pension! I was going to get WALL STREET RICH!!

With that thought in mind I started to concentrate on all I had learned about investing—its principles and its fundamentals. I laid out my objectives and my strategy. I determined the tactics that I would employ.

On November 1, 1972 I picked up the gauntlet that all investors must pick up when they accept the . . .

"Three Keys To Wall Street"!

When you accept the Three Keys, you accept the challenge to use them successfully!

It was on November 1, 1972 that I made my first purchase. I bought 2 bonds of Connecticut Light and Power, that were due October 1, 1980. The coupon was 3% on par value of $1,000. Therefore my income would be $60 per year. (Today my interest income is over $40,000 per year.) I paid $735 per bond. Total Investment $1470.

THAT'S THE START TO WALL STREET RICHES! ! !

It starts with $60 annual income!

Investors don't see the importance of a slow and cautious start. They want to start with the $40,000 annual income. BUT THEY DON'T WANT TO LOSE ANY MONEY!!

That secret I haven't discovered as yet. The way to start is to make a serious, dedicated attempt. You must segregate money for capital only. Proceed by totaling your net investment value each month and try to see that it increases each month.

A successful business practice is to set budgeted profit growth. It's difficult in investing because the cycle runs about ten years. However you would be amazed how my selling decisions are strongly influenced by this drive for growth each year.

A monthly check is the best reminder of my objective. If I fall behind some months, I will then tightly monitor my investment decisions.

In 1972 the stock market was in the doldrums. The banks were paying about 6%. My first thought was that I wanted to start investing with a minimum of risk . . . the Krumholz Factor!

I wanted to start investing with income to start so when I bought stocks, I would have some investment income to offset a potential loss. True it was only $60 but remember the very first investment principle, *PATIENCE!!* Take it easy.

It's a long road ahead. We have years before each bull market and we can't push the market up. You don't get rich quick in Wall Street and you don't get rich easy.

We are developing strategy. We are working towards a lifetime objective!

Now these bonds had a good investment grade rating and the current yield was 4.08%. Divide the $60 by your $1470. Since it would take eight years to maturity at which time I expected to receive $2,000, I would have a profit of $565. Divide that by $1470 and the yield is a profit of $70.62 per year which is an additional 4.8%.

The banks were paying 6%. I would get a total of 8.8%.

In addition, since part of the profit was capital gain, I would save taxes.

Assuming the total profit to be about 9%, that would mean that I took part of my capital and moved it from 6% to 9%. It's the same as though my $1470 became almost $2200.

I invested $1470 and became wealthy overnight! Did we not discuss money and how to manage it? Remember the first investment principle, "greed". Don't get greedy and don't get impatient. This is the way to succeed in investing. Perhaps not the only way . . . but it's the way I did it!

There are many principles illustrated here. The first is that I predicated my THINKING on my objective and my strategy. I did not invest in that bond for immediate profit. I expected to hold it for eight years until it matured. AND I DID!

That is not buying for the "long term" as you might think. There was a fixed maturity for "selling". It was to anchor a starting portfolio. It is different when investors buy stock for the "long term". They marry the stock! They never expect to sell!

I didn't look upon that $60 interest as income per se. I looked upon it as a $60 profit. I hope I am communicating the THINKING BEHIND THIS PARTICULAR PURCHASE.

With the little capital that I was starting with, there was not enough capital to think of INVESTING FOR INCOME. I started in 1972 with only a profit of $60 indicated for the year, but by the time I cashed in that bond, in 1980, I had made $74,427 as a small Wall Street investor.

My investment program was started with a bond instead of a stock for a very important point to remember about investing: *DON'T LOSE MONEY!!* (We have discussed the example of investing $10,000 to try to make it $20,000).

We found that if we lose 50% of the $10,000, we face

the task of making 400% to meet our objective. Don't forget this. You know how hard it is to earn more than a bank pays. You also recall our talk about switching from bank to bank. (Just as I am doing today, to pick up an extra fractional percentage.)

If it is that hard to earn money that you have to resort to switching banks, then how difficult do you think it is to invest profitably in the stock market or in the bond market? It merits covering this ground once again.

THIS IS THE START TO WALL STREET RICHES! Right here!

If it's that hard to earn an extra ¼% by switching banks, then. . . .

THINK! REASON! COMMON SENSE!

Surely your common sense will tell you to be most careful before you get involved with a stock! If you buy a stock at $10 and it loses $1, you lost 10%. Let me spell it out for you. . . . ten percent! And here we are talking about ¼% and a $10 gift from the bank.

Therefore your most serious consideration must be the amount of money you may lose.

THINK ABOUT THAT!

That is why my very first purchase was a quality bond to mature not too far in the future. (Eight years in investing is like planning to see a play two months hence). I did not want to risk a loss with my first purchase. It was necessary to make a positive step towards my objective!

Later that month I purchased one convertible bond, Wallace-Murray, 6½ s 5/1/91 for which I paid 100¼.

At the same time I bought one General Telephone & Electric convertible bond, 6¼ s 9/15/96 at 106 and I bought two Uniroyal convertible bonds, 5½ s 2/15/96 at 80½.

Here we've been talking about stocks and the stock market, chapter after chapter, and yet when I invest my money, it seems that I buy bonds. And we haven't as yet discussed bonds. Interesting!

You know the thrust of this book is to get rich by THINKING about how to make money by investing in Wall Street. Therefore it is critical that you know what and when and why.

So let's talk about bonds and why I bought them!!!

The Art of a Bond

Just as most investors don't really UNDERSTAND the nature of the stock market, many investors fail to take full advantage of a bond! . . . Let's just talk about that art.

Since a bond is a loan, it usually has a fixed rate of interest and a date when the loan is to be repaid. People are aware of giving a mortgage or taking a mortgage. They are familiar with taking loans and repaying them. They know of car loans and of business loans.

In these cases people know that there is a rate of interest and terms of repayment. However they are used to dealing on a one to one basis. There is you and there is the bank or finance office or charge account.

They are not accustomed to having these loans that they are involved with . . . sold or bought . . . back and forth . . . again and again . . . with strange people they have never spoken with.

They are not accustomed to having these loans traded! Investors fail to take into account the fact that there are people who specialize only in trading in bonds. These specialists trade bonds for "PROFIT" . . . not for the interest that bonds bring.

These specialists trade bonds as you and I might buy and sell stocks.

The Borrower is Called the Issuer

The corporations whose stocks are listed on the New York Stock Exchange are big. When some of them wish to raise money, they sometimes do so by selling additional stock.

Sometimes the corporations decide to raise money by selling BONDS. To know the interest rate and the maturity and other terms and conditions, it is necessary to read the indenture. This is the terms of the loan. It is the agreement between the company and the bond holder.

These bonds may be listed on the New York Stock Exchange *Bond Trading* or not. We are interested in those that *are*. Since the bonds are *issued* by corporations, they are called corporate bonds. When utilities issue bonds, they are called utility bonds. When the government issues bonds they are called treasury bonds. When states, cities and localities issue bonds they are called municipal bonds.

Different Bonds

Bonds come in different shapes and forms . . . just as stocks. That gives them different names. If a bond has assets pledged as security for repayment of the loan, it may be called a mortgage bond or it may be called a collateral trust bond.

If the bond is simply a promise to pay without any collateral, it may be called a debenture. Bonds may or may not be *first* mortgage bonds. If the loan is of shorter term duration, it may be called a note.

Different bonds have different names.

Convertible Bonds

The indenture is the terms of the loan. When the terms of a bond give the *bond owner* the right or the option to *exchange the bond for stock*, that bond is called a convertible bond. The bond owner has the right to *convert* the bond into stock.

The indenture may allow the owner other choices to convert to. It is not restricted to just that stock.

Straight Bond

A bond that lacks this convertible feature is called a straight bond.

Coupon Bond . . . Registered Bond

A coupon bond is one that has coupons attached to it. To collect interest, it is necessary to mail in each coupon to receive the interest. To receive the principal, it is necessary to turn in the bond, itself.

If you lose the bond, you are out of luck. The possessor is deemed to be the lawful owner.

A registered bond is a bond where the issuer has your name registered as the owner. The issuer will pay you interest and principal when due. If you lose the bond, you simply ask to have it replaced.

How to Buy Bonds

The bonds that launched me on the way to Wall Street Riches were the first two bonds which I bought: $2,000 Connecticut Light and Power, 3 s 10/1/80 at 72¼

WHAT DOES THIS MEAN? One bond is usually issued for $1,000. When I bought two bonds, the issuer now owed $2,000 to me! The key to remember is that this $2,000 never changes even though the *market price always does* and even though the loan is transferred.

This $2,000 obligation or loan never changes no matter how many years go by. Unless, of course, the indenture says otherwise. Therefore no matter what price I paid for them or no matter what year I bought them, Connecticut Light now owed me $2,000.

The *3* in *3* s 10/1/80 at 72¼ is the coupon rate. This is the annual rate of interest that is paid on the bond.

Buying the Bond

The, *s*, in 3 *s* 10/1/80 means *due*. It means that the bond, $1,000, is due and payable on October 1, 1980.

The 10/1/80 means that the bond will be payable on October 1, 1980. If it was 5/01/04, the bond will be due on May 1, 2004. The interest, however, is paid semi-annually. Interest is paid on the maturity month and day, and six months from then.

Thus with the 10/1/80 bond, interest would be paid every October 1st and April 1st. With the 5/1/04 bond interest would be paid every May 1st and November 1st.

The 72¼ is the price that I paid for one bond.

When bonds are traded, and when their prices are published in the New York Stock Exchange and Bond Trading, the last digit is omitted. For example to buy the Connecticut Light bond, I paid 72¼. Bonds have bid and ask prices just as stocks.

I paid 72¼ or $722.50 for each bond. If the bid were 98½ it would mean $985.00. If a bid is 101⅛, it would be $1011.25.

If I paid over $1000 for a bond, I would be paying a premium. If I paid less than $1,000, I would be buying at a discount. If I paid $1,000, I would be buying at par.

Therefore to buy bonds, you tell your broker that you "Want to buy five bonds of Con Ed at 98½. The bonds are the 9⅛ of 2004." You don't have to give the day and month.

Think About Bonds

Investors seem to feel that when they buy a long term bond that they must hold the bond for years and years until maturity. That's simply not so. They feel that way because a bond has a fixed maturity date somewhere in the distant future.

Let's consider a stock. A stock does not have a maturity date. It's forever! Conceivably that should be longer than any long term bond, yet investors don't think that way.

You definitely should consider buying a bond for a purpose and when that purpose is fulfilled, then *SELL IT!* Don't you do that with a stock? When you buy a stock, you don't marry it or shouldn't. Neither should you marry a bond!

What Kind of Bonds to Buy

The kind of bond to buy depends upon the purpose that you have in mind! We'll see as we go on.

When to Buy Bonds

NOW THIS IS THE ART OF THE INVESTOR!!!!!!!!

So let's talk some more!

THINK! AN INVESTOR IS INTERESTED IN WALL STREET ONLY FOR PROFIT! Therefore it is incumbent upon the investor to put capital where it can get optimum profits. Usually this is in the stock market.

Therefore I say that you buy stocks for PROFIT!

Many investors can't cope with the stock market and yet they are interested in income. These investors should buy and invest in treasury bonds. These bonds offer the minimum risk far as payment of principal and interest. So I say; buy *bonds* for income.

For this reason I say,

"BUY STOCKS FOR PROFIT . . . BUY BONDS FOR INCOME!!"

Therefore don't buy utility stocks for income. Buy them for profit! They are stocks—not bonds!

The Risk in Bonds

The investor is deeply concerned with the risk factor in dealing with stocks but the same deep concern applies to bonds.

When a rating of AAA or BB is given to a bond, it is *NOT* the *SAFETY* factor assigned to the investor. It is not the degree of safety given to that bond in the bond market. It does not assign the risk that the investor is taking as an investment.

That AAA rating *ESTIMATES* the *ABILITY* of the *ISSUER to make timely payments* on the interest and principal! Therefore the investor takes the same risk in buying a bond as is taken in buying a stock. The market price of both stocks and bonds are subject to supply and demand.

Although I say "buy stocks for profits. .buy bonds for income", there are times when an investor could buy bonds for profits but this should be done with that thought in mind!

Stocks vs. Bonds

We saw the stock market crash on October 19, 1987. For days afterward all Wall Street was stunned. Nobody was talking. Everybody spoke in whispers. It seemed Wall Street was confused and scared. The President immediately asked for a meeting with leading members of the Congress to resolve the budget dispute.

On the heels of all this I saw big advertisements in November and December . . . "Buy utilities for income," and "Buy utilities for defense."

I couldn't believe what I saw! Just why won't investors take it easy and THINK!! I don't know! I really believe that investors would think if they weren't misled by crutches!

Without a doubt, investors have the capacity to think. You don't have to be a brain to succeed in investing. But you do have to know how the stock market works and to understand it. We've covered that ground!

Let's think. They tell you to buy and hold utilities and others for income and for defensive reasons. This is my thinking. Stocks go up in a bull market. Stocks go down in a bear market. Therefore why should I buy stocks when they are falling down? Am I not supposed to buy them when they are going up???

Again, if stocks are falling and I don't have stocks, why should I have stocks for defensive reasons? What am I defending myself from? Why should I hold stocks and then have to defend myself???

Is there something wrong about my reasoning? If there is, then what I did through all of my investing career was wrong. So how come I got rich in the stock market? Evidently it worked for me! If it worked for me, why won't it work for you?

THINK! This is how I do it!!

WHEN STOCKS ARE FALLING . . . . I SELL!

WHEN STOCKS ARE RISING . . . . I BUY!

WHEN I WANT INCOME . . . . I BUY BONDS!

THINK! They tell you to buy stocks, for example, utilities for income. At this time they are only yielding 5% to 7½%. I could buy a quality bond yielding 9% or a treasury bond yielding 8%. Why should I buy a utility?

Oh! Utility stocks may appreciate.

Ah! So that's it!

You are not buying utilities for income, you are buying them for PROFIT. Therefore utilities belong in the STOCK MARKET and not in the INCOME MARKET!

If utilities are in the stock market and stocks are falling, just what do you think is going to happen to your utility stocks? OR DON'T UTILITY STOCKS EVER

GO DOWN? *Remember-that in a bad market . . . there is no such thing as a good stock!*

In December, 1987 I saw a published list of utility stocks practically all down with a few exceptions. Some were down 25%, 17% etc. *BUT DOWN!!*

Look how low the price of Gulf States Utilities fell! And how low the price of Long Island Lighting fell. Public Service of New Hampshire was on the verge of bankruptcy.

So THINK. Reason with me. We are average investors. Don't look for exceptions to the rule in the stock market. I know many of the answers. I've heard them all before.

The best defense, in fact, the only defense, is to sell everything when the market crashes!!

REASON! If you really want income, doesn't it make ordinary good sense to buy a two year treasury note? Guaranteed no loss! Guaranteed income! Isn't it smart to buy a five year or ten year treasury note for income?

Brothers and Sisters! Colleagues!

I was sitting on $150,000 in Treasuries plus other bonds and cash and ONE stock when the Stock Market Crashed on October 19, 1987. Just think how I sat and watched and listened to the flood of reports. I was completely relaxed. I felt I was a most successful investor!!

Uses of Bonds

I use treasuries to anchor my investment portfolio. I use them for income and for safety. I want to know that I can sleep secure in the knowledge that my annual income will always be there.

I use municipal bonds when I wish to minimize my taxes. I determine just how much taxes I want to save, then estimate the length of time my high income will continue and for how long a time I wish to minimize my tax.

When I buy treasuries and municipals, it is with the intention of holding them to maturity.

Straight bonds are bought when I want something more liquid. I could buy and sell these bonds on the NYSE without too much fuss. I use them when I want a better rate for a short time. I buy them for PROFIT, not primarily for income.

Convertible bonds are bought strictly for profit. I use these when I want to help defray the cost of margin interest. I also use convertible bonds when I wish to minimize the risk of holding stocks.

At times when the Krumholz Factor is a little difficult to ascertain, I will go with the convertible bond so if I have to stay with the issue longer than I had hoped to, at least I will be receiving interest.

This chapter does not tell all about bonds any more than previous chapters told all about stocks. How and when to buy and sell stocks and bonds are better learned when explained with case studies.

With each experience is a new twist, a new angle, a new thought. You are going to have to THINK without the benefit of hindsight, just as I did in these case studies. Therefore there is much to learn from them!!

12

How to Buy Bonds—For Profit!

I have outlined some of the many purposes and reasons for buying bonds. When to buy bonds is determined by the purpose of the investor. Sometimes the decision to buy bonds may be influenced more by the attractiveness of bonds rather than the purpose.

I was buying bonds near the year-end of 1972 because stocks had peaked in 1968 and were still in the doldrums. The cycle seemed to be more in the fourth stage of the last cycle than in the first stage of the new cycle. The stock market seemed always to be falling down.

Stock prices hit their lows in 1973–74 so I'm glad that I had patience with stocks. It appeared reasonable to avoid the risks inherent in holding stocks and to settle for a small gain or even a small loss with bonds.

The stock market was three years past its bull market high. From time to time it showed strength. There was a good market during the latter part of 1970 but each time that the Dow Jones approached the 1000 level, it retreated.

Consequently my thinking and my experience dictated that I shouldn't lead the market but follow it. I'd wait for the market to break through then I'd buy a rising market!! I was just thinking investment principles!!

The Interest Feature of a Bond

This is why I turned to bonds. The stock market was too unsettled and appeared to offer too much of a risk. My first bond was the Connecticut bond which was a "straight" bond. It was not a convertible bond. Then I bought several convertible bonds.

As we said, a convertible bond offers the owner or the holder of that bond the right to exchange that bond for stock. I bought one bond of Wallace-Murray, a 6½ s 5/1/91 at 100¼. I paid $1002.50.

There's an interesting difference between stocks and bonds. When you buy a stock, only the owner of a certain date gets the dividend. There's no splitting the dividend between the buyer and the seller of a stock.

Bonds work differently. Since they earn interest on a daily basis because they are loans of money, the seller receives interest up to the day that the seller receives the proceeds of the sale.

Thereafter the buyer starts to earn interest. The issuer, who is the borrower, pays interest semi-annually. If the trade is effected between payment dates, that six month interest is split between the buyer and the seller.

Therefore if I bought that Wallace-Murray bond in December and that trade settled one week later, let us say, December 12, I would have to pay the $1,002.50 plus the commission, plus the interest for one month and eleven days. I'd pay interest from November 1 to December 12.

On the following May 1, I would receive six months' interest. Since I owned the bond for four months and 28 days, I would get back the amount of interest that I had paid to the seller.

The Convertible Part of a Bond

The most interesting and important part of this type of bond is the convertible feature. Before the bond is issued, the indenture spells out the terms and conditions under which the owner of the bond may elect to exchange the bond.

Usually this is a straight forward fixed number of shares of the issuer's stock. For example, in 1987 I bought ten bonds of Tidewater, Inc., 7 s 12/1/10 at 44⅞. They were purchased on January 12, 1987.

Standard & Poor's publishes a bond guide as well as a stock guide. The back part of this guide lists convertible bonds. Referring to this guide, we find the listing of the Tidewater bond.

Under a heading labeled, Shares per $1,000 bond, there is the figure, 40.00. This means that you can exchange the $1,000 bond for 40 shares of Tidewater's stock anytime you desire to do so.

If the stock is selling approximately at $5 per share, the 40 shares that you would receive in exchange for the bond would have a value of $200. Therefore you wouldn't make the exchange.

Since I paid 44⅞, each bond cost me 448.75 plus the commission. If the stock that is selling at $5 per share appreciated to $20 per share, the forty shares that I would be able to get in exchange for my one bond would have a market value of $800. That's quite a profit.

My bond that cost me $448.75 would shoot up in value as well. Thus I have a choice to sell the bond or to exchange the bond for the appreciated stock which I could sell or hold.

THINK! It is interesting to note that the value of the bond would appreciate irrespective of interest rates or any other factor. The increased value of the bond is there because it is fixed to the exchange of the stock.

Effect of Rating on a Bond

Under the heading labeled, S & P quality rating, we find that the rating assigned to Tidewater is CC. That's terrible.

BUT . . . THINK! OUR WHOLE HOPE OF

ACHIEVING SUCCESS IN INVESTING IS BASED UPON OUR ABILITY TO *THINK* FOR OURSELVES!

We pointed out that this rating, while a factor, assigns the risk factor . . . to the *ABILITY* of *TIDEWATER, INC.* to meet the interest payments and to pay off the principal when due. It does not say *whether you should or should not buy the bond!*

However, I had a purpose in being interested in these particular bonds. In January, 1987 I had a big position in stocks. We were in a super bull market. Although the Dow and other averages were strong, other stocks were not keeping up with the averages.

At that time I was buying oil stocks and options on oil stocks and so I noticed Tidewater, Inc. The company is in the oil industry and is a low priced issue. Because it is a low priced issue, the stock would have the capacity to appreciate much faster than other stocks in the industry.

We discussed this in "buying stocks"!

This is where we have to do our own thinking!! We are *INVESTORS*. We are looking for profits. The timing was perfect for this investment. Oil stocks were on the rise and here we have a low-priced oil stock.

The technical indications were favorable but the fundamentals of the company were very discouraging. They were so weak that I couldn't buy the stock.

However, I noticed that they had *CONVERTIBLE BONDS*. I would never think of buying those bonds for income. But they might be an opportune investment for a short period of time. Therefore I invested in ten bonds!

THINK! No! I didn't expect the stock to move up to 20 from 5. But the bond was yielding over 15% and would probably trade in that area unless things got worse for the company. On the other hand, things looked good for the industry and, as stock prices appreciated for the industry, it could spill over into the price of the stock of Tidewater.

Therefore if Tidewater's stock moved from 5 to 6 or 7, the price of the bond would appreciate. They always do. I was looking to profit from this appreciation.

That is why even though the rating was CC, terrible, the rating in this instance was less of importance, than if I contemplated holding the bond for an indefinite period.

The bonds which I started my portfolio with in 1972 served a different need and a different time. Then the market was depressed and declining. In 1987 the market was strong and rising. I never would have touched the Tidewater bonds in 1972. The market cycle was different.

The convertible bonds that I started my portfolio with in 1972 were much higher rated than the Tidewater ones. I bought them because I wanted to start looking for profits. Those bonds offered less risk at that time than stocks.

The choice to convert the bond into stock gave me an opportunity for profits should those stocks rise. If a bull market ensued, I could convert the bonds and hold the stocks.

The percentage gain is greater buying stocks than their convertibles but that is the price of safety. My purpose was not to maximize profits, but just to make some profit. THINK! This is important.

YOU MUST ALWAYS THINK AS A SUCCESSFUL INVESTOR!!

In 1973 I prepared a one page introduction to bonds for my clients. It follows:

*   *   *

An Introduction To Buying Bonds

In reference to buying bonds you have to understand that there is no instant answer to simply taking your money out of the bank, and the broker's taking the bonds off the shelf.

When you buy that way, you never get the bonds that you want, or which really have value in relation to the market, or which really fit your needs, but you buy what is available. What you want is always in demand and is sold (almost always) immediately.

And so you have to seek and select and be ready to buy at the moment there is available those bonds which you had planned as being what you really wanted.

I will forward some material on bonds which you can slowly read and digest and when you are ready, call me again. You may have heard of AAA bonds. Let me inform you that in my own personal retirement fund, I have B bonds as well as AA bonds.

Learn a little about bonds and then make your decisions. I strongly recommend them as a base upon which to build your own investment fund for either growth or retirement.

* * *

Bonds and Portfolio Development

Watch carefully and think of the many thoughts and principles that I have written about and how I use them as I went through my first year in starting my pension fund. The years, 1969 to 1974, were not easy years for making profits. Consequently it was a good time to concentrate on bonds.

As you read the next letters, keep in mind what was happening in the stock market. Note that although I was buying bonds, I was always waiting for the time to swing into stocks where Wall Street Riches awaits those who will THINK AND USE THE ART OF INVESTING!

Note the dates of the letters that follow:

*   *   *

THE K FACTOR   SEPT. 3, 1973 . . . DJ 887.57

Wall Street Gambit . . . and it's Your Move!

"The bear market in stocks may climax in a buying opportunity of a life time", is the recurring theme that has been running through my mind this whole past weekend.

The idea first came to me in the early days of August but I had shrugged it off. A few days later it was back and as the hot August days tolled by, the idea kept gaining strength until by Labor Day, it was fixed in my mind. The torrid heat over the long Labor Day weekend did not deter me from concluding intensive research and study.

JUST WHEN THE CLIMAX MIGHT BE, I DON'T KNOW. BUT THIS IS THE TIME TO START!

The Gambit!

The stock market had been ruptured for nigh five years. Interest rates are soaring and bonds are losing ground consistently.

Saving banks have raised interest rates while commercial banks are offering 11% for money.

Interest rates are expected to go higher while money is expected to get very tight.

A business downturn is expected and a recession or depression is a distinct possibility and expected.

Corporations set record earnings and have increased dividends yet stock market prices go lower. They make new lows daily. Investors have tremendous losses and are totally discouraged . . .

. . .And so Wall Street offers a gambit! *STOCKS AT CHEAP PRICES?!? . . . OR . . . BONDS AT HIGH YIELDS!?!*

That's the offer . . . that's the gambit . . . and it's YOUR MOVE!!??!!

The move is to buy CONVERTIBLE BONDS! I have recently bought both investment short term bonds and convertible bonds. I expect to buy some more this following week.

Investment short term and convertible bonds are the first moves in planning any portfolio. This is the ideal time to get started as the stock market has cracked up for many years and a new cycle will begin sooner or later.

These are the convertible bonds I own or recommend.

(here I listed eight bonds)

As they may say in chess circles, I have accepted the gambit in bonds but have declined the gambit in stocks!

* * *

An eloquent and timely letter I believe . . . based strictly on the principles enumerated in this book. THINK ABOUT THAT!

I followed that letter twelve days later with this one. Please keep thinking of the art of the investor as you read this material. It will play a most important part in your thinking when you face similar decisions.

* * *

THE K FACTOR SEPT. 15, 1973 . . . DJ886.36

"The Stock Market is Old History"

Wall Street Gambit . . . and its Your Move

(Part 2)

I MADE MY MOVE!! September 6th, three days after I wrote my last letter, I bought one bond, $1000 Dayco Corp. and paid $692.63 to earn a current yield of 8.65%.

September 10th, I bought two bonds, National Industries and paid $517.54 for each bond to earn a current yield of 11.10%.

WHY AM I BUYING CONVERTIBLE BONDS INSTEAD OF RUNNING TO THE BANK FOR 8% interest???

IT'S HISTORY!

Stock Market History

Stocks rise and fall in a complete cycle and a complete cycle in the stock market may be said to have four stages: Accumulation; Rise; Distribution; Fall.

A cycle will end in a sharp drop in stock prices which may cover a period of years and from those seeds will commence the FIRST STAGE, ACCUMULATION, of a new cycle or new bull market!

The stock market from 1949 to 1968 covered twenty years. Theory has it that the longer a stage endures, the longer will the succeeding stage require to compensate.

Thus after twenty years and three stages wherein stock prices rose after stocks were accumulated and then distributed, it is now five years (1969 to 1973) that the fourth and final stage is in effect; which is certainly not too long a period to compensate for the excesses of the preceding twenty years.

Seeds of a New Bull Market

During these last five years, prices have proved disastrous to those who ignored their history. Some stocks appear to have about compensated. Many, the high multiple darlings and favorites, have not. According to history they still have to be chopped down.

While waiting for doomsday for these "darlings", there are secondary issues that may have started their period of accumulation for the next bull market. Not all stocks move together. Thus while some may be concluding the final stage of the previous bull market, others may be starting the first stage of the succeeding bull market.

Where Are We Today

I believe that we are in the lower end of the fourth stage of the bear market which commenced in 1949. I don't think that we have finished that. This means that I expect the market to drag on and that I expect a final plunge perhaps. And so I think that it is a trifle early to start to accumulate stocks.

It's not important that I anticipate the number of years because money can be successfully employed in the overlapping period of time between the end of the fourth stage and the start of the new first stage. It's not even important that I anticipate the price level of the Dow Jones Averages.

THE BIG THING IS NOT TO GET CAUGHT IN THE FINAL DOWNDRAFT OR CONVULSIVE GASP OF THE CONCLUSION OF THE MARKET NOW IN ITS DEATH COMA!

When to Move

Thus it is that before you manage money or invest in the stock market, that you have to know the market . . . THEN you have to understand the market.

THEN YOU'LL KNOW WHEN TO MOVE!

In this chapter we see from history that we are in the "falling" stage of a market cycle and at any time prices may plunge. Therefore, we see that this is *not* the time to move into stocks.

What to Move

CONVERTIBLE BONDS may be in the very tail end of their fourth stage or they may have just started to enter the first stage of the new bull market in convertible bonds.

CONVERTIBLE BONDS appear to be selling on their YIELD or INVESTMENT VALUE rather than on their connection to stocks which is their CONVERSION VALUE. Thus this could be the ideal time to capitalize on convertible bonds.

THUS WE SEE THAT THE MOVE IS NOT INTO STOCKS BUT INTO CONVERTIBLE BONDS!

The move, in my opinion, is now because if we are near the end of the last cycle, then the unrealized paper loss that I will suffer should not be unduly large. While if we are near the first stage of accumulation, then I'll be getting the maximum yield on convertible bonds which I can enjoy until such times as capital gains may cause me to decide to sell.

Which to Move

Selecting convertible bonds is more of an art and more difficult than selecting stock. After many, many months of constant study and selection, I have decided on which I feel belong in my small model retirement fund. I own or recommend these. They are the same as listed in my last letter. (The list of eight bonds are omitted here as they are not germane.)

* * *

That letter was full of sound and solid advice. It was most prophetic!!

This next letter introduces an advantage that we haven't discussed and continues explaining convertible bonds. It is written only two weeks after the last letter that you just finished.

* * *

THE K FACTOR SEPT. 30, 1973 . . . DJ 974.10

"The Profit in Convertible Bonds"

Wall Street Gambit . . . and it's Your Move

(Part 3)

In the first of three letters this month, I told you that it was YOUR MOVE! I made MY MOVE! Now stocks and bonds are making THEIR MOVE! My entire list of eight convertible bonds moved very well. City Investing convertible was particularly outstanding, moving up for a gain of 14½ points or $145 for the month.

NOW YOU KNOW WHY I AM BUYING CONVERTIBLE BONDS INSTEAD OF RUNNING TO THE BANK FOR 8% INTEREST!!

I'M WILLING TO TAKE THE RISK FOR POSSIBLE PROFITS PLUS 7%, or 8% or 11% INTEREST!

What is a Convertible Bond?

A bond is a loan, a debt that must be paid on its due date. It entitles the owner to receive interest semi-annually. Now if you add a special and unusual feature to a bond by giving the owner an OPTION FOR YEARS until the principal is due, to exchange the bond for stock at the owner's choice whenever the investor determines it is an advantage to do so, YOU HAVE A CONVERTIBLE BOND.

It's a convertible bond because if the owner elects to exchange the bond for stock, the owner would have CONVERTED the bond into stock!

Again! You buy a convertible bond! Any time that you want to you can exchange the bond for stock, even the same day that you buy the bond. (You will have to allow the necessary time for the paper work to be done).

You don't have to exchange the bond if you don't want to. Nobody can make you exchange it. You can keep the bond for years and collect the interest. However the company can call it and take it away from you if it is so provided in the indenture . . . just as they can call in any other bond.

Example of a Convertible Bond!

City Investing has a convertible bond which is described as 7½% due 12/1/90. This means that the company pays 7½% on a face value $1000 bond or $37.50 every December 1 and every June 1. The principal is due to be paid on December 1, 1990.

No matter what you pay for the bond, you will get the same $37.50 semi-annually from the company. No matter what you pay for the bond, the company will owe you $1000.

IN ADDITION, HOWEVER, YOU HAVE SOMETHING OTHER BONDS MAY NOT HAVE!

You have an option to convert the bond into stock of City Investing. If you do, you will receive 60.61 shares in exchange for your $1000 bond. This, let me remind you, is entirely at your choice and only if it's to your advantage!

Why You Would Want to Convert a Bond!

If you had purchased this bond as I recommended in my letter of September 3rd, and paid $930, the 60.61 shares of stock would have cost you $15.34 for each share should you ever decide to convert. This figure is obtained by dividing the price that you paid, $930, by 60.61 shares.

The stock closed September at 14¾. Just suppose the stock should move up to its 1972 high of 22. If you exchange your bond for 60.61 shares worth $22 that you paid $15.34, you would make a profit of $6.66 per share less commissions plus the interest or, let's say, the profit is about $300 plus 8% interest.

AND THAT'S THE MAGIC IN CONVERTIBLE BONDS, THE OPPORTUNITY TO MAKE A $300 PROFIT ON A $930 INVESTMENT WHILE GETTING 8% INTEREST WHILE WAITING FOR IT TO HAPPEN!!!!

From a practical point, you don't convert because the market reflects the increase in the stock once the conversion point is high enough. The bond would appreciate reflecting the increased price in the stock.

For example, the bond closed August, when I wrote my letter, at $900. It closed September at $1045, $145 higher. It's a simple procedure. You simply sell your bond just as you would stock and take your profit!!!!

Which to Move!!

As I said earlier, selecting convertible bonds is more of an art and more difficult than selecting stocks.

After many months of constant study and selection, I recommend the following as a package. Many of them I bought for my small model retirement fund!

Issuer	Bond	Rating	at 9/3 Price	Yield	at 9/30 Price
City Investing	7½ s 90	B	90	8.05%	104½
National Industries	5¾ s 88	B	50	11.1	52⅞
Cont. Mtg. Invest.	6¼ s 90	BBB	64½	9.04	69⅞
Dayco Corp.	6 s 94	B	68½	8.4	71
General Tel. & Elec.	6¼ s 96	BB	94	6.5	99
W.R. Grace & Co.	6½ s 96	BB	85	7.4	100½
Uniroyal, Inc.	5½ s 96	BB	69¾	7.6	74½
Wallace-Murray Corp.	6½ s 91	B	75¼	8.3	79½

COMMENT: In the table above under the heading of *Bond*, 7½ s 90, means that the company pays 7½% on a $1000 face value bond or $75 per annum and that the bond is due in 1990. The $75 is paid semi-annually.

5¾ s 88 means that the company pays $28.75 each six months and that the principal is due in 1988.

What About Long Term Bonds???

If you have something as valuable as an OPTION, would you want it to be over in two or three years or would you want it for twenty years?? Convertible bonds are bought for capital gains and the more years you have this opportunity, the better!

Buy Convertible Bonds!!!!!!!!

* * *

From what was said about convertible bonds and the additional explanation and description of the letters, you can see how bonds can be an effective medium for profit!

You can see that it isn't always necessary to run the risk of the stock market nor is it always necessary to take utilities up and down for years because of "income".

Certainly there is some indication that investing is an art. There doesn't appear to be any one way to succeed in investing. Consequently I believe that you can succeed if you will only *THINK* for yourself. But you do have to know and stay within investment principles.

13

The Early Stages of Portfolio Development

When to Start Buying Stocks

The first two years, 1973 and 1974, were the years when I started to build an investment program. They went quickly by. My net income was $4,167.91. That was good considering that those were declining years for the stock market.

I discussed and explained how I was concerned with avoiding losses and how this was accomplished with bonds.

If you were to concentrate on the market letters that I wrote, you would be able to discern from what I said and how I said it, that many of the stock market indicators were getting increasingly positive!

This is indicated once more in this next letter. Note how I once again use the phrase, "seeds of a new bull market" to imply the imminence of a rise in stock values! Another interesting point to mark is that now I am buying stocks!

A third point to think about is that the only stock that I mention has a CONVERTIBLE BOND which I own!

We have not completed discussing how and when to buy and sell bonds . . . nor stocks for that matter. It is not feasible to do so in one long and dry dialogue. We will do so as we go through some stock market cycles.

*   *   *

THE K FACTOR OCT. 8, 1973 . . . DJ 977.65

"Seeds of a New Bull Market"
Wall Street Gambit . . . and it's Your Move (part 4)

BUY UNIROYAL, Inc. (12) In the second chapter I explained how the "Seeds of a New Bull Market" may be in the winds so accordingly I have closely studied the stock of UNIROYAL, INC. and I heartily endorse its purchase at this price level.

You should note that Uniroyal has a convertible bond which is now yielding over 7% which I had recommended in the previous chapters.

I have a great deal of confidence in the financial strength of this company and accordingly recommend the stock to add the "growth" factor which I believe all funds should have!!

WHY UNIROYAL, INC.? The company's sales for 1972 was 1.8 billion.

The company owns $895 million in current assets and owes $326 million in current liabilities. Very, very strong financially!!

Earnings are estimated at $1.75 for the year, 1973. Six months earnings ending June, 1973 was $1.10 vs $0.95.

The company pays 17½ cents per share quarterly dividend and has been paying a dividend since 1943.

Products are automobile tires, chemicals, rubbers, plastics.

TECHNICALLY THE STOCK IS VERY STRONG IN MY OPINION. I interpret it to be in an accumulation area. It is in a very, very strong support area and I EXPECT it to move substantially higher!!!!

So It's Your Move Again!!

In my opinion it's time to move some money into the common stock of UNIROYAL, INC.

* * *

Although it was time to buy stocks, Uniroyal stock proved to be a loser. That's interesting! It only shows that even when you are right, you can be wrong! It was right to buy stocks but wrong to buy Uniroyal.

INVESTMENT IS AN ART, SOMETIMES IT GETS FRUSTRATING!

Early Stages of Portfolio Development

In the early stages of buying stocks and bonds, you must expect to take many losses before you settle down into a comfortable niche. You have all of your capital available and so many choices. Therefore it is important that before we reach the successful development of our investment fund, that I highlight this problem by an example.

For example, in June, 1972, a few months before I started my pension and retirement fund, I tried to profit from a stock that became a star almost overnight.

The letter that follows is appropriately entitled,

* * *

THE K FACTOR JUNE 17, 1972 . . . DJ 945.06

So This is Wall Street!

WALL STREET, the "boulevard of broken dreams", has two faces. One face is that of the serious investor, the middle class hoarder of solid, blue chip securities. The people who like to receive dividends and clip coupons.

Since late 1968, I have aligned myself with these investors and advised, "sell stocks, buy bonds." I enjoy a reputation for being conservative consequently, and my business has grown each year. Discretionary accounts which I manage are studded with telephone stocks and bonds.

As you cross to the other side of the street, however, approaching Broad and Wall Streets, you sense excitement. If you visit a boardroom, you'll feel the tense, pent up excitement that seethes through the watchers as their "faces" concentrate on the tape.

Each time their favorite glamour stock ticks up, you'll hear the rumble or the ejaculations that escape from these many, many faces.

Well, I decided to change my face for the first time in a long time. I'm going to walk along that "boulevard of broken dreams". I bought 150 shares of "glamour" for myself and not a single share for any of my discretionary accounts. (They'll have to call me and place the order themselves on their own responsibility.)

This other face of Wall Street is the one that I would say many of the investors take. This is the gambling side that overwhelms stock trading.

This is the fast buck side of the street. These are the investors who like and must have action!

They could be losing a great deal of money in their stocks but give them one "winner" and they'll be happy.

These are the people who buy a stock because "they like it."

WELL MOVE OVER PAL. I JUST BOUGHT A STOCK BECAUSE I LIKE IT!!

A NEW STAR IS BORN?? (44¼)

When I was a lad I read a book *"Tom Swift and His Electric Boat."* Today I read the newspapers, *"Curtiss Wright and the Wankel Engine"!* Both make fascinating and intensely interesting reading. Both grip my imagination.

Today's "fantasy" sounds like a take-off of yesteryear's taut and gripping novel. However, while Tom Swift excited and stirred my world of imagination and daydreams, Curtiss Wright stirs and excites my quest for grabbing the tail of a most glamourous Wall Street Star.

Risk Factors

Before I write any further, I want you to know that buying Curtiss Wright may be a considerable gamble. The stock has wide fluctuations and you stand to lose a considerable sum of money.

I know very little about the company nor have I done the research which I usually do before buying a stock. I don't know whether I'll buy any more or if I'll sell out and change my mind tomorrow.

I bought 150 shares on June 15th, 50 shares at 45¼, 50 shares at 44 and 50 shares at 42⅛.

The stock has a low of about 10 for these years since 1968 while its current high of 48¼ is the highest that I see going back to 1960. If it has been higher than that before that time I haven't bothered to find out.

Why I "Like It"

While I do tend to be conservative and I do like to receive dividends and clip coupons, I also am not averse to taking a "flyer" and try to make a fast dollar. And here is why I am taking a crack at Curtiss Wright.

Curtiss Wright is hardly mentioned recently without adding the "magic" name of the Wankel Engine. At first the name was mentioned in the newspapers rather sparingly, but as the stock of Curtiss Wright moved higher and higher, the Wankel Engine became more familiar.

Today I pick up the New York Times and there in very big print is an ad for, *WANKEL ENGINE STOCKS.* It is my opinion that the name of the Wankel Engine and its stocks will be with us for a long time and if it is, I want a piece of the action!

It Started Last Saturday

As a student of the stock market, I am continually on the lookout for stocks to buy. While many may cross my path weekly, very few get the benefit of my work. My time is very limited and, consequently, I husband my analytical time for those few that may lead to immediate and large awards.

Thus it was that last Saturday as I read the financial section of the paper, I noted that Heinicke jumped from 3¼, June 4, to 7⅜, June 11th. The reason . . . The WANKEL ENGINE!

If that stock can double (and I am somewhat familiar with the issue), and if American Israel Paper (holds some interest in the Wankel) can jump, then there must be something going on in Wall Street that I am missing.

So with a friend of mine, we went to my office on Saturday at 7 PM and started to look into Mr. Wankel Engine. I charted Curtiss Wright and as the chart started to develop, I became convinced that I was now looking at the new darling of Wall Street.

I make no predictions as to price but it is my opinion that we are only in the lower part of its high and that we haven't seen anything yet.

We have seen the airlines soar. We have seen the mobile homes roll high. We may hear the steady purr of the Wankel Engine stocks as they drive us all the way to the banks . . . or to the poor house.

But that's Wall Street, riches or rags, the "boulevard of broken dreams"!!

Good Luck!

* * *

This letter is a lesson in how to buy stocks. Note the stock does not necessarily have to be a blue chip. We buy a stock for its potential profit.

Note I didn't buy the stock in one lot. I looked at the high and low range which made me aware that the loss could be considerable. There are many reasons for buying a stock. This is a little different.

The Wankel Engine was to replace the standard four cycle engine that we use. General Motors paid some 50 million for rights to it.

Read the follow up letter after which we'll consider it in the light of developing a portfolio in its early stage.

* * *

THE K FACTOR JULY 2, 1972

Curtiss *Wright and the Wankel Engine* or Tom Swift and His Electric Boat or *How to Play the Stock Market*

In our first chapter, we left our "hero" driving a Wankel Engine on what he hopes is in the direction of the bank. He had just crossed over into Broad and Wall Streets and bought himself some glamour stock, CURTISS WRIGHT.

On Saturday, June 17th, after careful consideration of the risks and the potentials the stock of Curtiss Wright offered, he decided that this was a once-in-a-long-while situation and determined to start a "campaign" to accumulate the stock.

Being a professional Wall Street analyst, his conclusions led him to believe that the stock had only started on its long upward course and that the future market price might be four or five times what it was that day. In fact if the stock reached 80 by July 31st, he wouldn't be surprised.

How does a professional Wall Street analyst plan and conduct his "campaign". It doesn't just happen. It's planned. Perhaps we'll discuss it in a later chapter but right now let's get on with the conducting of the campaign.

Conducting the Curtiss Wright Campaign

Thursday, June 15, "Tom" had bought Curtiss Wright three times that day. He bought fifty shares at 45¼, fifty shares at 44 and as the stock continued its profit-taking, fifty shares at 42⅛. Its low that day was 41½. It closed at 42⅞. Two market days later it made a new high and closed at 49.

THE CAMPAIGN WAS WELL LAUNCHED!

"Tom" studied the market action the next day or two to try to determine whether profit-taking might set in. Wednesday night he concluded that the stock showed no indication of a "top" at this point and accordingly decided to accumulate more stock.

Friday, June 23, Curtiss Wright again made a new high, 52. Its low that day was 48⅛. Tom, now protected by a "paper profit", could afford the risk of buying at the "top". However since his profit was in 150 shares only, he had to cut back the size of his order to 30 shares. This he did by buying 30 shares at 49⅞.

Two market days later he bought 35 shares at 52½ and the next day, as profit taking came in, he increased his order to 50 shares and bought at 49. Two days after that as the stock moved to its high again, he cut back to buy 35 shares at 53, right at the top.

"TOM" WAS NOT AFRAID TO BUY AT THE TOP!

He now has 300 shares at an average price of 47⅜. Curtiss Wright is at 52 and a high of 52⅞ and no sign of a top. Accordingly, the plan is to keep accumulating small quantities, even 5 shares, as the stock keeps making new highs, and larger amounts, perhaps 100 shares or more if severe profit taking sets in.

Case Study

If any reader takes exception to the fact that I went into detail as to how, when and how much I have invested in Curtiss Wright, I apologize. I did so only at the suggestion of an interested party that I give my readers a Case Study of how I think and act and why.

I admit that I may lose my shirt in Curtiss Wright but I am prepared to . . . that is why I can take the risk. Do I expect to? Definitely not! I think I know when to get out and when to retrench.

By using a case history I am trying to teach several fundamental and important investment principles.

Investment Tactics

You don't buy more and more of a stock on the way down . . . but on the way up!

You don't buy 100 shares and forget it. Keep adding 5 shares, 35 shares, 15 shares . . . just keep adding as long as the trend is up!!!

*   *   *

The Case Study: Curtiss Wright

Soon after, the stock of Curtiss Wright started to drop. Using the indicators that we know of, primarily trend and volume, I liquidated with a small profit. The Wankel Engine turned out to be a big disappointment.

I was so sure! I was so convinced! I was *so* wrong!

Here was a case where I concerned myself with just

one fundamental of the company; it had the rights to the Wankel Engine.

The indicators were all so very positive. The trend was sharply up and the volume was abnormally high. If the engine turned out well, and so many companies had big money in it, I could do very well . . . fast!

As I kept buying the stock, I saw no top. The sky was the limit.

Note the price swing in just a few days, 42, 49, 53 and down again. The stock never made it. It dropped substantially after I took my small profit. Technical factors put me into the stock and technical factors PLUS investment principles (my second and third keys) took me out and saved me from harm.

How to Invest in the Stock Market

These letters are most instructive. They highlight so much of how we think and act in investing. Yes! This investment should be made by all investors each time it arises.

The answer is YES! BECAUSE WE THINK!

THINK! WE ARE INVESTORS! There may be many reasons that people buy stock but there is only one reason that investors do.

We buy only when there is a potential to profit within a reasonable time frame! Accordingly, although we study and learn when and how to buy, we only learned the art of investing.

You, the investor, have to apply it!

Nowheres do I ask you to memorize a theory! I don't know that there are any that have stood the test of time. You are not bound hand and foot by what I say.

Use Reason! Use Common Sense!

On the question: Wasn't the potential loss too great for a new portfolio being developed?

NO! We have enumerated the great care that we take

BEFORE we buy a stock. The letter may appear light, gay and flighty but due diligence was there!

Was I lucky to avoid the large loss that many took after the stock declined?

Heavens no! I usually avoid them! Study this book!

Incidentally before we move on, did you notice how I kept buying the stock using the "paper profits" to protect me from losses! I started buying 150 shares but cut down the size of each order as the price rose.

As the price dropped, the size of the order was larger. In other words, I bought more shares on profit taking than on the move up.

Although we went through chapters on how and when to buy and sell, the development of the many ideas and factors involved can never be completely explored.

Many are best developed if they are introduced by case studies from what actually did take place in the stock market. It's the history of the stock market that we learn from.

14

When to Buy "Junk" Bonds As An Investment

Just Plain Reasoning . . . or Thinking

As the stock market was bottoming out in 1974, I did some hard thinking! The top of the last bull market was in 1968. It was now six years later. That meant that the last cycle must have ended and we must now be in the first stage of accumulation which precedes a bull market.

Therefore, even though stocks had been in a steady decline since last year, there must still be a great deal of accumulating going on. As Wall Street says, "stocks must be going into strong hands". Investors must be buying stocks and locking them in the vault.

I had been accumulating convertible bonds. They pay interest and have potential for profits. The bonds that I had bought were too low priced to match the profits that stocks had to offer. Perhaps it was time to develop my fund potential by adding stocks.

But knowing that stocks should be sold in a falling market and not bought, I decided to hold off buying stocks until they found a support level and stabilized for a short while. The interim time was a good time to invest in "junk" bonds. I did that. . . .

With that thought in mind, I wrote the following letter which proved to be timely as 1975–76 proved to be the turning point in my investment career. At one point I made close to $100,000. I doubled my investment!

Note in the letter that I didn't know which direction stock prices were headed. It wasn't necessary to predict the stock market to be successful. Just to work at it!

* * *

THE K FACTOR SEPTEMBER 23, 1974

What Time is it on Wall Street?
A Private Letter by Jerome Krumholz

On Wall Street it's time to OPEN YOUR HISTORY BOOKS AGAIN! Wall Street is a devastated arena and while I wouldn't be surprised if panic selling materializes before the year is over, neither would I be surprised if a strong upward rally develops.

High interest rates and ravaging inflation are constantly in my thoughts and do figure heavily in my investment decisions. I am on the alert for any change in either or both!

From History Books!

While I recognize that the scene on Wall Street and economic uncertainties are literally ruining investors and money managers, I am confident of my interpretation of the investment picture and the opportunities which exist.

I do know this . . . that sex, eating, taxation,

investment and speculation are here to stay. The human race always has had its investors and speculators in one form or another.

So history will reveal that prudent, patient and thoughtful investors will prosper and flourish. Investments and investment opportunities will not die! Without investors Banks would perish! So to your history books!!

TAKE COURAGE AND LEARN FROM THEM!!

History Lesson

We learn from past stock market behavior that Wall Street never was a one-way street. Stocks go up as well as down! We have a bear market in stocks. We have a severe and precipitous decline since March of this year that is sheer breath taking and murderous, but this can only develop investment opportunities!

Therefore for the first time in several years, I have spent considerable time doing *new* research in attempting to ferret out investment opportunities. And I believe I have done so!!

Since July 17 for my own pension fund I have added these purchases:

REIT INCOME FUND stock at 1⅜, EVANS PRODUCTS bonds at 35 (yield 17.6%), the bonds of INSTRUMENT SYSTEMS at 33 (yield 20.08%), Boston Edison bonds to yield 12.1%.

Space prevents me from examining these issues but I'll gladly discuss them on request.

* * *

How to Succeed By Thinking

Space prevented me from discussing those purchases at that time but this was the time to profit from experience so I'll explain the thinking behind those purchases.

The opening paragraph asks the important *technical* question of when . . . timing! It's a stock market indicator. What part of the cycle are we in? However, even knowing the stage of the cycle won't prevent large losses. There's more to investing than that.

And so I comment that even though the stock market is in a steady decline, and since it is time for a change, I wouldn't be surprised if it happened at that point.

I then refer to another major indicator, interest rates, and point out that I'm constantly monitoring the many stock market indicators.

Investment Principle Number 1—Patience

Why did I make "CONTROL YOUR EMOTIONS" my number one principle? Because with control of patience, greed and fear, you can succeed. Without it you never will!

The next paragraph points out the PATIENCE it takes and the confidence that an investor has to have in the lessons that history has to offer.

History Lesson!

How often and when will investors learn this stock market lesson?? It is so eloquent and so fundamental that only GREED ERASES IT FROM THEIR MINDS!

How to Buy Junk Bonds

A junk bond may be deemed to be any bond that is of an unusual high risk. However an investor must think through the risk, aside from what others may think and say. We did discuss that in the purchase of convertible bonds.

Since I bought Evans Products bond at 35 which means that I paid $350 for a $1000 bond, the rating of that bond must have been quite negative. Wall Street evidently thought it was a case for the bankruptcy court.

However a study of the fundamentals of the company and a study of the technical trading in the stock of the company, indicated that if that was to be, it would be quite some time in the future.

Because an investor works for a profit within a time frame, that bond appeared to be an investment opportunity. Bonds in that price range have very sharp moves up and down. If the bonds were to appreciate from 35 to 45, there would be a very large percentage gain.

With the stock market being so very difficult then, it was a good time to invest in junk bonds.

Along with that bond I purchased the bonds of Instrument System at 33 (yield 20.08%). The fundamentals of this company were much more secure than Evans Products. In this case, the risk of loss seemed more remote and yet the yield was higher.

The key to buying junk bonds is to buy them when you don't expect news of any company action for many months. This will give you a chance to collect very high interest which I consider profit and not interest.

Also you buy them with the expectation of holding them for a few months or a year.

The Boston Edison bonds were investment caliber and I bought them as a delaying tactic to investing in stocks at that time. They were five year bonds which I bought with the intention of selling at a profit if they should appreciate.

Special Situations in Bonds

This selected instructive letter illustrates how it is possible to determine "special situations". We discussed special situations in determining what stock to buy. Here we see special situations in determining what bond to buy.

I bought the Boston Edison bonds that yielded 12.1%. Compare that yield against the yield of the junk bonds. It was about 5½% less than the Evans bond.

The thought arose that there can't be an imminent risk of bankruptcy with just 5½% difference. That was a major factor in concluding that the Evans bond was a special situation worthy of taking a risk for a limited time.

Compare the 17.6% yield of Evans to Instrument Systems 20.08%. I did the research and I make the judgment but as I saw it, the Instrument Systems company showed no signs of default as to the payment of interest. The principal wasn't due for a long time so I wasn't concerned with the principal.

The last item in the letter to be discussed is the REIT INCOME FUND stock that I invested in. I bought stock for 1⅜.

My portfolio had straight bonds. It had convertible and junk bonds. Therefore I was free of the risk in stocks. I wasn't buying stocks because the market was falling. But this was not the start of the fall nor was it in the early stage of its fall.

This was the perfect time to "Bottom Fish"!

Bottom Fishing

There are many theories and maxims heard in Wall Street. The problem is everybody hears of them but few know how or when to use them. Consequently they become what I call crutches.

Some pundits and investors, not knowing what to do or excusing their multitude of errors, call upon some maxim or theory as their apology.

While I call them crutches and fallacies, they are

based upon elements of truth or fact which at times prove useful. Let's talk about one called "bottom fishing".

When a stock is falling and investors have no idea whether it is going to meet support or whether it will fall still further, some investors will buy simply because they like the stock and decide to take a chance at any price.

They call it "bottom fishing".

There is a right time and a wrong time!!!

A second example of this might be after a stock made a new low and is trading at the new low for a period of time. Such a stock might be under distribution. If the investor buys in this situation, again the investor went bottom fishing.

You will encounter similar cases but this time the stock might be under accumulation. Again if the investor buys at the low, it is bottom fishing.

Therefore bottom fishing is buying a stock on or near its low. The ART IN INVESTING is to know how and when to do so. Don't use it as a crutch.

You probably gather by now that I don't think much of bottom fishing. I'm too interested in avoiding losses. My stated policy is that to succeed in investing it is essential that losses be held down. It is not necessary to buy stocks on the bottom. However there are times when bottom fishing makes good sense. YOU are the one to THINK WHEN!

Immediately following the Crash in 1987, a very noted fund manager stated that he bought stocks although lightly. He thought that he would take a chance to go bottom fishing.

I feel that he did a disservice to investors by making that statement. Perhaps because he controls billions of dollars, it may be appropriate for him to do so. He can hide the loss beneath that wealth. But investors are going to take that as advice to buy.

If investors don't take that statement as advice to buy,

then it will encourage them not to sell! Which they should be doing!

If you are a trader, if your purpose is to speculate in the many swings of the stock market, then we are not on the same wave length. I doubt if an investor should invest when the stock market is going through the worst crash in stock market history.

THINK—THINK! I keep repeating many times and many ways that stock market history is prologue to stock market riches. Study stock market history and you have *HINDSIGHT*.

Apply what you learned from history and you have stock market *FORESIGHT!!* And so I coined the phrase. . . .

"USE HINDSIGHT TO GUIDE YOU TO FORESIGHT WHEN BUYING"

If you love the stock market enough to study its past behavior and match it against that pundit's advice to bottom fish in the worst crash in history, then you will need nothing else to succeed. You won't buy! You will sell!

Going back to that letter in 1974 when the market was bottoming out, I decided that the time was appropriate to bottom fish. That was why I bought that stock. It was time for stocks to rise again!

However the stock market was falling so I kept my patience until December 23rd when I went bottom fishing again. I bought 100 shares of International Tel & Tel at 12⅝.

Why Bonds Are Needed in a Portfolio

The stock market bottomed out in 1974 and at the end of the year I had a portfolio of straight bonds, convertible bonds and some stocks. I also had problems.

My capital investment was $44,500. The cost of my investments was $57,325.18. I owed the broker money since I started to buy on margin. Margin is using credit.

That was not my problem. My problem was that the market value of my portfolio was $47,062.55 which left me with an unrealized loss of $10,262.63.

To offset this loss, however, I had a realized net profit of $4,167.91 for the first two years of my program. That would give me an indicated equity of $38,405.38.

A loss of $10,262 on an investment of $44,500 is 23.06%. Now that's a problem. However that loss was offset by the interest income from the bonds. Therefore not only did the bonds keep me above the loss level set by the Krumholz Factor but it helped prevent a greater loss by taking money away from further stock investments which had declined.

This experience indicates how *THINKING about money as capital to be invested* differs from always thinking of buying stocks and holding stocks and the stock market.

Since I understood the stock market and investing very well, I had confidence in what I was doing. I was well aware of my losses. They were under control. I knew the Krumholz Factor in each and every investment.

I was prepared for these market fluctuations. Yes the market was falling so I had to expect these setbacks. The market was just doing its thing. It was moving up and down . . . up and down. This was the time it was falling. How unfortunate for me. I needed a great deal of patience and understanding!

As I explained in how to buy stocks and when to buy stocks, as my stocks started to move up, I started to accumulate those that were moving up.

When the year, 1975, ended, the cost of my portfolio totaled $127,003.37 and the market value was $129,917.25. The gain was $2,913.88.

My net income for the year was $12,001.04!

I was on the move!

NOW'S THE TIME TO THINK

Let's think about HISTORY! My case is not historic. Nor was the stock market historic then. But both my case and the stock market then are history.

AND THAT'S WHAT WE LEARN FROM . . . HISTORY.

So let's continue to look at my various experiences on my way to Wall Street Riches! Let's think *now* about the stock market *then* so that you may be able to repeat the same investment know-how in the future which will enable you to make profits in the stock market.

You will know what to think about. You will be prepared to think. The stock market will never quite surprise you.

A Look at History

To start with, technical analysis indicated to us that the stock market cycle was in a stage of accumulation. It's safer to buy in this stage than when stocks are tumbling down.

We started with straight bonds. We added convertible bonds and only then followed with stocks. Those stocks that started to move up were accumulated. Thus the principle: "Buy a rising market, not a falling star".

Now you see why if you want to succeed, you must exercise patience and restraint. Don't jump into a crashing stock market because you and others think that rich, sophisticated, experienced professional investors suddenly lost their minds and decided to crash stock prices to let you in on a good thing.

A stock may rise to become a "star" and a Wall Street darling. When that star starts to fall, don't buy it. The chances are that you will pay a dear, dear price for that "bargain". That's no time to buy stocks.

The thought might have entered your mind as to where I got money to have such a large portfolio by the end of 1975 since my equity just a year earlier was only $38,405. I borrowed it. *MARGIN!* You know that dirty word that every one avoids talking about.

Margin is anathema to the investor . . . unless of course you know how to use it. Just as investors don't know when to "buy for the long term" or when to "buy stocks for dividends", they don't know how to use margin. The art in investing is to know when to use what!

Me, I never consider myself fully invested unless I am on maximum margin. In 1985 my net worth was just shy ½ million dollars but my portfolio had a market value shy of one million dollars. I owed about ½ million.

MARGIN?? If it weren't for margin, I never would have made it!!

MARGIN IS AN ASSET! USE IT WISELY!

THINK! It's really so simple to succeed in investing, if only you will but think. Use common sense. Use reason. Think for yourself. If you understand the stock market and how it goes about its business, you will be able to do all these things without losing sleep.

Don't borrow money when a gambling craze is sweeping the country such as the one which swept through the stock market in 1986 and 1987. Use margin when you know the market is relatively stable. I have told you how and when to know when that condition exists.

THINK! Throw away your crutches. Learn basic investment principles, facts and history and you'll do OK.

The stock market was on the rise starting in 1975 so I used margin to build a portfolio. My margin is not a permanent loan. I use it for a temporary time.

I use margin for a temporary purpose. If I start to lose money, I'll cut back on my margin so fast that the stock market wouldn't fall fast enough to catch me. Picture that! Study my margin position during the 1982–87 bull market.

January 1, 1982 I owed no money.

1985 I owed $494,666.

February 28, 1987 I owed $161,954.

September 30, 1987 I owed no money.

October 19, 1987 The greatest stock market fall ever!

So in 1975 as the market started to rise, I really started to use margin and I ended the year by increasing my net worth by $24,596.87. My net income was $12,001.

I made an additional contribution to my Koegh and capital investment account during the year which brought the total that I had committed to the fund to $47,369.42. So the year was a good year.

It may be fine to grow at 8% or 10% per year but you won't get rich that way. After you THINK your way through the stock market for many years, you will be able to average 18% or more each year.

However you must have years when you will double your money. Only that way can you make substantial sums. Therefore while 1975 was a good year for me, I was still looking to double my money.

Unfortunately you and I must practice that first important investment principle, "Control Your Emotions" Fear, Greed, Patience.

We must have patience to wait for the bull markets to start rolling. The retail business has its big season during the holiday season at the year end. They have it big once each year.

We, however, are in a business that has a much longer cycle. We have to wait many years. As much as you and I would like the stock market to go up, we have no effect. It would be nice if it were a little more obliging. But, we investors must be patient . . . and wait.

However we don't wait idly. We have preparatory work to do. We know the stock market and what to expect. Don't we?

Let's go to work. Let's tie in bottom fishing, margin,

and everything else we know about Wall Street and see if we can't double our money in 1976!

December 31, 1975 completed the first three years of my investment program. After three years of consecutive net income plus unrealized profits plus the additional contribution to my capital account, my net worth was $66,352.95.

15

How to Double Your Money With Stocks!

Going Through the Work Process

International Tel & Tel is a large company and well known. It has many shares outstanding and it has large sales and a large capitalization.

By capitalization we refer to the capital that the company raised to do business with. This is the money that the company received from the sale of its common and preferred stock that it may have issued, plus the amount of money it may have raised through the sale of bonds.

In December, 1974, the stock was depressed and had been in a down trend for many years. Looking around for a stock to invest in, ITT (International Tel & Tel), caught my eye.

The stock had peaked at $67 per share in 1971 and was in a steep and steady down trend since. The stock made a low of 14 in October of 1974, rallied to 17 in November, and now in December of 1974 made a new low below 14.

Thinking through the decision on ITT, my first glance at the upside potential indicated that ITT should have no trouble in doubling in a good market.

Considering the downside risk, the question is how much lower can it go? At that time I didn't know. But it was worth BOTTOM FISHING!!

Before doing that, however, I had work to do.

Case Study—International Tel & Tel

To do my research on ITT I went to the library. This library has several services for reference. This time I used Standard & Poor's as my source. They publish a series of four volumes that contain a single page sheet on all the listed stocks on the NYSE (New York Stock Exchange).

There are other volumes for stocks listed on the ASE (American Stock Exchange as well as information for O-T-C, over-the-counter stocks).

First I reviewed the single page sheet on ITT to digest the fundamentals of the company. Then I refer to another volume that S & P (Standard & Poor's) puts out.

This is a large volume that publishes all the latest news about public corporations. It often contains news that the single page lacks.

If I am still interested in the company under study, in this case ITT, I will then refer to a third volume which contains the history of corporations in detail from their inception.

This last volume will give the details of bonds, other debt, as well as other information that you may be interested in knowing. This volume is especially useful when interested in bonds.

Now if I like what I find, I make copies of the various data to take back to my office. Back at the office I really go to work. During the preliminary process that I just described, many a stock has been left at the library.

If I'm interested sufficiently to make copies for my files, then I really get down to serious work. I will concentrate on the fundamentals. If they prove satisfactory, then I have to think about the decision of how much to buy and when to buy. This is a technical decision.

For the technical decision I closely study the trading activity of the stock for the past several months. I save the daily and weekly stock pages of the New York Times so when I want to backtrack for this information, the reference material is right at hand.

I go back several months in order to develop a feel or an understanding of the volatility of the stock. In order to know what abnormal volume is, it is necessary to find out what normal volume is.

I copy the daily and weekly volume of trading. Frequently I trace the monthly volume. I study to see how the volume has effected the price of the stock. You see I am studying the HISTORY of that stock.

I want to know just how much volume it takes and how often that volume comes into the issue. I want to know if there is evidence of buying support after each sell off.

It is necessary to get an idea of how sharp the trend is and how long that the trend has been in effect. I want to know if the trend lines are being tested. I want to know if the stock is now trading in the middle of the trend or if the stock trading is near the trend line.

I want to know; did the current price, break the trend line? I would like to know if volume, indicating support, is evident if it did break the trend.

I get all this information from researching the trading activity of the past few months.

Making Charts

Since I can't retain the details of all my research in my mind, it is necessary to make charts. Isn't a picture worth a thousand words? Isn't a picture worth a thousand dollars? How about $100,000 dollars?

How about half a million dollars? . . . because that's what I accumulated utilizing pictures or charts! In the case of ITT it was worth thousands and thousands of dollars! Charts are scoffed at because they are used as crutches. But, they should be used as pictures of what has taken place AND what will probably happen in the future.

There are many times when charts are misinterpreted. There are many times when they may be false indicators. But what Wall Street theory isn't? What investing principle isn't? Why don't the writers scoff at the latter?

If you are not successful interpreting any given chart, work with charts of a different stock.

So here we have ITT hitting new lows. Everything points to it as a buy and yet it keeps hitting new lows. In this case we'll use BOTTOM FISHING! I don't know where the low is. To protect myself I'll use the Krumholz Factor. I'll set my loss!

Buy Them on the Way Up

On December 23, 1974 I bought 100 shares of ITT at 12⅝. The low turned out to be 12. Lucky? Of course! But didn't they say that about the millionaire farmer who had no time to stop to chatter because he was busy working.

The early part of January is usually a good time for the stock market. It usually rallies at that time of year. It didn't disappoint me and was quickly on its way, bouncing off its four year low!

Well by now, you know how I think and what I say and I always do what I say: *BUY THEM ON THE WAY UP . . . NOT ON THE WAY DOWN!*

January 10, 1975, I bought another 100 shares of ITT stock at 15⅝.

The thought arises: why not take the profit on the 100 shares that was purchased at 12⅝? This in turn raises the question again of when do you sell a stock?

I only sell a stock when I think that it is going to go

down. By that I mean when I think that the up trend has been reversed and that the stock is at the beginning of or in a down trend. I don't sell because profit-taking comes into a stock or when it is just doing its job of up and down.

I have no formula for taking profits. I usually let my profits run. In fact as you see, I do the opposite. Not only did I not sell ITT on the rise but I bought more of it.

The follow up question is when do you buy? I buy when I think that the stock is going to go up.

If a stock is in a down trend, I won't buy it. If I think that the down trend has stopped or is broken, then I'll buy it.

International Tel & Tel was in a definite down trend. This appears to be contrary to what I have been advocating. But a close study of the down trend revealed that the stock was on the bottom of the line forming the trend.

This is technical as has been discussed. Also by buying it I was "feeling" for the bottom. I was feeling for a trend reversal.

That's Bottom Fishing

So here we are with ITT rallying off its low. At the price of 15⅝, I saw no sign indicating that the market or the stock was going to retreat or pull back. Consequently following through on my reasoning, since the stock appeared to be in a rising trend, I bought some more!

Now here is where the Krumholz Factor comes into play and is so important to the success in investing. I could afford to buy 100 shares at 15⅝ which I did on January 10, 1975 because if I was wrong, and ITT dropped back, I was protected by the profit in the first 100 shares.

If the stock did drop back, I could get out about even or so. Remember that we aren't in this business to squeeze out 8% or 10%. We are in this business to get rich.

If you sell just because you have a profit, you won't cut it here. You must stay with investing guidelines.

January 29, 1975 I bought 500 shares of ITT. Note how I bought them. I bought 200 at 18¼, 200 at 18⅝ and 100 at 18¾. The stock was on a rise! The higher it went, the more my earlier purchases protected me from too severe a loss.

I now had 700 shares of International Tel & Tel. That's how to buy stocks. This was one of the times to buy! The campaign was in full swing. I was working with "their" money! I wasn't risking my capital. I was risking my profits. That's one of the many "secrets" of success.

March 5, 1975 I followed up by buying 200 shares of ITT at 18⅞.

November 25, 1975 I bought 200 more shares of ITT at 21¾. The stock, of course, moved up and down . . . up and down . . . up and down during this period.

When I wasn't sure of the direction or the trend, I just held . . . and watched . . . and waited . . . THINKING all the time!

International Tel & Tel closed 1975 at 22½. During my campaign I had accumulated 1100 shares.

In the meantime while I was conducting this campaign in ITT, I was buying and selling other securities as my thinking dictated. Filling in all the details would not be as constructive as following the ITT campaign to its completion.

REMEMBER IF YOU DON'T SELL, YOU DON'T GET RICH!

There is a time to sell! Let's find out when!

How to Manage a Portfolio

The month of January, 1976, proved to be another good January for the stock market. International Tel & Tel closed the month at 27⅝. February, ITT closed the month at 28⅞. Then followed the usual . . . up . . . down

. . . up . . . down . . . cycle that the stock market and stocks go through.

However on June 21, I bought 200 more shares of the stock at 26⅝ and the very next day, I bought another 200 shares at 27⅜.

NOTE THAT I DON'T BUY ALL AT ONE TIME!

I never know what the market is going to do!

I just THINK my way through!

All the time, all the way I am watching my technical indicators. I'm watching the volume, the trend, the range, the volatility.

I'm also closely monitoring the fundamentals as they make news. I'm clipping out earnings reports, large sales or orders, backlog, and just everything with the name ITT on it. I do have thousands and thousands of dollars at *RISK*.

IT IS MY MONEY! MY CAPITAL! MY LIFE SAVINGS!

Everything about the company goes into a file on ITT! So you see, yes, there is this work that you must do. If you just buy a stock and wait for someone to ring a bell to tell you when to buy more or to tell you when to sell, you'll have many surprises in store for you as well as a fractured bank account!

The Streamlined Portfolio

The year, 1976, ended and my position was 1600 shares of International Tel & Tel. My cost was $34,378.47. The market value amounted to $54,200. The stock had closed the year at 33⅞.

THINK . . . This all started with the purchase of just 100 shares at 12⅝. Investment $1,262.50. This and the Krumholz Factor.

Many investors who bought 100 shares at the time I did, had a profit of $2125 on their International Tel & Tel stock. I had a profit of $19,821.53. We all bought the same stock at the same time! Interesting!

It is now about two years since I started this campaign in ITT. I didn't buy the the stock for the long pull. I didn't buy it to trade. I bought it because I thought it might go up.

I'll sell it when I think that it might go down. I won't fall in love with the stock even though I have a profit of almost $20,000, and I won't marry it!

I'm going to sell it! It's paper! I'm going to sell it as I intended to do when I first bought it!

THINK! Are you learning about Wall Street?

Are you learning how to double your money?

The stock market is fun when you are really making money!

Results of Streamlining

International Tel & Tel wasn't the only campaign that I had going. Two others of interest were American Investment Company, a loan company, and National Industries, a conglomerate. Both companies had their stock listed on the New York Stock Exchange.

I first bought American Investment on June 6, 1975. I bought 100 shares at 3⅜. I bought 700 shares later in the month and in December I purchased an additional 3200 shares for 2½ and 2⅝. Total 4000 shares costing $11,213.

On November 4, 1974. I bought 400 shares of National Industries at 3⅝. In November, 1975, I bought it several times for a total of 2700 shares. At the end of 1975 I had 3100 shares costing $19,661.

I also had 2400 shares of Mid-Continental Telephone costing $30,522 as 1975 closed. So I was conducting four major campaigns at once.

Note that instead of accumulating a basket full of stocks, I conducted a streamlined campaign. Many investors would have been holding twenty or more stocks.

I had just a few. That's my investment strategy when I wrote;

"DON'T DIVERSIFY BUT STREAMLINE"

Concentrate on a few. It is less timely and more rewarding. It is easier to work hard on just a few. It is very discouraging if you have to spend a whole day just to keep up with the news on twenty or more stocks.

The commission is less, too. Instead of selling ten different stocks and paying commissions on 100 share lots, sell a single lot of 1000 shares. You save on commissions.

Again, if the stock market crashes, you have to worry and watch twenty or more stocks. You can't watch them all, so you do nothing. If you have four large holdings, it is easier to think and act clearly as you should.

And so the year, 1976 ended. And this year we finally did it. We doubled our money. My net worth at year end was $121,060.94 My net income for my fourth year was $16,326. I still had large profits which I had not taken as yet.

At year end the market value of my pension fund was $202,795. Of course I was on margin . . . borrowed money! As 1976 was winding down, I realized that for the twelve month period between 1975–76, I would approach my first $100,000 profit in the stock market.

Wishing to share my profits with my two grown children, I set up a trust with $12,000 taken from my pension fund. I would manage the trust for them.

In 1959 when I more than doubled my money, I took all the money and bought my house. That left me with no capital to continue investing. This time it was different. This time I was able to withdraw money but still remained with capital to continue investing.

The trust was for eleven years.

From the profits of the trust plus $8,000 which I withdrew from my pension fund, I set up an investment fund for my grandchildren.

When the trust reached its termination date, eleven years after its inception, $24,939 was distributed. This, of course, would have been substantially more if the profits over many years had not been distributed.

And the partnership for my grandchildren amounted to $49,017 on December 31, 1986.

So you see, I was lucky more than once!

I have no theories about investing in the stock market or about investing in bonds. I have no hang-ups either! I think and reason and when that fails me, I just use plain old-fashioned common sense.

Many money managers follow the doctrine of always being invested in the stock market. They manage funds by switching between "aggressive" stocks and "defensive" ones.

Needless to say, I don't agree with that approach. Again, with money constantly coming into funds from investors, it may succeed for them.

I don't profess to be the only successful manager in the stock market. But certainly that approach is anathema to me. I don't see how an investor can succeed that way.

Those crashes and those crippling down trends, even if of short duration, are severe. They cause large losses and set investors back many years of endeavor.

Therefore let's see how to think and reason our way through down trends using International Tel & Tel as our illustrative example. We'll learn from history . . . we'll learn from a real experience . . . as it happened . . . as we thought it through!

To prepare to sell . . . to prepare for down trends . . . once again brings us back to what Wall Street is all about! Investing in Wall Street is not a science. Investing in Wall Street is a business!

It's an art! A beautiful art. A challanging art. It is a fascinating art. But above all it is a most difficult art. It's not the art of the painter or that of the composer or author or builder, as we said before.

It is the art of interpreting and understanding the stock market. It's like the painter only in that it takes but one brush stroke to spoil a good piece of art. It's like that of a composer only that it takes one shrill note to spoil a Beethoven symphony.

A computer can only give out instantaneous responses and answers. Whether the answers are correct will depend upon the quantitative and the qualitative inputs.

And so I say that Wall Street investing is an art. It's a most difficult art. We read so many different opinions on what to buy and sell that we just throw up our hands and ask, "Who do you believe?" One analyst will recommend a sale of a stock that another analyst is saying is a buy.

This art is different from most others. In this art, the "artist", the investor, must not permit the slightest emotion to be expressed in the completed art.

This is an art of decision-making and, no fear, hope, anxiety, patience, greed or any other emotion dare be expressed in the making of the decision.

This is an art of cold emotion, of icy nerves, of steel backbone, of strong determination, of calculated risk, of planned strategy, of pre-determined objectives.

There is certainly no room for obstinacy in this art. There is no place for rationalization or excuses or crutches.

THIS IS THE ART OF WALL STREET INVESTING!

Yes all artists have bad days. So will you. It's part of the art to know and to expect this. In a good market, you don't need a Wall Street expert to tell you what to buy. All you have to do is to close your eyes and, if there is a stock for sale, buy it.

You will make lots of money . . . until the next bear market . . . when you will give it all back with some of your own money thrown in.

16

How and When to Take Profits in Long Term Stocks

Preparing to Sell

We had launched a campaign and had been accumulating International Tel & Tel stock from late 1974 at 12⅝ until we saw it close on December 31, 1976 at 33⅞.

Were we ever going to sell?

Had we fallen in love and married that stock?

Did I write this book for naught?

To sell that sweetheart was going to be difficult. That was why it was necessary to go through all this preparation and training of the mind.

To sell would require the body of principles and discipline which we have so exhaustively discussed. It would take all our fortitude. We were prepared for quick and decisive decisions.

Investors agree that the selling of stock is the most difficult part of investing. Because it is so very difficult I repeat that: "If you don't sell, you'll never get rich!"

This task of selling is so insurmountable to many investors. The reason is because the decision to sell stems back to their buying approach. We have discussed this, too, but let's look at it in the light of this case study. What might the situation be of some other investor?

The chances are the investor would have been quite invested when I first bought ITT because the buying approach for most investors is to buy and hold stocks.

Therefore to continually add buying power to the portfolio from time to time, the source of funds would probably originate from savings or the maturity of some bonds. Or perhaps there might be some cash available.

Again the average investor goes in for a portfolio that is diversified and, frequently, too much so. Hence the investor probably would not pick up more than 100 or 200 shares of the ITT stock when I did, especially with the stock market being in the bearish state that it was.

Later when ITT appreciated from 12⅝, I bought 100 shares at 15⅝. I don't think that the average investor would have bought at that time after paying 12⅝. And as I continued to accumulate the stock, I doubt if the average investor would have done the same thing.

Now you might suddenly think to ask this question. I said that my first interest in considering whether to buy a stock was whether the price could double.

When I bought ITT at 27⅜ did I consider that it might double? That's an interesting thought because it seems to belie what I said earlier.

Now this is where your own good thinking must come into play. Don't take everything I say as gospel because I can't explain everything I do. I try to. This is a case in point.

I consider the potential of a stock doubling in value only before an initial purchase. After that, I accumulate. I campaign. I am no longer interested in percentages. I am now interested in total dollars.

The smaller the risk, the more will I invest!

My approach to buying is entirely different from most

investors. When I consider an initial purchase, I have a campaign in mind. Other investors make a purchase as a one shot deal.

What investors never take time to think about is that bull markets are far and few in number. Consequently when they are in a bull market, they have 100 or 300 or so shares of each stock. When *I'm* in a bull market I have thousands of shares of each stock.

Again investors buy many stocks in which they lose money, as well as buying stocks which appreciate. I do the same thing.

But in a bull market they still have their same winners and losers. Me! I weeded out the losers. I sold them at losses and put the proceeds into the winners.

Finally *they* approach buying as collectors. They want a box full of paper. They have no thoughts of selling when they buy stocks.

When they do change their minds about holding a stock, they just don't know when and how to go about it. They don't think it through. It's an emotional call.

I, of course, know in advance that I am buying with the intent to sell . . . hopefully at a profit. I don't refer to investors as collectors in a derogatory sense at all. I use the word, collectors, to force investors to face up to the difficult task of succeeding in investing.

Therefore when I bought ITT after my initial purchase, I was not interested in doubling my money. I am not averse to making any small profit or building a big profit.

However with my first purchase, I had doubling my money in mind. But once the trend was established to be up, then I jumped in with both feet. Remember I only sell when I think that the trend is reversed and the stock may go down. But as long as the indication is up, I'll keep buying and buying and buying.

Therefore when ITT closed out December 31, 1976 at

33⅞, I had an unrealized profit of $19,000. The average investor who bought when I did, originally had a nice profit. I, with the same stock, had substantially more!

When the time comes that the stock market gets choppy and stocks start to fall, not *after* the fall but *as* they fall, the investor might let this ITT profit in 100 shares melt away.

BUT WOULD THIS INVESTOR LET $19,000 MELT AWAY??

THINK! SHOULD WE REALLY RUN THAT RISK? . . . and let THAT happen? It's just that we work at cross purposes. It's just that we think along different lines!!!

How to Sell

I never know if I'm making the correct decision when I buy or sell. Frequently I'm so uncertain and fearful that I make my right hand grasp the wrist of my left hand and force it to pick up the telephone to call my stock broker to place the order. (I'm lefty).

But with a $19,000 profit on the line and volume failing to move stocks higher (Volume is a major indicator as we discussed), I can't afford to worry whether selling is the correct decision. IT'S PRUDENT AND IT'S REASONABLE!

It's Good Thinking

I sell! I sell to cut losses and I sell to take profits! I sell to preserve capital so I can play again . . . later . . . on my terms . . . when I want to play!

There is another reason that makes selling difficult for investors. And that, too, is in their whole approach to buying. When they buy, it is without the conviction or confidence that I have.

They buy usually on someone else's recommendation.

Consequently when some of their stocks appreciate, there is no one there to tell them when to sell. They just don't know when to let go. They have no confidence.

They are afraid to sell because they are not sure if their next selection will prove profitable. In fact they are afraid that their next selection might turn out to cause them to lose money.

The Selling Decision

The decision to sell International Tel Tel first crossed my mind in October, 1976. The stock market had bottomed out at the end of 1974. As 1976 approached the year end, it marked almost two years of rising prices.

Also as the months of 1976 ticked off, the market was backing and filling; that is, it was moving sideways. This creates a "blackout" as I call this kind of action. A "blackout" has great significance.

Historically it precedes a major move. The longer the time of duration that it takes to form, the more volatile the move.

From what I understand about stock market behavior, the Dow Jones average could "break out" and become 1982 or it could "correct" or "pullback" as it did on previous occasions.

Several times before, the stock market tried to break out above the 1000 level only to fall back creating large stock market losses for investors.

We don't have to predict the stock market. We must follow it. Also all stocks don't top out with the averages. Therefore I closely monitored ITT aware of past history lessons and knowing just what it was that I wanted to achieve.

I already had 1600 shares but as ITT made a new high in August, 1976, I bought 200 shares at 31. For the month it's high was 32⅛. Now I had 1800 shares!

Nerve? Fear? I first bought the stock at 12⅝! My

thinking was that the stock was in a rising trend. Although I was concerned about the stock market, itself, still I can't work on emotion.

My thinking and understanding must always make the decision. The stock is rising! Buy a rising stock not a falling star. After ITT made a new high in September at 33¼, the ides of October arrived and ITT backed off.

Aware that the stock was on the upper level of its up trend, knowing that stocks go up and down, studying the fact that ITT moved from 12⅝ to 33 in less than two years, with heavy volume and not too great a price move up, isn't it "reasonable" to expect a down move??

Am I predicting it?? No! Expecting it! Yes!

THINK! When *DO* you sell? Well what was the objective when you bought? Was it to sell at a profit?

THINK! GREED! Isn't greed the reason for not selling? Do we know where the top is? No!

BUT THINKING PITS REASON AGAINST GREED

Under these circumstances I have accumulated such a large profit and such a large position that I must listen to reason when it says, "so it'll take a little longer to get rich. Sell and take your profit".

On October 5, 1976 before the ides of October can usher in its historic decline, I placed reason over greed and sold the 200 shares that I had purchased in August at 31. The selling price was 31¾.

Now do you know when to sell? How much to sell? You think it through. If the decision is tough, you stop reasoning. Use common sense. Just don't be greedy. Don't be emotional. Be a *THINKING INVESTOR!*

Of course I didn't know that the year, 1977, was going to be a tough year for the stock market. However ITT ended 1976 on a strong note at 33⅞.

My net worth at December 31, 1974 was $38,405.38, 1975 . . . $66,352.95, 1976 . . . $121,060.94.

International Tel & Tel roared into the new year of

1977 to make a new high of 34⅞. However in February, it just churned in a trading range closing down at 33⅛. When a stock weakens, I always have to consider selling. Now I considered my position and estimated that I had about $18,000 in profits in ITT.

The stock market itself, had been strong for two years. The move up in ITT had been relatively sharp. There had been no real long corrections. I know that stocks go up and down.

The stock was on the upper level of its major up trend. Not only am I concerned with the Krumholz Factor which deals with total loss potential but I am also very much concerned with not letting profits slip away. I just don't have a tolerance for taking stocks up and then taking them down. This is my thinking and this is how I reason. No deep thoughts. No esoteric devices or formulas. No gimmicks. No hard and fast rules to memorize.

Just plain reasoning with stock market indicators. And that is all they are . . . indicators! Don't get frustrated with them. They only make suggestions. If you don't like the suggestion, don't take it.

To Sell . . . Ask the "Crossroad" Question

I don't know where the top is. I don't want to miss any further rise in the stock. But neither do I want to take a stock down again. This resulted in the "crossroad" question".

When I'm in doubt whether to sell or not (and almost always I am in doubt), I ask myself these questions.

"How will you feel if you sell and the stock goes way up and you settled for only a $19,000 profit?"

. . . and . . .

"How will you feel if this is the top and you take the stock down again?"

In other words "Make your choice now. Don't live with regrets tomorrow."

On many occasions not only did investors let their profits melt away but also let their investments turn into losses which in turn called for the crutch, "hold for the long pull". I can live with a $19,000 profit but I can never forgive letting profits melt away!

Now here are the rules of the game.

"You know", I say to myself, "You can't predict the stock market. You know that you can't tell from minute to minute what stocks are going to do. You know that you have been wrong so many times."

"So why don't you be smart enough to recognize the limitations of being a plain human being? You know that you only have the choice between whether to sell and take your profit or stay and gamble on a rise."

I know from past experiences that I will feel badly for a day or so if I sell too early. But I *never* forget the times I stayed too long. They are the ones that still hurt.

Therefore I developed this thinking and trained myself ever after to follow that thinking. When I face that choice I ask the "crossroad" question and then *I SELL!!*

In time I developed this investment practice. When I sell, I never look at the closing price of that stock that day or for years afterwards. I have a very good reason for that.

If I see the closing only to find that I sold too early, I won't sleep that night. Each time I look at the higher and higher price in the papers, I will keep getting anger pangs.

What do I need that for? It will only interfere with clear thinking that will be required on decisions to follow. It's imperative! Leave emotions out of decisions!!

So you see investing is a matter of training and thinking and reason and logic. It's a matter of common sense! Now you should know that although I don't have a single solid reason for selling . . . no one rings a bell at the top . . . (usually) . . . and says now is the time to sell, I know when to get out (usually).

I believe that if you develop your thinking similarly that you should be able to be successful in your investing in stocks and bonds.

Therefore when February, 1977, approached the end of the month, and it appeared that ITT would close down for the month, I decided to cash in my profits.

ITT might be at the beginning of a long down trend. It might reverse its two year up trend. There is a very important technical tool that I used but which I haven't elaborated on because if I get involved in discussing technical analysis and fundamental analysis this would be a book of 1000 pages.

This book is a guide! I want to give you sufficient knowledge for you to succeed. Should you want to learn more, then this book is your textbook to higher learning.

But briefly the important tool was the combination of studying closing prices, (ITT was closing down on the month), the volume, the trend and the "blackout".

We discussed all but closing prices. The indicator in this case is that when prices close down on volume, it may be a reversal to an up trend and vice versa.

Studying the history of stock trading, I learned that the effect of a "blackout" is to tend to offer resistance when a stock tries to penetrate that vast area of trading.

This can work either up or down. Or if a trading area develops into a "blackout" area, then it may fail to continue its direction.

It was this combination of major technical indicators that caused me to reason along the lines that I just expressed.

Do you see how fundamentals and the forces of supply and demand work hand in hand with investment success?

In a similar vein the stock market averages were face

to face with the resistance level, 1000, on the Dow Jones Industrial Average. Again while I don't predict the stock market, I use indicators to alert me to approaching danger.

On February 25, 1977 I decided that I had achieved my objective. I was going to sell what I bought for a profit. I was going to do what I trained myself for. I sold four calls on ITT at 3¼ and received $1,249.68.

I don't want to elaborate on options (a call is an option) because you don't need them to invest successfully. Don't use them because you will lose a great deal of money unless you have long years of experience in the stock market. I use them very infrequently.

I wanted to start selling out ITT. I wasn't sure that this was the time. Therefore instead of selling my stock, I sold a buyer options to buy 400 shares at $30 per share.

I would receive $12,000 if the option buyer elected at a later date to buy 400 shares from me. The buyer had until April 30, 1977 to decide.

If the buyer of the options did not exercise his right to buy, then the contract would expire on that day and I would have made $1,249.68. That's what the buyer of the options had paid to me for the right to buy.

Why would I, the seller, want to give a stranger this right? Because the stranger paid me for the right to call 100 shares for each option. One call option is the right to buy 100 shares of stock.

Since I sold four call options, I sold the right to buy 400 shares of my ITT stock. I sold it @ 3¼ or $3.25 per share, thus I received that less the broker's commission and so I received $1,249.68.

In effect what I did was to buy time to decide whether to really sell out. That was my purpose in selling the calls or options. If I had a change of mind, I could repurchase those options at a profit or loss. Either way it was worth the money to gain the time that I needed to decide.

Taking Profits

The same day, February 25, 1977, I also sold three calls at $8 on the ITT stock. The time frame was the same but the agreed contract price, which lets the buyer purchase as many as 300 shares, was $25 per share. For these three calls I netted $2,349.03.

You see by selling these calls I was locking in profits. Should the market decline, I would at least make profits by selling call options.

Should the market for ITT stock rise, I would have some time to repurchase those calls. If not, then at least I would have received a larger profit by selling.

It boils down to another maxim that I coined; "I would rather make an investment where the choice is between making a *great profit or a little profit*, than having to make a choice between *a great profit or losing money.*" Give me the sure profit all the time!

Three days later, on February 28, 1977, I sold four more calls. This time the contract ran to July. I received $1,506.70 for these calls.

Since ITT closed down for the month of February, I continued liquidating the stock. This time, however, instead of selling calls, I decided to short the stock, itself.

I sold 400 shares short at 32¾. I received the net amount of $12,972.78.

17

When and How to Take Profits Using Short Sales and Stock Options

What is a Short Sale

I really don't want to go into short selling but since I use it from time to time, I will explain it. You don't need it to succeed. That's something else I leave to give you the thrill of discovery should you want to go deeper into the study of the stock market.

When you own stock, you are said to be "long" stock. The statement from your stock broker will list all the stock that you own but which is in the broker's possession. That is your "long" position.

The stock certificate in the bank vault is "long" stock. Consequently when you do sell your stock, you are considered to have sold "long"!

Nobody says this when you place the sell order. You might be asked, "Do you have the stock?" "Do we have the stock?" Nobody says anything about it being a long sale. But that is what it is!

Now many investors, at times, see a stock that they

feel is going to decline. Playfully they will say that the stock is heading “south”. They would like to sell the stock but they don’t own it.

Well how can you sell something that you don’t own? Wall Street has an answer!

How to Make a Short Sale

The broker says, in effect, “If you want to sell that stock, we will borrow the stock certificate from someone who owns it and lend it to you.” With that borrowed stock now in your possession, you can proceed to sell it! When you do, you made a “short” sale!

In actual practice to make a short sale or to sell stock short, just call your broker and say, “I want to sell 10 shares of XYZ short at the market” or at a fixed price.

You might have to wait until the person taking your order checks their back office to see if they could borrow the stock. With most brokers and most stocks, they don’t have to check the back office. In most cases there is no problem to borrowing the stock.

That is short selling!

Therefore instead of selling call options, I chose to sell ITT short. After the shortsale my position in the ITT stock was that I was “long” 1600 shares. I had sold 11 options and I was short 400 shares. My net position in ITT was that I was long 100 shares.

Get it? I had 1100 long stock in reserve in case the 11 options was exercised and the buyers wanted to buy that stock from me in the future. I also had to hold 400 shares to “cover” my short sale.

Consequently, it was still in my interest to have International Tel & Tel continue its move up.

Short Sales vs Stock Options

Selling options has this advantage over selling the stock short. When I sell calls, I immediately receive the money. This reduces my margin debt to the broker which in turn reduces my interest charges.

When I sell stock short, it does not reduce my margin but the proceeds of the short sale are kept in a separate account receiving no interest.

Also it costs less commissions to trade options than to trade an equal number of shares of stock.

Then again ITT is very liquid and its stock has more trading than the options.

Too, the bid and asked prices have usually a ⅛ point difference in the stock while the options often run between ⅜ to ⅝ of a point.

Consequently when I am keeping a very sharp eye on my investments with the idea of making major changes in my portfolio, I tend to swing from options to the short side or to the stock, itself.

In the meantime the stock market had reached a little over 1000 but was declining. Now this is a major force in my thinking.

I say that in a falling market that there is no such thing as a good stock. Of course you can't use this as a crutch any more than you can use the talk of "hold for the long term" as a crutch.

The Call Options Are Exercised

All sayings and principles have implications but you stand alone! No one is going to return your money to you. You have to do the THINKING! It's your money! It's your responsibility!

In April, 1977, ITT started to rally and to move up. But with the stock market moving down, I decided to try to lock in some more profits.

On April 1, I repurchased the three calls that I had sold. I lost $201.38 on this transaction. On the same day I sold four calls and received $1,024.98.

In effect I now had a zero position in ITT. It no longer mattered to me whether the stock went up or down. My calls plus my short sales totaled 1600 shares and could be offset by the 1600 shares that I owned.

The stock continued its upward path in spite of a weak stock market. On April 18, 1977, the buyer of the four calls exercised the option and called 400 shares. I fulfilled my part of the contract by selling 400 shares at $30 per share.

The proceeds of the sale of this 400 shares plus the premium I received for selling the 4 options totaled $13,100.26. My cost for those 400 shares was $10,933.35 so my profit was $2,167.01.

April 29, 1977 the buyer of another four options elected to exercise the calls and paid me $30 per share.

On this transaction my net proceeds from the sale of the options plus the sale of the stock totaled $13,410.66. These 400 shares had a cost of $9,193.65 which resulted in a profit of $4,217.01.

This left my position in ITT with 800 shares against which I had sold four calls and 400 shares short. Again it was equivalent to a liquidated position but I still kept my choices open.

When the month of May started, I was in a dilemma. The dilemma that all investors face. The stock market is now moving up and ITT is moving up.

Understanding the stock market, we know that not all stocks make their highs at the same time as the stock market. Most do but many make it before and some after. Perhaps ITT was going to be one of those that make it later.

This was not based on hopes but on facts. ITT was moving up and was near its two year high. Was I going to "fight the tape"? Never!!

The tape on ITT said that the stock was moving up so on May 3rd, I decided to resume buying. I could either buy 400 shares and increase my margin and my interest expense or simply "cover" my short sales.

To "cover" means either to deliver stock that you own

long or else buy back the stock that you shorted or that you sold short. I also had the choice of buying back the calls that I had sold.

I followed this up three days later by now buying or repurchasing the options that I had sold. On the short sale I lost $731.80 and on the options I lost $715.04.

I told you I lose money frequently. It's the price of success. It's the insurance that guarantees me a profit after it is all over. This is not a major mistake. It's the cost of doing business.

THINK! In June, 1977, ITT made a new high. The stock traded at 36⅜. I bought 300 shares on June 17 at 35½, June 21 I bought 200 at 36⅛, June 23 I bought 100 at 35⅞ and June 27 I bought four calls.

When June ended I went from a completely liquidated position to one where I owned 1400 shares plus 4 calls. Back to my 1600 original shares plus.

You see how I don't predict stocks. 36⅜ proved to be the top for ITT until the year 1983. If I now had to hold that stock for the long pull, I would have had to wait six years to get my money back!!

THINK! My capital would have been tied up for all those years. I would have been starved for profits for six years. Is that investing? Can you now see the fallacy in holding for the long pull?

What better time to contemplate the evil of "buying for the long term"? What would you do for the six years?

To buy other stocks you would need fresh money. If you need new money doesn't it tell you something? Doesn't it tell you that you are not managing your money correctly?

Doesn't it scream . . . "HEY YOU! YOU'RE NOT MANAGING YOUR MONEY PROPERLY!!"

THINK! I am embarrassed to tell you that I bought the stock right at the top. But I told you that successful investing is an art and not a science. I have no magic. I just think!

In spite of my embarrassment do you think for a minute that I was upset? No! Why you ask? Because I expect to do that at times. I understand Wall Street. I know the stock market.

I know that stocks go up and down. I know that I can't predict the stock market. Yes! I made profits year after year. I missed just about all the crashes and I think I got in near all the lows.

That is in spite of buying stocks at the top or perhaps selling near the bottom. I got whipsawed many, many times. To be whipsawed is to buy a stock at the top then sell it when it's down, then buy it again after a top only to sell it once again near a low etc.

I did it in 1986–87 and that was in a roaring bull market but before the Big Crash. I did that in spite of all my experience and success. That's what this book is all about; simple thinking of our limitations and expectations.

We deal only with probabilities in the stock market. A probability is no more than a guess. In my case it is an educated guess. It is a very considered guess. You, too, can think your way through . . . but you must work and you must think.

Yes. It is very difficult to sell. You can see, too, that sometimes it is difficult to buy. All this buying and selling of calls and short sales were devices I used to delay a final decision to liquidate.

If I simply had sold the 1600 shares, the campaign would have ended and I would not have followed ITT any more. I used the short sales and stock options just to keep the campaign alive.

In hindsight, it would have been better for me to have ended the campaign. But the fact that I didn't, affords you the opportunity to see how and when to take profits and how to carefully approach the selling part of investing.

Sometimes these devices work against you. At other

times they can make many thousands of extra profits. The main thrust is that it keeps you psychologically happy and comfortable with what you are doing. It keeps you thinking constructively.

In August, 1977, the stock market was in full retreat. It was only in June that I bought all that ITT stock at the top. Investing can be quite vexing at times. What am I going to do now? Let's find out!!

WHAT TIME IS IT ON WALL STREET FOR ITT?

IT IS WEDNESDAY, August 17, 1977!

The time of day is 9:25 A.M.

I have only 25 minutes!

I go to my file cabinet and thoughtfully open the third drawer from the top which is labeled, "Research". I slowly remove the file that reads, "ITT", still lost in deep thought.

Placing the file on my desk, I sink into my armchair behind the desk and open the folder to the top page. I start carefully reviewing all the quarterly earning reports for the last several years. Slowly!

Then I concentrate on the quarterly earnings just for the current year. The earnings trend is definitely up.

Soon I glance at my watch. It is now 9:32. I have only 18 minutes left.

I turn the next page and study the material there and then the next page and the next page. These pages are clippings pertaining to the latest developments in ITT.

It is now 9:39 and there are just 11 minutes to go.

With time hurrying by, I quickly spread some of what is the most important fundamental data before me covering my entire desk top but leaving the center of the desk clear.

I again go to the file cabinet and extract my chart on ITT. I place this technical indicator on the desk holding center stage and concentrate very, very intently on it.

I look at my watch. It is now 9:51. I am one minute

late. I must make a very important investment decision. If I'm right, I'll save thousands and thousands of dollars! A wrong decision will cost me as much!

Usually, I place my orders at 9:50 A.M. to make sure that my orders are in before the opening. Wall Street starts trading at 10 A.M.

It may be Wednesday, August 17, 1977 and the time of day may be 9:54 A.M. but for thousands of dollars the big question is . . .

WHAT TIME IS IT ON WALL STREET FOR ITT?

Is it time to buy?

Is it time to sell?

Is it time to hold?

International Tel & Tel closed yesterday at 33⅛! I reach for the telephone to dial my broker. I have made my decision!

I wasn't going to "FIGHT THE TAPE!" The stock market was going down and this time it was taking ITT with it! I sold 300 shares at 33¼ and the next day I sold 300 more at 33¼. The same day I sold my calls. I lost $2,442.65 on those transactions.

Four days later, on August 22, I shorted 400 shares at 33 and another 400 shares at 33⅛ the next day. Again I'm using the short sale to keep the campaign alive rather than sell my long stock.

Keeping the Campaign Alive

On August 31, I was long 800 shares and short 800 shares. I "stopped my losses" but kept the campaign open! You see, I hate to sell too!

The next three months, September, October, November, I stood pat. ITT made a new low in September of 28⅝ on much volume.

This was the major indicator that the bull market for ITT had ended. The volume for September was the largest volume for a very long time and the stock was down.

Also the trend for the stock had reversed. So now we have two major indicators MAKING VERY STRONG SUGGESTIONS!!

The stock market stabilized in September, October, November and ITT seemed as though it would move up for a rally. I decided to keep the campaign alive a while longer and so I bought 200 shares at 32¼ and covered 200 shares that I was short. I lost $35.76 on the short covering.

Five days later, on December 7th, I covered another 300 shares for a profit of $402.06 and on December 20th, I covered another 200 shares for a profit of $506.31.

And so through a very difficult year. The Dow Jones Average traded down about 200 points which was about a 20% loss. I had a continuous struggle to determine whether to maintain a campaign in ITT. It isn't always that difficult.

I started the year with 1600 shares of ITT and ended owning 1000 shares and short 100 shares. I had taken profits on 700 shares or about 43% of my holdings.

The 1000 shares of International Tel Tel had a cost of $20,751.80 and a market value of $31,750. The stock closed the year, 1977, at 31¾. The 100 shares that I was still short I had sold for $3280.48. ITT represented about 20% of my portfolio.

My net income for 1976 was $16,326 and my net income for 1977 amounted to $14,893. The total net income for the first five years, 1973–77 inclusive, totaled $47,387. That's about 25% per year on the money that I invested.

Much of those five years I was investing in weak markets. There was really just one short period of time where there was opportunity to make large profits, 1975–76, and I did take advantage of that opportunity.

Managing Many Stocks

The management of one stock, ITT, is not managing the portfolio. There are other investments and other campaigns to be concerned with. How does an investor cope with many stocks in managing a portfolio during good markets and bad markets?

That's the history to study. You are going through history when you review the ITT case. The importance of this review is to note my many mistakes and losses so that you should know that taking losses is NORMAL and paves the way to WALL STREET RICHES!

Therefore let us briefly chronicle other stocks in the portfolio to see how we managed the portfolio.

Managing Several Stocks

As the stock market declined in 1973, to finally bottom out at the end of 1974, I bought the ITT stock. At the same time I bought 300 shares of American Investment Company for $1018.07, 1000 shares of National Industries for $4030.38, 200 shares of Mid-Continental Telephone for $2258.36.

I also bought five other stocks to round out my stock investments. They were 700 shares of C I Mortgage for $997.20, 200 Uniroyal, Inc. for $2120.63, 1000 REIT Income Fund for $1706.60, 200 Madison Fund for $1419.83, 100 General Public Utilities for $1052.83.

Note that I had eight stocks and each had about the same amount of capital invested to start! But I didn't accumulate all eight. I only conducted campaigns in some for the reasons we have discussed in prior chapters.

Therefore it is worth chronicling the campaigns in the stocks of the American Investment Company, AIC, and National Industries, NI, to reinforce what and how you should think in buying and selling while managing the entire portfolio!!

AIC was a consumer loan company whose stock was

listed on the NYSE. NI was a conglomerate, a company that had several diverse businesses. This stock, too, was listed on the NYSE.

On January 1, 1975 when I owned ITT, I had 300 shares of American Investment Company, AIC, which cost $1018.07. The 1000 shares of National Industries, NI, cost $4030.38.

I sold the 300 shares of the American Investment in February which closed that position.

At the same time I bought 1500 shares of NI raising my position to 2500 shares having a cost of $11,380. I'll leave the pennies off henceforth. NI closed February at 4½. The market value was $22,250.

That month I didn't touch ITT. National Industries closed March at 5⅜.

Now this is 1975 when the stock market started its rise into 1976.

In June, with ITT being higher and NI closing higher at 6¼, I was protected by these profits to allow me to purchase 4000 shares of American Investment for $14,094.

In July, I took profits in AIC and sold 700 shares. The stock ended July at 4⅜. I also took profits in NI. I sold 1000 shares and the stock closed July at 6¾. I also took a little profit in ITT.

In August I sold another 900 shares of NI at a profit. That left me with 600 shares. I also sold 2000 shares of AIC which closed at 3¾.

In September, I sold 500 shares of AIC and it closed the month at 3¼. I had 800 shares remaining. I sold 200 shares of NI for some more profit.

In November, I bought 2700 shares of National Industries which gave me a total of 3100 costing $19,661.

In December, I purchased 3200 shares of AIC which gave me a total of 4000 shares with a cost of $11,213. The stock closed the year at 2½. The market value was $10,000.

National Industries stock closed the year, 1975, at 6⅝. The market value of the stock amounted to $20,537. The cost was $19,661.

In 1976 and 1977 I didn't do much with National Industries. The stock never did take off as I had thought it might. It hovered around six dollars and seven dollars much of the time.

I bought and sold it as it gave indications first one way and then the other. I finally decided to end the campaign in May of 1977.

Another Stock Doubles its Value

American Investment Company proved a very profitable investment. It closed 1975 at 2½ but it closed 1977 at 5¼.

In February, 1976, I sold 3200 shares and the stock closed the month at 4¼. I sold the balance of 800 shares in March.

In November, I once again bought the stock, 3400 shares for $13,013. In December, I bought another 2600. Now my total shares amounted to 6000 having a cost of $24,843. It closed the year at 5⅞. The market value was $35,250.

In 1977 I bought and sold American Investment Co. several times. I closed the year at 5¼. I had 10,3000 shares costing $47,342, while the market value was $54,075.

Note how the campaigns in ITT, NI and AIC differed. With ITT I frequently used short sales and options to keep the campaign open. Since NI didn't fulfill its projections, it was ended in early 1977.

With AIC the campaign was ended and then a new campaign was started three months later. This time it was started with more stock and a bigger capital investment. I had the experience of the previous campaign to benefit from and profits to protect me!

The year, 1977, ended with the campaigns still going in ITT and AIC.

THINK! While I use one stock as a guide to others, each stock is different. Each stock has its own TIME TABLE!

18

How to Cope with a Stock Market Crash— The October Disaster of 1978!

When To Take Profits

The year, 1978, started out with the stock market continuing a decline that had started in September, 1976. The trend was down on the Dow Jones Industrial Average even though there was some support the prior three months.

This support, however, did not indicate that the down trend was going to be reversed. The campaign that was taking place with International Tel & Tel had been going on for three years.

We know that stocks usually go up and down. ITT made a new high in June, 1977 and here it was six months later and still no new high. Evidently the stock was undergoing a "black out" stage.

THERE WAS A LOT OF TRADING IN A LIMITED PRICE RANGE TO CAUSE THIS. Buyers couldn't overcome the supply of stock offered by sellers, who evidently were taking profits!

You see. Since so many sellers were taking profits, doesn't it appear that they think that the stock is fully valued?

We are discussing technical developments. Let's add another one at this point. Usually in the early part of January, the stock market rises. This Wall Street phenomena has been commented upon by many writers.

This gave rise to the theory we sometimes hear and voice, but as January goes, so goes the year! If January closes up, the stock market will have a good year. If the month closes down, then the year will be a weak one for the stock market. I like to see a good January for that reason.

I let that thought influence my decisions as the year marched by. Consequently when January of the new year, 1978, proved to be particularly bad and sharply lower, I sold 200 shares of ITT at 29 on January 30th.

I followed that by selling 200 at 28⅞ the next day and another 200 the very next day again. This last price was 28⅝. Note that I didn't sell the 600 shares at one time.

You see, I'm never sure that I'm right. Also, I am reluctant to sell a winner. Thinking through selling decisions isn't a science. It is difficult but it must be done.

The stock market rallied sharply in April and then continued this move upward for several months. I rested on 300 shares long and 100 shares short.

However, American Investment did very well. I had started the year with 10,300 shares and the stock closed January at 5. In spite of the week stock market, this stock moved higher so in February I took profits on 1500 shares.

It closed the month of February at 7¾. At the end of the month I had a balance of 8800 shares.

When to Take Profits

In march I sold another 1300 shares of American Investment and the stock closed the month at 8⅜. In April

I took profits in 1500 shares. On April 30, AIC closed at $8 even.

In May I took profits in 1500, June 2900 shares and in July 1100 leaving me with 500 shares. It closed July at 7½.

When to Add New Stocks to a Portfolio

While I was taking profits in my compaigns, the stock market started a rally in April that lasted through the summer. I took my profits a few months too early.

However there were strong indications that my stocks were meeting resistance so I couldn't risk losing profits. But since the stock market itself was rising, it made sense to switch from my stocks which were vulnerable to stocks that had less of a risk potential.

Therefore in April, I purchased 3000 shares of Genovese Drug which is listed on the American Stock Exchange. The stock cost $15,419 and closed April at $5 per share. The market value was $15,000.

At the same time, through researching Genovese Drug, I encountered Adams Drug. Adams Drug, ADG, was listed on the New York Stock Exchange. This is a good trick of what and when and how to buy. Try the same industry. I stumbled on ADG in 1946.

I invested $15,610 and bought 4000 shares of Adams Drug stock.

When to Buy? Buy a Rising Market

In May I added 2500 shares of Genovese, GDX, and the 5500 shares I had at the end of May cost me $30,136 while the market value was $32,310. It closed at 5⅞.

During May I added 5600 shares to Adams Drug. My total at the end of May was 9,600 shares costing $42,835 while the market value was $50,400. ADG closed at 5¼.

In June, I took some profit in GDX by selling 1000 shares. But I added 500 shares to Adams and I bought a third drug chain buying 600 shares of Cunningham Drug which closed June at 9¾.

So you see how to buy stocks. One Drug chain led to another undervalued situation.

In July I hedged a little by selling 1500 shares of Genovese Drug and 400 shares of Cunningham Drug. However in August I added 2800 shares to the 200 I had in Cunningham Drug.

Notice how often I swing back and forth to avoid too large a loss. My investment in the new campaign in these three drug chains at the end of August was Adams, 10,100 shares costing $45,187 having a market value of $60,600.

Genovese Drug totaled 3000 shares, costing $15,419 and having a market value of $17,625. Cunningham Drug consisted of 3000 shares costing $32,462 with a market value of $34,500.

The reason that I was liquidating some campaigns and starting others was because I was liquidating when risks increased and buying when strength was indicated!

The October Disaster of 1978

The stock market was declining through March when suddenly in April it erupted with record volume. It peaked in June but then dropped in July.

In August, it once again moved sharply higher on tremendous buying. And so on August 31, 1978 I found myself with a $51,250 profit for these eight months.

I was satisfied with the way things were going and made no changes in September. I expected to make much more by year end.

The Dow Jones Average closed on Wednesday, October 11 at 901.42. The next day, Thursday, The DJ average closed down a modest $4. 68 and on Friday it closed up 35 cents. A rather uneventful week in the stock market.

Suddenly, on Monday, October 16, out of nowheres, it seems, stock prices dropped $21.93. The volume for that day was over 24 million shares but not enough to cause undue alarm. I was anticipating an approximate decline of the DJ of some $75 from 900 to 825.

The next day, Tuesday, the market closed down $8.83. The volume increased sharply to some 38 million . . . AND NOW . . . FOR THE FIRST TIME ALL YEAR . . . I WAS ALARMED!!!

That day, with only a drop of $8.83 in the stock average, I lost more than I expected as a norm.

THAT NIGHT I DIDN'T SLEEP AT ALL!!

WHAT TIME IS IT ON WALL STREET??

IT'S TIME TO PRACTICE THE ART OF INVESTING

THAT NIGHT, TUESDAY, OCTOBER 17, 1978, I DIDN'T GET A WINK OF SLEEP!!

WHAT TO DO?

Now here's where exercising and training your mind to be a successful investor pays off! This is a situation that will repeat itself. This is the time where studying investment lessons and principles will keep you on the road to Wall Street Riches.

TO STUDENTS! Q. WHAT DO YOU DO IN FALLING MARKETS?

A. *S E L L ! ! ! !*

And so the next morning I SOLD. Perhaps I should have liquidated my entire portfolio but I didn't. I did sell heavily the next day and the days that followed.

No "hold for the long term" . . . no "buy defensive stocks" . . . no "buy utilities for income" . . . no crutches!! By November I was sold out! The only thing in my portfolio were those two bonds that I first bought to start my fund!

Oh yes! I had some profits for the year!

My net income for 1978 amounted to $17,238. My net worth was $123,869.44. This was the only crash that I failed to avoid. I lost much of my profits in it.

Perhaps I was too greedy and stayed too late into October. Perhaps there weren't enough volume days of falling prices to help me avoid the crash. But at least once I was caught in it I wasn't going to magnify my error. I just had to "STOP MY LOSSES!"

Six Years of History Lessons

I don't know where time flies faster than in Wall Street! It seems to me that I'm always waiting for the next day to see what opportunities await me . . . or if my stocks moved up.

Therefore before we continue into the next phase of the stock market cycle, let's review what history revealed to us during our recent experiences.

Importantly how did we cope in this October, 1978, disaster? I had over a $50,000 profit going into October. Most of the year I was careful. But in spite of the warning indicators, this time I elected to reason and stay with the market. I was greedy. I expected more than $50,000 by year end. I didn't want to give up trying for that.

Too, it gets discouraging to buy and sell. So I thought that I would carry the portfolio through a small pull back. The trouble with that crutch is that the pull back some times turns out to be a disaster.

Consequently as the market started to crash all about me, I said the devil with reason, give me just plain common sense. It said . . . the market is crashing . . . the trend is down . . . the tape says down . . . so I ran!

THINK! The first lesson is "Control Your Emotions". Don't get GREEDY! . . . Also don't ignore warning indicators. They are not infallible. Yet without them you can't succeed!

It is in the History Books

The year, 1978, showed how successful "streamlining" a portfolio turned out to be. Once a stock started to rise, a heavier committment was made in that issue.

As the stock built profits, there was little need to be concerned with the Krumholz Factor. Now the fund was working with "their" money. The concern was with protecting profits. That's easier to live with.

Now it's "their" money and "your" profit! It's no longer the reverse, "your" money and "their" profit. Now you buy the Mercedes! Now you buy the yacht! You see! It's all in the THINKING!

REASON AND COMMON SENSE!

You can't beat that!

Taking a Trading Vacation

Among Wall Street traders there is a saying that will save you lots of money. They say take a trading vacation. It is good for you.

Many times investors get whip-sawed. It is best in such situations to get away from the stock market even if it is only for a few days. You will feel more enthusiastic when you return.

Another good time to take a trading vacation is right after a stock market crash. It's even better if you sell out before the crash and then go on vacation. A crash is also a good time to "Turn your portfolio over just like a new lawn!"

When I sold out during the October, 1978 crash, I decided to take a "trading vacation". I had all that cash in the bank and I was pretty exhausted from being tested by the stock market!

So while I was on that trading vacation, there was one very important history lesson remaining to be learned. What do we do about the many mistakes?

What to do About Mistakes

We all make many mistakes! But the idea is not to magnify them! Don't punish yourself for being human. So you didn't see the crash coming. But if the stock market did crash, then use common sense and acknowledge it. Don't use the crutches that Wall Street hands out.

If you sold and you were wrong, you will still sleep the night after and all the nights to follow. But if you didn't sell and you lose more and more, then you'll also lose sleep that night and the next and the next.

If you were prudent and sold and stocks went higher, then you have the choice to re-enter the market . . . not with that stock perhaps, but with a choice of many others.

On the other hand, if you lost money and are locked in . . . Good bye . . . give this book to someone who still has capital left!

Don't concern yourself with the opinions of others. You only make money when you are in control of the stock market and not when the stock market is beating you about the ears!

Why You Should Sell

THINK VERY HARD about what I am going to tell you about selling at this point. After I sold out during that disaster in October, 1978, this was my thinking.

All my Wall Street experiences are behind me. All my mistakes are behind me. I am clean . . . I am fresh . . . I have capital . . . I have no hang-ups . . . I have no allegiance to any stock . . . I am not bogged down with a lethargic utility stock tempting me with its dividends.

The stock market is my oyster. I'll roam it . . . I'll study it . . . I'll play with it . . . WHEN I AM GOOD AND READY TO PLAY AGAIN . . . ON MY TERMS . . I'LL PICK THE STOCK.

I don't need to pick a stock to MARRY! By gosh, I'm free again! I am an investor!

When you are in control of your capital, you feel strong, powerful and secure! You are in control of the situation. Not only the stock market but the world is your oyster.

You are free to look around, scan the stock pages, read the news, read financial magazines in luxury. When you finish a successful campaign, you enjoy reading about all the happenings in the business world.

You are going to pick the time and you are going to pick the stock! Keep an open mind and don't bring any preconceived ideas of which companies are "good" and which are "bad".

It's this feeling of exhilaration that you should always remember so that when you are in a crisis, you will want to return to it. It will help you to turn over your portfolio "as you would a new lawn".

When you sell out completely, it's such a good feeling after the initial letdown, that you will feel reborn. Even if you sell at a loss, you will still be exhilarated knowing that you have the capital to make a fresh start.

With this feeling . . . with this thinking . . . you won't use crutches!

Do you know what's wrong with holding a utility because it pays a good dividend? It's wrong because it is tying up your precious capital, your *source of wealth.*

Your capital may be tied up in a 7%–9% trendless utility when capital should be employed trying to earn 100% per year!!

If you feel that you are better off earning 8% in a utility rather than getting 5% from a bank, AGAIN YOU ARE WRONG because with cash in the bank you have complete freedom to move into the stock market. With capital tied up in a utility, you first have to decide to sell the utility to raise the capital.

Is that the objective of the investor? To put capital into a 9% utility until death do you part? Or was capital put into the stock market to make huge profits for retirement and pleasure?

A long time ago I coined a phrase, "Don't buy stocks

for income. You buy stocks for profit. You buy bonds for income!" That's what this game is all about.

THINK! Why must investors perpetuate their mistakes? Why must slogans be the "Conventional Wall Street approach to investing?"

WHY CAN'T "COMMON SENSE" BE THE "CONVENTIONAL WALL STREET" DOGMA?

Wall Street never tells the investor to think! They give you theory, crutches and excuses. They'll tell you WHY the stock market crashed in 1987, but not how to avoid it. Did they avoid the crash with their money?

Why should they now tell you how to invest yours?

It is really fascinating to read other opinions, especially from those who are supposed to know . . . those who manage billions of dollars . . . those in high and prestigious places . . . those who make the news . . .

Fascinating, yes . . . but utterly worthless! Isn't it really amazing that so often the financial papers will print contradicting opinions on what seems so simple a choice of whether to buy, sell or hold?

Often I see material where one broker recommends what another says sell. A very strange state of affairs! A most amazing paradox!

19

Wall Street Has a Timetable

What Time is it on Wall Street

The hands slowly moving across the face of the clock on the old church on Broadway in the financial district of New York City are a warm and familiar sight to those of us who frequent the area and watch the jam-packed streets during the business hours when the stock exchanges are open for business.

The eyes of thousands of passerbys have looked up to see what time it was as they hurried by.

Alongside the church is a small churchyard and cemetery. There are benches in the cemetery for those of us who have a moment to spare to sit and rest.

As your eyes rove around while sitting on the bench, you see many graves with small weather beaten headstones. You eyes can't resist sweeping in a circle as they move from one stone to another.

You can't help but forget the stock market for a moment as you return to the "real world". You can only sit for a moment or two before you will get an irresistible urge to approach closer to the headstones to read what is written there.

I remember being there one day in the summer of 1948. As I passed from stone to stone, I stopped to read one that hypnotized me. I'll never forget it. That was forty years ago and I still remember what it said.

It read, "Stop stranger as you pass by . . .". I'm not going to finish it because it haunts me from time to time and I don't want it to haunt you.

But I remember being fascinated by it. It was logical I thought. It was reasonable. It was so true. That writing splashes ice cold water on your excitable emotions and causes you to think with more reason and logic.

It helped re-enforce my decision to be reasonable in my stock market decisions and objectives and less emotional. It reminded me that the real world has no sympathy for losing investors.

On Broadway the old church clock may have helped thousands of us with the time of day but to investors who are involved in the "Wall Street Game", it is totally useless.

The "Wall Street Game" has an entirely different timetable. Wall Street has its own clock! Wall Street doesn't have clock hands. IT HAS ITS OWN INDICATORS TO TELL US THE TIME!!

But I never forget that small gravestone with its haunting saying. When I'm faced with difficult investment decisions and wondering whether the indicators on Wall Street are suggesting that it is time to sell or time to buy, my mind sometimes reverts to that old familiar and friendly clock over the church entrance and to that old and small churchyard.

And so it is that when I write market letters, I write that Wall Street has a timetable. In those letters I frequently ask the question.

WHAT TIME IS IT ON WALL STREET?

There is a time to buy! There is a time to sell! There is a

time to hold! There is a time to buy stocks! There is a time to buy investment bonds!

There is a time to buy convertible bonds! There is a time to buy tax-exempt bonds! There is a time to buy utility stocks!

There is a time to use margin! There is a time to stay out of the stock market! There is a time to take a trading vacation!

THIS TIMETABLE IS THE WAY TO WALL STREET RICHES!

SO THINK! The stock market crashed in 1978 and I sold out and took a trading vacation. The timetable suggests that after a crash, stock prices will decline for a long while. There is no hurry to get back into stocks.

It wasn't until the end of March, 1979 that I made my first serious attempt to get back into the stock market. On March 23, 1979 I bought 300 shares of Adams Drug at 3¾ and on March 27, I bought 1100 shares of Genovese Drug at 4⅝.

These two issues appeared to me to be special items. They were both family owned and growing slowly.

They were in a good industry. They both had big prescription departments. Their management styles were different. Genovese expanded using money generated within the company. It used its profits for opening new stores. It had little debt.

Adams Drug had more debt and expanded by using its profits and borrowing. Adams Drug also expanded by acquiring other drug chains.

Therefore I had two interesting and promising situations on my hands. My thinking was that in time, Adams should be able to go to $10 per share and that Genovese should be able to appreciate to $12 per share.

The downside risk seemed very little on Adams Drug and a little more so on Genovese Drug. I couldn't see Adams below $3 and Genovese could decline to the same level. Since Genovese Drug (GDX) had a bigger percentage risk, I had to watch the Krumholz factor more in the latter.

Well you know how to buy stocks. You buy a little at a time watching for a pull back. You don't want to lose too much money. I kept buying Adams Drug (ADG) every few days until the end of April.

On the end of April, I had 10,000 shares that cost between 3¾ and 4. On April 4 I bought 1200 shares of GDX so on the end of the month I had 2400 shares that cost between 4½ and 4⅝.

There was a third issue I bought at the same time.

How to Buy Stocks in Down Markets

The stock market didn't have startling moves in 1979. The market just moved . . . up . . . down . . . up . . . down. It's quite difficult to accomplish much in that kind of market.

Even though the market had crashed in 1968, it appeared to have stabilized towards the end of March of '69. That's why I thought there was a good chance to profit with these stocks.

Holding 10,000 shares of one stock, ADG, all I needed was a one dollar rise and I have a $10,000 profit. I didn't need anything else from the rest of my portfolio to have a year that would beat the bank's interest.

What if Adams rose to $8 in 1979? I have had stocks appreciate three and four times quite frequently in the past. Unfortunately those were the days when I could only afford to buy 100 shares.

Adams at $8 would give me a $40,000 profit! On a $40,000 investment! If, instead of Adams, you invest $40,000 among eight stocks, then how much can you expect to make?

Let's look at it another way. If you have eight stocks instead, in order for you to get a point rise in each of those stocks, you would need a bull market of sorts!

Usually you get one good bull run each ten years. With a stock like Adams Drug or Genovese Drug, I had many chances in that time frame! However you must not hesitate to set a loss limitation before you buy!

Once you understand the stock market . . . once you have no fear of the stock market . . . once you are acclimated to taking losses without losing a night's sleep, then you should try to profit from your knowledge and ability during any part of the cycle.

But you must know what you are about . . . you must always be THINKING!!

I had no success with those drug stocks. To limit my loss, I sold 1300 shares of Genovese at 4½ losing commissions. That was in July. I also sold 6000 shares of Adams at $4 which about covered most of my commissions.

Over the summer I started a campaign in the stock of Simplicity Pattern. I accumulated 3500 shares for a total cost of $40,459.

In August I was back again in Adams with a buy of 4000 shares and I also bought 4000 shares of Genevose Drug. The end of September, I had 8000 Adams, 6500 Genovese, 6000 Liberty Loan and 3500 Simplicity Pattern.

By year end I cut Adams to 2000 shares, Genovese to 5000 shares, Liberty Loan to 800 shares. I didn't touch Simplicity. I had about $50,000 in cash.

For the seventh successive year there was a net income. It amounted to $10,758. The total NET FOR THE SEVEN YEARS TOTALED $75,383. I estimate that to average about 22½% per year. Outside of the period from 1975 to 1976 they were difficult years for investing.

My net worth declined about $7,000. Net income is always different from changes in my net worth because my portfolio carries over unrealized profits and losses from year to year.

For that reason net income never truly reflects how much is made or lost each year. However its accumulated total reflects the result of many years, since sooner or later I go into an all cash position.

The 1980 Timetable

The history of 1980 again establishes the fact that reason and common sense will prevent losses from crashes and down markets.

The Dow Jones Average tried once more to surmount the 1000 level with me hanging onto its coattail, I had several campaigns going subject to severe losses.

Adams Drug dropped to 2¾. Remember I didn't expect it to go below three dollars. Genovese dropped to 3¾. Here, too, I expected a possible low of three dollars.

Thanks to the Krumholz Factor I didn't have blocks of stocks. I did add 4000 shares to Simplicity Pattern. It had a lesser risk factor than the drug chains.

When 1980 ended, I had 500 shares of GDX, 1100 shares of ADG and 7500 shares of Simplicity pattern. The latter cost $77,396 and the market value was $64,687. There was a small profit in the stocks of the two drug companies. I did hold $39,000 in cash.

I had to wait for telltale indicators to tip me off when to restart the campaigns in the drug companies. I spent most of 1980 trying to make money with Simplicity Pattern.

For the first time since I started my pension fund in late November, 1972, I had a net loss for the year (1980). It amounted to $656. However my net worth increased by $1100.

The Stock Market Tries Your Patience

During the first half of 1981 the stock market hovered near its top. Quite a "black out" picture had been formed. That signified a major move.

With $77,000 in Simplicity Pattern. I wasn't going to

give the market a chance to test my Krumholz Factor. My thinking was that the issue was getting too vulnerable. It was taking just too long for the stock to show its value.

Therefore I started liquidating the campaign in March. I sold 2000 on March 19, 3500 on March 20, 1000 on March 23. You see all the time I was giving the stock a chance to demonstrate that I was wrong.

I continued selling until I had 200 shares left. That was just in case I wanted to renew the campaign. It was something to keep me interested and watching.

In July, I didn't see anything that the market was doing that would indicate a move to a new high in the averages. I decided to end my interest in Simplicity stock. I sold the last two hundred shares. I lost $1,402 on an investment of $77,396.

At the same time I decided to get out of Adams Drug in July. I sold 1000 shares holding 100 shares. I started the year with 500 shares of Genovese and added 6500 for a total of 7000 costing me $42,915.

The stock market maintained its downward course unwaveringly. It just backed away from that "black out" area as I feared that it would. It hovered near its low through January of the next year, 1982.

Seeing the "trend' being down and knowing not to "fight the tape", I sold the last 100 shares of Adams and sold off 5300 shares of Genovese. I held 1700 shares of the latter.

There was a profit in the Adams stock of $1,601 and a loss in the Genovese stock of $2,581. And that's the Wall Street Timetable! Up . . . down . . . up . . . down. It tries your patience! My 1700 shares of Genovese cost me $10,667.

The year, 1981, proved to be the second and last time that I had a net loss for a year. It amounted to $6,506. My net worth, however, increased, to $127,320.

Although I had a net loss for the year, it proved to be

the darkness before the light . . . the last thunderstorm before the brilliant sun.

We didn't know it but we were just before the light at the end of the tunnel! WE WERE ABOUT TO ENTER THE GREAT 1982–1987 BULL MARKET! Before we do let's rest a moment and THINK!

THINK! You haven't had to memorize a single sentence in this volume and yet think of how much you may have absorbed. I believe that what I say is reasonable and that you will have learned through osmosis basic truths that can help you achieve success in your investment program.

I believe that you now have sufficient knowledge and understanding about successful investing that you may even anticipate what I was going to do in 1982–87.

I expect that frequently you will anticipate how and when I am going to do it. My friends and family know what I did just by reading what happened on Wall Street.

When they hear of a crash, they just know that I must have sold out before the crash. When the market has a sustained move up, they just know that I must be making money. That's confidence built upon my years of successful investing!

If they knew that without reading this volume, then surely you must have an advantage that should prove rewarding to you.

Just one last thing. We have covered tremendous ground. We spoke about buying, selling, how, what and when. I have illustrated the thinking process using historic cases that I experienced.

There are nuances, of course, to buying and selling that I can't hope to describe. I am giving you all I can. But it would take another volume or two if I covered every buy and sell decision that I made.

Investing is such an art that if we worked together, we wouldn't always buy and sell exactly at the same time or at the same price. The difference is not significant because we would both wind up rich. We would both think it through to a winning solution.

Therefore in working with me through the 1982–1987 market, we will cover the last three parts of the cycle. We covered the first stage, the accumulating part in the years, 1977 to 1981.

Think carefully as we go through the next five years as many nuances will probably arise. Also I will introduce other indicators and factors that will help you succeed.

Have this thought in mind. We covered the first part of the stock market cycle, the accumulation stage. Those years 1977 to 1981.

It sounds simple, the accumulation stage. It sounds as though all you have to do is to accumulate stocks. But we saw how difficult it really is. Therefore realize that the years, 1982–87, is the second stage, the bull market that we all wait for. You'll see the problems that exist there.

The third stage takes place at the top of a bull market and continues as the market falls to start the fourth and final stage of the cycle.

Remember, too, that the distribution stage and the falling stage go hand in hand for a long while. As the fall continues in time, the distribution will lighten up. During the fall many rallies and bear traps ensue.

Therefore 1982–1985 will be the bull market rise. The years, 1986–1987, will probably be the distribution stage. The fall was probably ushered in by the Great Crash on October 19, 1987.

Strange as it may appear to many of my readers, the stock market average may have risen hundreds of dollars, but I doubt if the majority made the same bull market gains.

Behind all those wild moves was one heck of a group of "program millionaires" who overpriced stock values tremendously. Behind those rising markets I started to "distribute".

The Crash in October, 1987, indicated to me that the fall had started. But we'll analyze what was happening when we get to that year.

NOW THINK! I have repeatedly stated that there are many dozens of factors that are to be considered but that they all funnel down into one *TECHNICAL* factor which is the *TREND!* All these factors are gathered so that you can render either a buy decision or a sell decision.

In essence what I stated was that the objective of investing is to buy low and to sell high. Not to buy at the bottom and to sell at the top. Consequently all these factors result in a buy-sell decision but not as to when!

WHEN MEANS TIME! Time means that there is a timetable. That's what this chapter is about.

20

How to Get Rich . . . Buying Stocks 1982–1985

One last reminder before entering the Great Bull Market. Keep in mind the Wall Street Timetable. If 1982–85 represents the second part of the cycle and if 1986–87 is the third part of the cycle, then you figure out what to expect after the stock market crashed in October, 1987.

The Start of a Bull Market

The stock market entered the new year, 1982, in a down trend. The month before, in December, it made a high for that quarter after which it trended down.

A bull market was the last thing in my mind. Notice that I did not predict a bull market or even suspect that one was on the horizon. I had no reason to expect one.

My thinking was that we are again in a down trend and I'm not going to "fight the tape". It was reasonable to expect the market to test the 750 level. In December, the previous month, the Dow Jones had approached the 900 area.

Last year it was at 1000 for the fifth time. From 1000 to 750 is a 25% decline. Those with stocks and little buying reserve, faced quite a set back and a major threat as I saw it. Note all these things as we continue this historic route.

Recognize that all the losses that I suffer are of small consequence at the end of the years and particularly at the end of bull markets.

No Magic . . . Just Thinking

I'm going to roll up my sleeves at this point so that you can see that I have nothing up my sleeves . . . no magic . . . no gimmicks . . . for getting rich!

I'm just going to continue doing what I told you to do throughout this book. I'm going to do the same thinking. I'll reason and when things get out of hand . . . when I feel threatened . . . I'll stop using reason and resort to plain common sense.

I entered 1982 with a net worth of $127,320.36. The only stock I owned was 1700 shares of Genovese Drug having a cost basis of $10,667.08. That averages to $6.275 per share. In the next two years, stock dividends reduced that basis to $2.89 per share.

January, February, March, April . . . I was cool and loose. I was very, very patient.

The stock market made a new low in March. I didn't "bottom fish". I was patient. My capital was idle. It was resting. I was liquid. No gimmicks.

The market rallied in April right into May! On May 3, 1982, I bought some high yielding utility bonds and on the 5th, I purchased another six bonds.

I didn't know how many months I might have to wait before I bought stocks so I wanted to increase my yield in the interim. May 28 I bought a few more bonds. Remember I was looking for a declining stock market.

The First Harbinger of a Bull Market Is:

A Major Technical Indicator—VOLUME!

Stocks dropped in June. And the very first thing of significance that I noticed in 1982 was that there was tremendous buying in Genovese Drug, GDX, that month.

The buying put the stock up to 8¼ which was the best price since 1980. This was a positive indication but didn't result in any action on my part. I did want to wait to see what developed.

The stock market, after doing its job of . . . up . . . down . . . made a new low in August. Genovese, on large volume, made a new high in July of 8⅞. It traded between 7¼ and 8¾ in August. Thus the stock traded on its high range even though the stock averages made a new low!

AUGUST, 1982, A HISTORIC DATE! The start of the greatest bull market in history!!

Me? I was oblivious!

I'm just another investor in the stock market. I have no connections. I don't see that this market is any different from those between 1976 and today. 1982 shapes up as another difficult year for investing in stocks.

THINK! Then a second unusual happening came to my attention. The volume of trading in the stock market leaped tremendously for a second week! With the increased volume the Dow Jones had a range from approximately 788 to over 870! A huge move up!

The Second Harbinger of a Bull Market Is:

A Major Technical Indicator—The TREND

This was followed the following week by a similar large amount of volume and the Dow Jones advanced to 908 dollars before closing at a lower level. Three successive weeks of large volume and this time the average advanced to 940, closing about 925!

Now history teaches us that when stocks rise on large volume, it is bullish. When they decline on large volume, it is bearish.

Is there anything smart about that? No! Most every investor soon learns that. SINCE I'M AWARE OF THAT I *THINK* ABOUT THAT AND I *ACT* ON THAT!

THAT'S WHY I BUY WHEN BULL MARKETS START AND SELL BEFORE STOCKS CRASH!!

Thinking about this last indicator gets me to think about another indicator. The stock market since about the month of September of last year was in a trading range that was between roughly 780 to 900 on the Dow Jones Industrial Average.

This repeated up down, up down movement created a "black out" picture. History indicates, as we said before, that a move away from this black out is usually very strong and definitive up or down.

As a thinking person, it was reasonable to expect that since the trend was down until the middle of August, that if there was to be a penetration through the lower level, 780, then I could expect the stock market to continue down to perhaps below 600.

Therefore this move up by GDX and this latest strong move up by the average isn't what I was expecting. This is a very good time to emphasize that I don't predict the stock market.

I'm just a reasonable person who has a good understanding of Wall Street and its ways. I don't lead the stock market. I follow the stock market! I'll demonstrate that to you shortly. That's why I think that you can too!

When the stock market in August reversed its down move and started on its rise, I did nothing about stocks. In fact I bought ten more utility bonds on September 2nd.

THINK—Are you thinking of what I was thinking then??

THINK—If this were to happen next week what would you do??

I was thinking of these *TECHNICAL INDICATORS:* My stock, GDX, broke out to a *new high on volume!* Bullish! The stock market broke out on the upside from a "*black out*" area! Bullish!!

Volume on the stock market was magnificent while accompanying the *up move!!* Bullish!! The *down trend was broken!* Bullish!!

The big volume on the stock market was not just one week or two but *several weeks!* Bullish!! After five weeks I could see that the *trend was now up!* Bullish!!

Now! Now! Now is the Time to Think

Are these indicators of the "Wall Street Timetable" trying to tell me something?? Are they trying to tell me that the "Wall Street Clock" has turned from Sell to Buy??

"WHAT TIME IS IT ON WALL STREET?" "DO YOU KNOW?"

Mind you I'm not thinking bull market. That thought hasn't entered my mind at this time. I'm not even conjecturing how high this move may carry. I don't even know if the Dow Jones can penetrate the 1000 level after failing so many times.

I don't know or care about such matters as they are of no moment. The stock market can only go up or down. I'm an investor. I'm only interested in trying to buy to sell at a profit!

I'm thinking very hard. What am I going to do? I'm trying to reason through these investment indicators. Should I take profits in Genovese or should I buy Genovese? How many times have we struggled with that question these many past years?

I'm trying to tell the time on Wall Street!

After reviewing the indicators, a FREE AND OPEN

MIND can only conclude that they were strongly suggesting that on Wall Street, it is time to BUY!!

On September 21, 1982 I entered the Great Bull Market! I purchased 500 shares of Perry Drug, PDS, at 9⅜. The 500 shares cost me $4,733.

What did I do next?

Of course! The next day, September 22, I bought 1500 shares at 9½ for $14,360. This is a good time to rest and reflect a while on how THINKING got us to this point.

Note that I didn't buy 2000 shares of PDS at once. I bought 500. I slept on it. I liked the idea so I went back for 1500 more.

Don't worry about commissions and ⅛'s and ¼'s. We are investing for big money. We pay the insurance to avoid big losses and to avoid getting locked in!!

Reflect how we just think about *the same factors*. Note that we don't memorize anything. We stick to our purpose.

The stock market never has run away from me yet and it won't run away from you either. Don't worry about missing buying opportunities. There are loads of them. Just don't take big losses.

In the preceding years we went through buying stocks during the first stage of the cycle. Now we are starting to see how we buy stocks in the second stage . . . in a bull market!!

In response to the question, "How and what stocks to buy and when" did you by chance wonder why I bought Perry Drug now when in prior years I was buying Genovese and Adams Drug?

Why didn't I start a new campaign in Genovese at this point? Why did I introduce a new stock to my portfolio? What about the "don't diversify but streamline" concept?

How to Buy Stocks in a Bull Market

The "when" part we have just gone through and will continue with as the market rolls on. What stocks to buy I'll answer now.

I explained that in the early part of my research, after I am attracted to a stock, that one factor I always look into is the relative value of that stock to others listed.

I'm looking for an undervalued issue. And of course my major concern is the risk. As my decision approached the buy stage in September, my first thought was Genovese. It was the one stock that I had. You would expect me to buy that first.

But you must remember this important understanding of Wall Street. I haven't discussed it before. *The stock you own today is not the same investment value tomorrow?*

Stock prices are in constant motion. Just as atoms and molecules keep bumping into each other to and fro, so do stocks. In many instances the relative values of stock prices to each other are never the same two days straight.

If the change is slight, then you have no problem. If the change warrants it, then you have to reconsider and rethink your position and your attitude. And that's what this book is all about!!

Therefore when the time approached to make a buy decision on GDX, I had to go through the process again.

The Key to What to Buy

To find the relative value of Genovese Drug, it was necessary to look at stocks in the same industry. If GDX was the best investment, then I would compare it with some other stocks. That's the operating procedure.

In the case of Genovese and Adams, I looked at Perry Drug among others. I found it to be a larger company with more promise for the future. Its fundamentals stacked up better in my opinion.

Next I studied the technical situation. What were the lows and the highs on these stocks? Where were they trading today?

I found that Perry Drug had a trading range between

5½ and 9. It was still in its trading range but near the top. It was selling for about the same price as Genovese.

However Genovese Drug had moved up substantially and was trading above its normal range. The trading range for GDX was from 4 to 8.

Perry Drug closed September at 9 and Genovese at 9¼. If those two stocks declined, I would suffer a larger loss by buying Genovese. *The key to buying at this point was the Krumholz Factor!*

Since my chief concern is the loss factor, I decided to go with Perry Drug. The stock had the potential to multiply with Genovese.

That's how I bought Perry Drug and not Genovese Drug!

There is still another important reason for buying Perry. This, too, answers the question of what to buy. It's a good idea to buy a stock in the same industry as a stock that you already own.

If one moves, then you have an earlier indicator to let you know to expect that the other will follow suit! I very successfully used this idea when I first started to invest in 1946. I followed the aircraft manufacturers then.

After one aircraft stock advanced, I would switch to another that lagged. This indicator is not very useful in other stages of the market cycle but is excellent for use in a bull market!

In October, the Dow Jones went to 1050 on still higher volume. GDX made a new high to 12 which doubled my investment at that point. PDS went as high as 11⅛ with volume now coming into the stock. What is volume? A technical indicator!

THINK! What Time Is it On Wall Street? How many years were stocks being accumulated? It's time to think that maybe we started a bull market.

From October 14 to the 22nd I bought 30 more bonds. With this rising market I had more confidence in the safety of these bonds.

THINK! I had Genovese years ago and it did nothing. Now the same stock is 12. What's the difference?

The difference is the Wall Street Timetable. *WHEN!*

THINK! Using hindsight, instead of buying those last thirty bonds, wouldn't it have been more reasonable to have put that money into stocks?

Of course! That was the time to buy stocks and to forget about bonds. In fact it would have been a good time to switch from bonds into stocks.

It proves what I contend, that I'm not always right. But I'm always consistent in that I take the safer course. I'm an investor. If I am good at it, I'll grow.

Perhaps a little slower but again it boils down to the question of making a little vs making a lot . . . or taking bigger risks than I was comfortable with at the time.

Between October 22 to the 25th, I bought 4000 shares of Adams Drug, ADG, between 6⅝ and 7. The cost was $27,238.

Why back to Adams Drug and not GDX or PDS?

Of the three drug stocks, Adams was the only one that showed an up trend since March. That is it showed a very decisive up trend. Too, each time that the stock moved up it was accompanied by large volume. That indicates buying!

THINK WITH ME! This, I reasoned, indicated that the stock was a laggard and could appreciate much more *on a percentage basis* in the immediate future than the other two!

Also it would give me a third stock in the same industry. By watching three stocks I would have an early alert of impending moves and direction!

THINK-THINK! All plain reasoning and knowing what to think about!

Adams Drug closed October on its high of 7½. Although I was buying the bonds and Adams stock, I still had a lot of thinking to do! I thought that I wanted to have a larger stock position. Still, I had to be cautious.

I noticed that Perry Drug had recently issued a bond that was convertible. So my thinking went this way. The stock paid a very small dividend. The bond interest was substantially higher. I was using margin and the rate of interest was about 10%. By the end of the year the interest on margin was as high as 15½%.

Secondly, I never know when a stock is going to correct or have a pull back. In that case the bond will lose less value than the stock.

Finally, I reasoned that the optimum time to buy a bond that is convertible is when it is selling a little over par or over $1000. At that point the bond will tend to rise equally in value with the stock as it appreciates.

It was an ideal time and spot for investing heavily in convertible bonds! Therefore I decided to buy them. So on October 19 I bought twenty bonds at 106. The 106 is $1060 for each $1000 bond.

October closed and I had 4000 shares of Adams Drug at 7⅜, 1700 shares of Genovese Drug at 10⅞, 2000 shares of Perry Drug at 10 and twenty convertible bonds of Perry Drug. I also had a lot of straight bonds. I WAS IN THE BULL MARKET!

ARE YOU THINKING! Have you noticed that I am using MARGIN!! Note how, when and why! Notice that the Krumholz Factor is protecting me in all this buying!

Note that it is also protecting me against the risk of using margin. Note that I am risking my profits and THEIR money! Note that I am "streamlining". Note, too, that I am campaigning.

November saw record volume days for the stock market and with it, new record highs for the Dow Jones. I didn't stop to think in terms of a bull market. I just did my job which is to think about my portfolio.

As long as the trend is up . . .

STUDENTS! Q. WHAT'S THE ANSWER?

A. You are right! . . . *B U Y ! !*

In November I bought another thirty bonds of Perry Drug over a period of several days. There were none for sale at 106. I had to pay 114 and 115. That is $80 and $90 more for each bond! I now had 50 Perry Drug convertible bonds for an investment of $55,067.

I also purchased 7 convertible bonds of Beefsteak Charlie and 100 shares of Suave Shoe. I now recognized that there was a rip roaring bull market on fire and though I had several campaigns going on, I wanted to take advantage of a bull market! They are few and far apart!

My margin debt was piling up!

THINK! I didn't buy thousands of Suave as I did in other instances. I bought 100 shares. I didn't buy 50 bonds of Beefsteak Charlie as I did Perry.

Each stock and bond is a specific investment and a specific case. The fundamentals and the technical factors of each are different. You must think through the risk of each investment.

Plain thinking and control of greed indicates how much to buy. Plain thinking will do the trick. Try not to think under pressure. Think in a relaxed manner. Again watch the Krumholz Factor, control your emotions and you should be okay.

December was another big volume month for the stock market. It closed the year in a strong manner near its high. I did no buying in December.

I have a very big question for you!

WHAT DID I DO DIFFERENT THIS YEAR FROM ALL PREVIOUS YEARS?

THE ANSWER . . . I did not sell in all of 1982! This establishes the fact that I have no formula for selling. I only sell when I think that a stock will decline or to stop losses. In 1982 the Krumholz Factor level was never reached as in previous years.

This is the time to consider the pros and cons of my

principle; "Don't diversify your portfolio . . . Streamline it!!" It is making me Wall Street Rich!!

The average investor, when looking to accumulate stocks, would buy one stock in many industries. The word for that is "Diversification". Should some industries turn down, the others may not. Consequently some of your stocks may decline but hopefully the others will not.

But now instead of monitoring several issues as I do, other investors would have to monitor many issues. As often happens they have so many that they don't bother to monitor any.

I have three stocks in one industry where one stock cued me as to when to buy the others. For example I started to buy Perry Drug because I had an interest in Genovese. Now I have two stocks "watching the store" for me!!

You see throughout this book I'm only talking reason and common sense to you. Yes the year, 1982, was a record year for the stock market. My net income was only $9701 but that was because I didn't sell to take profits.

The only thing I did sell was $20,000 Treasury notes. I needed the money to buy 20 Perry convertible bonds. The treasury notes are part of portfolio managing which I have not discussed.

My net worth increased for the year by $63,363. It totaled $190,683 . . . a record high! The market value of my portfolio reached a record $303,167. The cost was $260,201. I owed the broker $112,484.

My pension fund was a balanced fund at year end.

A balanced fund is one that consists of both stocks and bonds. Mine was as follows:

I had $53,915 in treasury notes . . . $58,438 in bonds . . . $61,700 in convertible bonds . . . and three campaigns in drug stocks totaling $129,112. That was it basically.

I expect to retire with this fund. I understand the stock market and I have a deep, deep respect for it and what it can do to me in just one single day. I can tell you stories that I know of and which I have read that would fill volumes.

Suffice it to say . . .

"I'D RATHER BE PRUDENT THAN RIGHT!" Of course many in Wall Street would say that with this portfolio that I'm not prudent. That, too, is a matter of opinion.

21

How to Triple Your Money—With Stocks and Bonds!

T*HINK!* How are you going to manage your investments in 1983? I'm going to manage mine the same in 1983 as I did in 1982 and as I did in all the previous years.

No different. It'll be the same thinking. The same reasoning. The same principles and guidelines. If reason won't work, then I'll use common sense.

I'm not going to take you through every trade because by now you know what to think about and how to think. I'll only take you through things that you should know and not fear.

In 1983 I was selling continuously. I sold lots of stock. In theory its best not to sell until the end of the bull market. But I never know when the market is going to have a major correction and I was determined not to let my profits vanish into thin air.

I wasn't going to wait seven years for a bull market and then waste two years of a bull market. That would be bad investing practice! Therefore reason dictated that I sell and so I sold.

Mind you, it was not to take profits. Not to cash in. But to PROTECT profits. But I did not hesitate to buy when reason dictated that.

How to Use Margin

On February 28, 1983, I owed the broker $146,703. On March 31 my margin rose to $246,639. In April it dropped to $209,120 which indicated that I had sold on balance.

In May it rose to $297,091 . . . June, to $339,473 and on July 31, 1983 I owed the broker $365,811 on margin. It's my profits but "their" money!

It is important that we know "What Time It Is" when we use margin. It is the time of the Great Bull Market!! The second stage of the cycle.

My net worth rose to a record $462,080 on July 31. On December 31, 1983 it was $420,219. I started the bull market in 1982 with $127,327. I more than tripled my money. And that was holding bonds as well as stocks!

Although my net worth or my equity had a sensational rise, my net income was only $19,168. Even then it was a record net for my fund. As I said I wasn't selling to cash in. I only sold where and when I felt threatened.

You see it's not what your paper is worth, it's what you cash in that will ultimately determine your success in investing. I still didn't cash in my paper!

To complete the picture of how to manage your investments and triple your money, consider my portfolio at July 31, 1983. I still had $50,000 Treasury notes. I sold most of my utility bonds to buy stocks (remember I said that was the thing to do last year). The value of my Perry bonds about doubled in value. As the stock went up, the bonds went with them. On June 30 the bonds were trading at $2000 for each $1000 bond. I about doubled my money with bonds.

I tried a campaign with International Tel & Tel again. I had 2900 shares trading at 45¼. It was worth $131,225. Remember it was 30 to 36 when I invested prior.

I now had 6700 shares of Perry Drug selling at 27 worth $180,000. My cost was $83,098. I had 5100 shares of Adams costing $40,974 worth $103,275.

With Genovese Drug I was busy buying and selling. On July 31 I had a cost of $43,713 which was worth $85,100. I had 17,000 shares of Umet Corp. selling at 4¼. I was short stock. I was short calls. These latter were used as I had explained in another chapter.

I BOUGHT AND SOLD AS REASON DICTATED!

In December I lost $40,022. My margin was cut back by $56,761. You see when the market declines I get nervous. When I get nervous, common sense tells me to protect my profits.

When we started this book I was talking about buying two bonds for $1400 to $1500. Now I lose $40,000. They were both dictated by the same principle . . . The Krumholz Factor!!

The Achievement of Wall Street Riches

The year, 1984, was a tough, tough year. It tested my patience, my nerves, my ability to think and reason. It tested my common sense. Oh yes, it tested my greed! It also tested everything that I wrote in this volume.

January, 1984, started as most Januarys seem to do. It started in an up mood. It was so strong, in fact, that it tested the new high of the stock market.

But then it started to decline. It didn't seem to be a normal easing of prices but rather large declines. It seemed like a fall because volume was near record for several weeks.

THINK! What does a thinking investor do in such situations? You don't reason. You use common sense. Get out! I'm sitting with about $300,000 profit and I'm an investor. I want my profit.

I SOLD! I hope that you knew that I would and I hope that you will, too, in similar situations.

On January 1, 1984, my portfolio was $476,981 and I owed the broker $56,761. January 31 my portfolio was $214,956 and the broker owed $199,424 to me!!

When to Sell

This is one other time to sell. Did I think that the bull market was over? No! But I never think in terms of bull markets or bear markets per se. I think only in terms of profits and losses.

The market was long overdue for a correction. That means that the market was due for a fall. How long or how much the correction would be, I didn't know or care. I only know that when the trend appears to be down, I want out!

By February 28 I was practically out of the market!

On March 31, 1984 I had $255,000 in treasury bills and notes. Reason reported to me that the indicators said that we were in a roaring bull market. All my understanding about Wall Street said that we were in a roaring bull market.

But common sense said, If you don't sell, you don't get rich! If it's a choice between the two, always use common sense. So I decided to lock up part of my profits! To make sure that they were locked, I put them into those treasury items.

However, when the market showed signs of a "black out" by the end of March, and some indications that the market might find support, I started to buy. With every purchase I established a Krumholz Factor.

The market continued its decline into June and July and then had a very sharp move up in August. It had a large trading range right until the end of the year. It kept me busy buying and selling.

The Investor's Function

When I sold in 1983 it was to PROTECT my profit! When I sold in January and February of 1984 it was to TAKE my profit! I had completed my functions as an investor!

I was now ready to start investing once again. You

don't necessarily start at the first stage of a cycle or at any particular part of it. You start whenever you have the capital to do so.

However I didn't get anywhere the rest of the year. I finished the year with $185,000 Treasury bills and notes, 20,200 shares of Hallwood Preferred stock, 7⅞, value $159,075, 1000 shares of Genovese Drug at 12¾ worth $12,750 and many thousands in bonds.

The total portfolio was $450,206. I owed the broker $66,471. My net income was $268,092. I had to withdraw about $100,000 from the fund, some $85,000 for income taxes and $15,000 for a personal expense.

The year, 1984, again established that you don't have to predict the stock market to get Wall Street Rich. Just don't trust the stock market. I never did. I have the deepest respect for the devastation it has caused and will continue to cause.

Investing is a Business

In February, 1985, the stock market made a new high. It went over 1300 and on big volume. A new high and big volume are two indicators giving the time on Wall Street.

THE BULL WAS ROARING!!

In July the market again made a new high. The Dow was now about 1568. From September to December it was straight up. There was big volume in the fourth quarter.

What was I to do in 1985? You know by now that when the market goes up . . . you buy! Let's once again examine how to go about the business of investing. It is best seen via my margin account.

Working With Margin

January 1, 1985 I owed the broker $66,471. By the end of January it had increased to $142,500 . . . February it was $231,685 . . . March it was $228,522.

In April I owed $164,411 on margin. In May and June it was about the same. But in July it reached $468,351 and August 31 it peaked at $494,666. I owed almost ½ million dollars!

Let's rest!

THINK! Am I mad to borrow ½ million dollars to invest in the stock market . . . Especially when it is on a record high?? Every few years I ask my wife, "Am I a gambler?"

THINK! Was it reasonable to go into liquidation not too long ago and pay $85,000 in taxes? Wouldn't it have been better to utilize that money to work with? Does it make sense to pay thousands in commissions and interest on funds borrowed?

THINK! At my age, supposedly in retirement, I don't need any more money. I have more than I can reasonably spend. What the heck am I doing in the stock market and why in heck am I borrowing ½ million dollars to speculate with?

Well I have a philosophy of life and a value system that my mom taught me as I was growing up.

My mom taught me that money is not as important as people. Work for it because you need it. But real life is concerned with people. And so I love people all over the world.

I believe that there are only two ages in life. You are either mature or immature! Your birthday does not enter into it. Therefore if you are mature and healthy, you should not think that you have arrived at the end of your life. You haven't died yet!

Consequently, if you have 100 birthdays and you can think . . . and you want to be an investor . . . buy stocks and bonds. Don't sit back and bemoan the fact that you are so old.

When I playfully told my wife that we had a one million dollar portfolio and asked her was she nervous that we borrowed ½ million dollars to put into the stock market, she replied, "A little".

We both laughed. I was a "little" nervous too. You see how human I am. But I know Wall Street and I understand Wall Street. AND I'M AN INVESTOR! I did what an investor is supposed to do!

Surprise

August 31, 1985 I owed the broker $494,666. Thirty days later he owed me $757.83. All I had in stocks was $9462. From maximum optimism (shown by maximum debt) to no confidence (indicated by no debt)! That's what it takes to survive in the stock market. I never had that confidence after that!!

In November I did start to buy again and by year end my fund totaled $661,187 and I owed the broker $223,917 on margin.

Why You Must Only Rely on Thinking

For 1985 my net income was $74,848. Now while that may sound okay, I was very disappointed. It's good if I only consider that my own capital was about $47,500.

But if you consider what my capital was to start the year, then you understand my disappointment, especially in a bull market!

However, there is really a difference between this market and other markets that I have experienced and studied. I really think, and it is only my opinion, that the bull market of the 80's lasted from 1982 to 1985 when the Dow Jones Industrial Average reached to about 1570.

The unprecedented jump from about 1550 to 1950 and then to 1975 was the result of program trading and trading in futures. Portfolio insurance, too, had a role in this.

The range of trading and the huge volume convinces me that were it not for these new trading vehicles, the stock market never would have gotten as high as it did without several major corrections.

Certainly it never would have gotten to 2700! I say that because there were too many secondary issues that did not reflect such a stock market average.

At this time I made a very, very costly mistake as an investor.

Although reason told me to buy the stocks in the averages, I couldn't bring myself to do so because I felt that they were overvalued. I knew that they were subject to the risks inflicted by the program traders.

If I were to buy stocks in the averages, I felt that I would be gambling and no longer investing. That's why I didn't buy. Program trading is a constant threat to investors. It is *not* investing!

It should not be allowed on the same stock exchange with investors. Let them buy stocks and use them on their own separate exchange. Program trading permits millionaires to skim off money from smaller investors.

Surviving Program Trading

In 1986 the stock market approached 2000. In spite of the sharp, historic rise it was one helluva see-saw. The program traders had a picnic.

I started the year with the right stocks. I was loaded with utilities. That was the time to buy them. But with the gyrations of the stock market, probably caused by program trading, it is difficult to idly stay month after month with loads of stocks.

So I bought and I sold. I went with the tape! I went with the trend. I ended 1986 with just one big campaign. It was a utility, Northern Indiana Public Service. I was holding 20,500 shares. It was at 11¾ valued at $200,685.

The company was having financial problems but it didn't faze me.

In that volatile market it reasoned to be a good buy. However this campaign ended the next year with nothing much accomplished.

When the year ended I owed the broker $63,552. For 1986 my net income was $31,001. Another disappointing year for me.

22

How to Stay Wall Street Rich!

Another Look at the Big Crash of 1987

I said that if you don't sell, you won't get rich! Now I say that if you don't sell before or during stock market crashes, you won't STAY rich!

The year, 1987, was ushered in with euphoria. Most everyone was sanguine. Me! I was thinking!

THINKING? This is the crux of this whole book! Common Sense! I was thinking that in the last two years . . . two big years of a super bull market . . . with my capital and my expertise . . . that I should have become a millionaire!!

WHAT HAPPENED? WHAT DID I DO WRONG?

WHERE DID I REASON INCORRECTLY?

I don't know the answer for a certainty. It seemed that all the talk and concentration was on the stock market averages, on the option and future markets and on all the takeover stocks.

It seemed something new had been added to the stock market. The stock market suddenly seemed like a strange place to me. I had the feeling that this was my first time buying stocks. I felt like a newcomer.

Of course, even though I didn't make the large sums

that I had expected, neither did I have a losing year. Again the stock market will always be here.

There was one thing I sure wasn't going to do. I was not going to get caught up in the crazed gambling taking place on Wall Street.

I didn't know what I had done wrong the last two years, but I did know what I had done right for the forty years that preceded. And that's what I was going to continue to do!

THINK! January, 1987, roared in with every bull charging and leaping ahead. The stampede was on!! The stock market shot up out of a catapult.

2100 on the Dow Jones Industrial Average before you could blink! I maintained my steady objective. I had the one big investment that could give me big money should it move. If this bull market was for real, then this stock should go.

The end of March saw the Dow average almost make 2400!! I increased my margin. I was buying. My profit for the three months was $27,203. Thirty days later I had a loss of $14,104 so far for 1987. A swing of some $41,000.

I found this very annoying. 2400 on the Dow and here I was after four months with a loss? That's what this book is all about. THINK! ASK YOURSELF FOR RESULTS! REVIEW YOUR METHODS AND WHAT YOU ARE DOING!

From a high debt due to my broker of $161,954, I cut it to $6,685 by April 30th. The key to think about is that I didn't get angry or stubborn. Yes, I was annoyed but I never stopped thinking and reasoning.

Thirty days later the broker owed money to me! There was $88,005 due to me and I had cash in the bank of $70,258. When I saw that I was losing my profit and when that profit became a loss, I sold out one half of my one big holding. The balance was closed out in May! End of campaign!

I had been bullish on the oil stocks for many months

and I had bought several of them as well as call options. But when they backed off, I lost confidence.

Therefore in July and August, I owned only 1980 shares of Utilicorp United and 600 shares of Mobil Corp. Mobil Corp. had me talking to myself many times!

I did nothing in September! I just watched!

I had no idea whether the stock market would go up to 3000 or crash down to who knows where. Even while doing nothing my portfolio lost $7513 in value.

It's Time!

What kind of a bull market am I in?? It might be a bull market for others, but its my money and it is not doing so well. That is sending me a message! I can't convey this message to others if they will not listen. Isn't that what I said in the prologue?

At September 30th, I was just about at the break even point for 1987. Nine months and the Dow Average hundreds of dollars higher and I'm left out of it. Do I have to predict the stock market? NO! I just have to think!

I watched the stock market start October with a gain of $42. The next day was Friday, October 2, and the market closed down $1.79.

On Monday the market was down 89 cents but on Tuesday, October 6, the market fell $91.55. The volume was very high. In my market letter I said I told a friend that when the market has several days of over 200,000,000 shares on the down side, it would be time to sell! That would be a new record for volume.

But the next day the market held. There was no follow up to the big down day. We had big single down days before so while I was uneasy, I didn't expect anything spectacular at the moment.

When the market dropped $34 Thursday and $34 Friday, the Wall Street Clock started to ring out the hour! The Dow stock average dropped $10.77 on Monday, October 12. It was up the next day $36.72 but fell Wednesday $95.46. A second $90 down day!

THE VOLUME . . . 207,000,000! THAT is big volume!

Thursday, October 15, another $57.61 down on 263,000,000 shares!!

ARE YOU WATCHING YOUR INDICATORS?

On Friday, October 16, 1987 the Dow Jones falls $108.36 and THE VOLUME. . . .

A STAGGERING . . . AN AMAZING . . . AN UNBELIEVABLE – *338,000,000 Shares!!*

Let me spell it our for you. . . .

Three hundred and thirty-eight million shares!

For Whom the Bells Toll

They toll not for me! They toll for thee!

They say in Wall Street that there is nobody to ring a bell when the stock market is at the top. That may be true sometimes. That my be true most times.

But if you use the Wall Street Timetable and its indicators, then more often than not, you'll have your own private sentinel ringing the bell for you when you'll need it most!!

IT DID FOR ME!! LET IT RING FOR YOU!!

After watching carefully all of September, I sold 200 shares of Mobil on October 1. That left me with 400 shares. I took a loss of $503.

Not knowing that a CRASH was about to descend upon me, I added 300 shares of Utilicorp, my utility stock, at 17. This was October 6th.

By the 14th, when the stock market was going through its second $90 day sell off, my "sentinel" started tolling the bells. I heeded cautiously and sold off 200 more shares of Mobil Corp. My loss was $1493.

I still didn't expect a crash. I only knew that the TREND, *that* technical indicator was down *and* that my losses were approaching the Krumholz Loss Level. *Another* tolling of the bells!

I still didn't do anything for my clients because I still didn't know that a crash was on its way. I try not to sell for them as often as I do for myself. I try to protect them first by testing the waters myself. Many times I have sold only to make a quick reversal as I have pointed out through the book.

So on Thursday, October 15, I sold 200 shares of Mobil for a loss of $1785. Friday, I did nothing while the market fell $108 on 333,000,000 shares.

BUT ON SATURDAY I KNEW! I HEARD THE "SENTINEL" LOUD AND CLEAR! I could just picture him on top of the steeple jerking the rope as fast and as hard and as often as he could. The bells clamored!

He was frantically screaming at the top of his lungs, GET OUT! . . . GET OUT! . . . IT'S OVER! . . . IT'S OVER!. . . . as the perspiration rolled down his cheeks.

That was the first time that the thought of a crash entered my mind as I said in the market letter. It was not until I had time to study the market action over the week-end that I first realized what those early October days of high volume and falling prices were telling me!

Yes! They were telling me the time!

WHAT TIME IS IT ON WALL STREET???

It was time to run for the hills! The CRASH IS HERE!! You have no time left. You have until Monday, 9 A.M., to get out. After that you are on your own. Don't reason! Use common sense! Protect yourself and your clients!

The rest you know. That, too, is history!!

Before the market opened I called my clients and said sell everything at the market. Make sure that you place your orders before the market opens for trading!

I only had one utility so I sold half that day and the balance the next day for about ½ to ⅝ lower. My loss on that stock amounted to $4,279.

October was a better month for me than September when I made no trades. I made $601 in October and I managed a profit during perhaps the worst crash in history. Now you know how to avoid crashes. You monitor the trend and volume.

As of this writing, I haven't prepared my tax return for 1987 as yet so I don't have my net income for the year. However I do have the value of my portfolio which is $481,931.84. The gain for the year is $11,406.32.

So after starting 1982 with $127,320.36, I wind up a five year bull market with an increase in my net worth of $354,611. My profit is greater because this is after taxes and personal withdrawings of over $100,000.

That would reflect a gain of $454,611. I roughly estimate about 357% for the period. Of course I don't know how many thousands of dollars I paid in interest over this period but it was substantial.

On December 31, 1987 I had 150M in Treasury notes, 135M Municipal bonds, 54M junk bonds and $143,000 in cash. January 1, 1988 I am ready to start all over again!!!

23

The Secret Indicator Hidden by the Stock Average

In this volume I have told you a great deal of what you have to know to succeed in investing in Wall Street. You have a lot of hard work before you, but I trust you now know what must be done.

You know what to think about, and where and how to go about getting the information that you will need. But please be aware that if you don't give it 110%, you won't make it. There is no margin for error.

This book is not finished. I have additional important information for you. I have another technical indicator for your Wall Street Clock. It will help you determine the stage of the market cycle and help you in deciding when to buy and when to sell.

THINK! Every day the papers publish a list of the new highs and new lows made on the New York Stock Exchange. You will find them in a small box in the financial section.

THINK! Of what significance can this be to us?

I reason that the stock market goes up and down. It does this so often that it would be very confusing were it not for other indicators to guide us.

Without outside indicators it's difficult to get a sense of trend.

Hidden by the stock market averages are the number of new highs and the number of new lows made every day. Although the market may go up and down, a stock doesn't make a new high one day only to make a new low the next.

If a stock makes a new high, it is safe to assume that same stock is in demand and consequently a "safer" risk. *We use this bit of information in what and when to buy.*

Similarly when a stock makes a new low, it is reasonable to assume that there is an over supply. There are more sellers than buyers. The stock then is a very large risk. That's why in a crash don't bottom fish!

Did everything fall into place?

Well, a bull market is not created by one or five stocks making new highs. A bull market is created when more and more new highs are made.

That's what was so strange about the bull market in 1986, 1987. There were many new highs. But not as many or as often as you would expect with the Dow Jones leaping by the hundreds. That was probably because the program traders use the averages. Therefore those stocks made the new highs.

THAT'S WHY YOU MUST ALWAYS DO YOUR OWN THINKING! It's history but never quite the same!!

It wasn't too long ago that a move of $15 on the Dow Average would create excitement. Now it seemed that every month the Dow would be up another hundred points. The way the averages were bouncing, I expected three times the number of new highs.

Therefore, when you note that more and more new highs are being made, it is reasonable to accept that as a confirmation that the stock market is in a rising trend and will continue that trend for an unusually long time period. This should help you to buy early in a bull market!

Let's swing to the sell side. If you notice that the new

highs are decreasing and that the new lows are increasing, then look out! The stock market is heading for a fall. It is heading for another October 19, 1987.

I would have liked to have mentioned this indicator in much of my other discussions with you but there is so much information to discuss that even by osmosis a newcomer just couldn't absorb an unlimited quantity.

Listed are the new highs and lows that I selected for a few days. I chose four Mondays before the October 19 crash. I listed the day of the crash and some days after the crash.

Monday, September 21, there were 25 new highs and 58 new lows (and that's a bull market?). Monday, September 28, 78 highs and 53 lows. (For a bull market I would expect 78 highs and maybe 3 lows).

October 5 there were 83 highs and 39 lows, October 13 there were 8 highs and 112 lows (on this one indicator, alone, you could have headed for the exits)!!

8 new highs and 112 new lows in the biggest bull market in history??

The crash on October 19 resulted in 5 highs and 327 new lows! October 26 . . . 0 highs . . . 467 lows!! Tell me friend, were we still in a bull market?

November 2 . . . 1 high, 34 lows; November 9 . . . 2 highs . . . 46 lows; December 18 there were 1 high and 41 lows; and on December 28 there were 0 highs and 37 lows.

THINK! How many new highs after October 19th? I count 4 for four days.

THINK! On October 19,the day of the crash, there were 327 new lows. After the crash, one week later, there were 467 new lows. And 2–3 days after the crash, they were telling investors to buy, bottom fish, don't panic.

THINK! If they were right, then I was wrong.

What do you think?

THINK! I said that the bull market was over. Did I

know that for a fact? No! Did it really matter whether it was? No! If I was wrong, I'd be among the first to know it!

No stock market ever got away from me for long. And this one wouldn't either . . . even if I wrote that the downside major objective is 1000. I change my mind every time the tape changes its direction.

DON'T FIGHT THE TAPE!

The Ides of October

Early in December, 1987, the stock market rose over 100 dollars to make a new record high for such a move in any one week. This strong display for the bulls was followed the very next week by another record shattering day, a rise of some $108.

THINK!

If the market was shattering records now, why is the Dow Average under 2000?? With such fanfare should they not be over 3000 somewhere? What were they doing under 2000?

THINK!

When the Dow Average made its record 2700, what was the volume figures before and after? Did the market leap when the volume approached 200,000,000? How many 200 million share days did we really have on the march up from 1000?

We had six days in July with over 200. Then on August 11, the volume leaped to 278 million and the next day the Dow Average touched 2700 on 235 million. The Average still didn't close at 2700 as yet.

Finally on Monday, August 17, the Dow Average closed at 2700 *but the volume was a mere 166 million?* That's not good! *A new high without new high volume is bearish!!* This was August.

BEWARE OF THE IDES OF OCTOBER!!

In September the volume settled down to the usual

150 million, 188 million etc. And then, of course, came the forewarned crash in October.

To Complete the Cycle Come the Bear Traps

How would you interpret the volume, trend and cycle indicators after the crash, now that you studied them leading up to the crash? Also, since we added the new high-low technical indicator, use that as well.

In November the volume tended to just hang in there. However, on Monday, November 30, the Dow Average fell some 77 dollars and the volume shot up in a single day to 268 million shares (shades of October).

Was this a time to buy stocks? Wasn't this the falling part of the cycle? Wasn't that a reasonable assumption?

For two weeks in December, the Dow Average made record moves up, and the volume only hung around the 200 million level with but one day making 276 million.

Was this a bull market?

THINK! In December the market was gasping at the 1700, 1800, 1900 level. For every seller there is a buyer but doesn't that work the other way, too? For every buyer isn't there a seller? We have discussed this aspect!

To me there were still more sellers than buyers! That's why the average struggles at 2000. If the averages were at 3000, I would then say that there were more buyers than sellers!!

So the Dow Average might rally to 2200–2300. Big deal! The program players would rip millions from the investor who would be losing it!

My reasoning was that with no new highs on December 28, 1987 and 37 new lows, the bull market was over . . . at least for 1988. Reasoning told me that stocks were in the falling stage of the cycle and wouldn't stop until the new lows shrank considerably.

There was now an overlap between the third stage, the "distribution", and the fourth stage, the "fall", of the stock market cycle. Every time that you get a rally, you will find that "DISTRIBUTION" will take place. This is the BEAR TRAP!

This market shouldn't make a run to 3000 before all the distribution is over. And that should take a long time! Stocks, today, are in "weak" hands. That's because investors who were caught by the crash are now waiting to dump millions of shares.

There is another factor that makes investing more difficult today than in the past. That is the takeovers that are in vogue. They confuse the picture as to what is happening on Wall Street.

If you buy a stock based upon investing guidelines, only to have someone accept "greenmail", there could be a disastrous loss. The loss could be far below the Krumholz Level simply because one man decided to accept "greenmail".

The bull market may have ended but your job hasn't. You have the task of avoiding the bear traps that inevitably follow the end of bull markets. Too, you have the task of planning your strategy for the next cycle!

After the Crash of 1987

In preparing for a fresh start, I decided to take a trading vacation from the stock market. I had barely looked at the stock pages for months and I still hadn't bought any stock.

Instead of talking stock let's reflect a moment. Isn't it true that you and I may have had similar experiences? Our first introduction to the stock market was someone first telling us about some stock and so we bought it.

What was the thought in your mind? My only thought was that "it sounded good" so I bought it! That's all! I did not think in terms of "long term". I really had no objective.

Way back someone told me that a new car, Kaiser-

Frazer, was coming to the market in 1946. I should buy the stock. Then I discussed the idea with my wife who permitted me to take our entire savings of $2000 to purchase that stock.

I never did but that's how I got interested in the stock market. However, I did use that $2000 to invest in other stocks and went on to make over ½ million. Now I estimate that my annual tax-equivalent interest to be about $45,000.

Selling?? I NEVER THOUGHT OF THAT!! I thought of buying. Isn't that how society indoctrinates investors? Everybody buys stocks! Do you ever see large advertisements to sell stocks? Do you ever see mutual funds advertise in big letters, SELL STOCKS?

We are taken in as "small children", indoctrinated to buy and then have our money taken away from us.

In return they hand us cliches and crutches. Oh yes! And lots and lots of "paper"! Plenty of "paper"!

When new investors are introduced to Wall Street, they are immediately told what to buy. Buy a utility. Buy General Motors. Buy ATT (who hasn't heard of that one?) Buy an oil. Buy a chemical. Buy a mutual fund.

Buy . . . buy . . . buy . . . Sell? Who sells stock? If you walked into a stock broker's office and said that you had $100,000 and wanted advice, just how long do you think it would take that broker to invest that $100,000?

I don't know. I have a client who retained me in June, 1986, with that sum. It is over a year and a half and all he has invested is about $16,000 . . . and that's in bonds!

It's true that he bought stocks, Mobil, Schlumberger, Utilicorp etc. and was out before the crash but I don't think he ever had more than $50,000 invested at any one time!

It's easy to buy stocks, get the dividend, and then lose money!! Everybody does that! The trick is . . . FIRST not to lose money . . . THEN get WALL STREET RICH!!

THINK! Just buy stocks and lock them up??

What a terrible way to teach a person a new skill . . . a new profession!!!

If you wanted to become a doctor, would they put you into an operating room with a scapel in your hand before you had learned and say, "Cut! Proceed with the heart transplant!"

Or would they prepare you for your objective?

Construction? Should you want to build a house, how would you start? Either you would hire someone to do it or you would learn how to do it youself!

Investing! It's as difficult or perhaps even more so then medicine or construction! How many successful investors do you know? How many doctors and lawyers do you know?

So before you *think* of buying your next stock, learn the business of the investor and where it all begins. It begins in understanding Wall Street and not in any specific stock. It begins in learning the how's and the why's of the stock market and not in any one particular stock.

THINK! What moves the stock market? Why does it move? Now that you know that, try to buy a stock that is low, to sell when it is high. That is what you must learn. That's the research and the work that you have to do.

I feel that my trading vacation is coming to an end. I'm tempted to buy some low priced stock that can double in one year. But I remember from the history of the last two years how disappointed I was with my profits.

Therefore I started 1988, the year after the Big Crash, holding bonds and lots of cash. My interest income for 1988 is expected to be about $42,000. That's not bad since my original investment was about $47,500.

In the meanwhile I'll start some research.

How to Invest After the Big Crash

What I am buying now are straight bonds. They mature between 3 to 8 years. If the market value declines, then I'll hold them to maturity. I have other bonds that will mature sooner and that will furnish the money for the stock market when I am ready.

I just started to buy convertible bonds. They give me a call on the stock market for rallies etc. In the meantime the yield is substantially higher than investment grade bonds.

Also while I didn't hesitate to buy \$40–\$50 stocks during the bull market, now I am looking at only \$3–\$5 stocks. I'm looking for the big percentage play.

Again in the bull market I didn't hesitate to purchase 10,000 or 20,000 shares of a stock; now it will be 300 or 1,000 or perhaps 2,000 shares. We are in a different phase of the stock market. Be careful! Watch your loss factor!

INTERESTING ISN'T IT? WE'VE COME FULL CYCLE ONCE AGAIN! I'm making a fresh start in my fund with what I started with originally. I started in 1973 with 2 investment type bonds, then added convertible bonds. That's what I am doing again. History repeating its teachings!

One last caveat! Beware of what you see, read or hear. The financial magazines and other media are replete with headlines and full page stories urging you to buy stocks.

After every crash there is a massive media explosion to "buy now". Look how cheap stocks are! Only yesterday they were twice as much.

They load you with fantasies about dollar averaging, buy for the long term . . . etc. . . . We went through this! Soon even I don't know what's happening. They speak so convincingly, so knowingly, that even I wonder if I know what it's all about.

THINK! Did they get rich *as an* investor? Or did they get rich *from* investors? And they are telling you what to do?

THINK! It's *your* money! It's *your* responsibility! Only *you* must conclude which stock to buy and whether you should sell! But you must learn to do it!

The Time?

It's now 10:28 A.M. It's Thursday, December 31, 1987. Soon the clock on the old church down in the Wall Street area is going to ring out the old year and tell the people passing by what time it is. It's a New Year! Happy New Year!

But wait!

WHAT TIME IS IT ON WALL STREET???

Is it time to buy?

Are you going to let them tell you?

OR ARE YOU GOING TO TELL THEM???

Index to Selected Instructive Letters

WRITTEN TO CLIENTS

Index

C

D

S

T

U

V

W

See next page for ORDER FORM

ORDER FORM

Abben Publishing Company
Box 463, Flushing, N.Y. 11365

Please send the book:

The K Factor
A Proven Stock Strategy

by Jerome Krumholz

I wish to have it as a permanent reference.

Enclosed is my check:

for the book	$23.95
for sales tax (N.Y. City sales tax is $1.98).	
for shipping..............................	1.00
total of check enclosed	

You need not remove this page.
Just send your order to the publisher
with your name and address.

40, 110, hitlen | dazzling, sterpe 219 | 233 sideways movement | selling short 242